VIOLENCE

Xerox College Publishing
Waltham, Massachusetts • Toronto

GEORGE F. ESTEY
DORIS A. HUNTER

BOSTON UNIVERSITY

Violence

A Reader in the Ethics of Action

Dedicated to our students
who are confronting
the problems of an
ethics of action.

Library of Congress Catalog Card Number: 70-163782
ISBN: 0-536-00667-9 Printed in the United States of America.

Acknowledgments

Robert Ardrey, "The Violent Way," condensed from *The Social Contract,* by Robert Ardrey. Copyright © 1970 by Robert Ardrey. Reprinted by permission of Atheneum Publishers.

Bernard Beck, "Talking Violence Blues," from *Dialogue on Violence,* edited by George Vickers, copyright, 1968, by The Bobbs-Merrill Company, Inc. Reprinted by permission of the publisher.

Bruno Bettelheim, "Violence: A Neglected Mode of Behavior," *The Annals.* Reprinted by permission of the author and The American Academy of Political and Social Science.

Loren Eiseley, "The Last Magician," from *The Invisible Pyramid,* by Loren Eiseley. Originally appeared in *Playboy* Magazine. Copyright © 1970 by Loren Eiseley. Reprinted by permission of Charles Scribner's Sons.

Jacques Ellul, "Christian Realism in the Face of Violence," from *Violence: Reflections from a Christian Perspective,* by Jacques Ellul. Copyright © 1969 by The Seabury Press, Inc. Published by The Seabury Press, Inc., New York.

Romain Gary, "The Baiting Society." Originally appeared in *Playboy* Magazine. Copyright © 1969 by Romain Gary. Reprinted by permission of the Robert Lantz-Candida Donadio Literary Agency.

Herbert Gold, "Random Violence: Is That Man Coming Down the Street to Kill You?" *Look* Magazine. Copyright © 1970 by Herbert Gold. Reprinted by permission of the author and his agent, James Brown Associates, Inc.

Hermann Hesse, "To Children," from *Poems,* by Hermann Hesse, translated by James Wright. Copyright © 1970 by James Wright, copyright 1953 by Suhrkamp Verlag. Reprinted by permission of Farrar, Strauss & Giroux, Inc.

Morton Hunt, "Man and Beast." Originally appeared in *Playboy* Magazine. Copyright © 1970 by Morton Hunt. Reprinted by permission.

Lucy Komisar, "Violence and the Masculine Mystique." Reprinted from *The Washington Monthly* by permission of the author.

R. D. LAING, "The Mystification of Experience," chapter 3, pages 57–76, from *The Politics of Experience.* Copyright © 1967 by R. D. Laing. Reprinted by permission of Penguin Books Ltd.

HAROLD I. LIEF, "Contemporary Forms of Violence," from *Science and Psychoanalysis,* vol. 6, edited by Jules H. Masserman, M.D. Copyright © 1963 by Grune & Stratton, Inc. Reprinted by permission of the author and Grune & Stratton, Inc.

HERBERT MARCUSE, "Solidarity," from *An Essay on Liberation.* Copyright © 1969 by Herbert Marcuse. Reprinted by permission of Beacon Press.

THOMAS MERTON, "Is Man a Gorilla with a Gun?" from *Faith and Violence: Christian Teaching and Christian Practice.* Copyright © 1968 by University of Notre Dame Press. Reprinted by permission.

TRUMAN NELSON, "No Rights, No Duties," from *The Right of Revolution.* Copyright © 1968 by Truman Nelson. Reprinted by permission of Beacon Press.

REINHOLD NIEBUHR, "The Conflict Between Individual and Social Morality," from *Moral Man and Immoral Society* by Reinhold Niebuhr. Copyright 1932 by Charles Scribner's Sons; renewal copyright © 1960 by Reinhold Niebuhr. Reprinted by permission of Charles Scribner's Sons.

MORRIS RENEK, "Reflections on Violence as a Literary Tool," from *Story* Magazine. Copyright © 1967 by Scholastic Magazines, Inc. Reprinted by permission of the author.

DONALD L. ROGAN, "Salvation Through Revolution," from *Campus Apocalypse: The Student Search Today,* by Donald L. Rogan. Copyright © 1969 by The Seabury Press, Inc. Published by The Seabury Press, Inc., New York.

ARTHUR M. SCHLESINGER, JR., "Existential Politics," from *The Crisis of Confidence.* Copyright © 1967, 1968, 1969 by Arthur M. Schlesinger, Jr. Reprinted by permission of the publisher, Houghton Mifflin Company.

FREDERIC WERTHAM, "The Goddess of Violence," from *A Sign of Cain,* by Frederic Wertham. Copyright © 1966 by Frederic Wertham. Reprinted by permission of The Macmillan Company.

Preface

Today's students seeking answers to an ethics of action are not only involved with intellectual questions but are also caught up in an emotional atmosphere which ranges from the sweet euphoria of "All we need is love, love, love" to immediate, brutal satisfaction because love is vain. Two film documentaries of the rock culture, *Woodstock* and *Gimme Shelter,* depict this emotional vacillation. The movement from love and peace to murder negates, for many students, Henry David Thoreau's plea to simplify. They are confronted instead with the complexity of both nonviolence and violence.

In *Nonviolence: A Reader in the Ethics of Action,* we presented the complexity of the issues involved in a commitment to nonviolence as an ethics of action. In this volume, *Violence,* we attempt to do the same task, not by oversimplifying the intellectual and emotional factors involved in violence but by introducing some of the factors which make the problem of violence more complex than is usually realized.

Students ask the important questions, but seldom find material for the answers outside upper-level philosophy or religion courses. Although there are hundreds of readers for freshman courses in English and the humanities, only seldom do they present the issues in other than isolated essays. As we noted in the Preface to *Nonviolence,* "It is our contention that freshmen not only are capable of considering ethical questions, but that they are deeply interested in exploring such questions, not merely for historical interest, but because they are seeking appropriate means to define their own ethical stance as they deal with problems on their campuses, cities, states, and nation." We have seen no reason to change our view of the abilities and interests of freshmen since publishing that statement.

This reader, a collection of essays drawn from a wide range of disciplines, is designed specifically for freshman courses in composition. It will be useful in humanities courses, probably as a supplementary text, and may find similar use in natural and social science courses as these begin to extend their interests beyond the experimental and theoretical into the ethical realm. We have not diluted the difficulty of the materials or the concepts presented in them, for we are aware of the growing sophistication of the entering student. However, even the relatively naive student should have little difficulty in comprehending the major points considered here.

We have kept editorial apparatus to a minimum. Comments and questions, which should elicit either wide-ranging class discussion or reasonably well-focused essays, are found in the sections headed "Projects." Bibliographies of related readings enable both student and instructor to explore these questions further. Where possible, we have included films that raise similar concerns. The dilemma of action presented through these readings has been relevant for centuries: it is not less relevant in America today. We hope that this book enables some people to confront their ethical choices effectively, and perhaps earlier than would otherwise be possible.

G.F.E.

D.A.H.

Contents

PART I
Definitions of Violence

The logic of the rebel is to want to serve justice so as not to add to the injustice of the human condition, to insist on plain language so as not to increase the universal falsehood, and to wager, in spite of human misery, for happiness.

ALBERT CAMUS
The Rebel

Introduction

We usually assume that we know the meanings of the words we use. However, events of the last decade suggest that certain words are either changing in meaning, or that the meanings are so confused as to require constant attention to definition. When national publications report that various groups are seriously debating whether bombing buildings is "violent" or whether kidnapping government officials is "violent," then we should begin a book exploring violence with a section on definitions.

Bernard Beck, an assistant professor of sociology at Northwestern University, first tries to clear away some of the confusing elements surrounding the word "violence." He then provides a general discussion of the concepts of "person," and "rights of person." By relating "violence" to these concepts, Beck gives us a useful beginning point for examining "violence" without engaging in impossible tasks, such as determining motivation. Beck thus attempts to keep "violence" in a social context, between persons.

Harold Lief, a physician, is Professor of Psychiatry at the School of Medicine of the University of Pennsylvania, and Director of the Division of Family Study. He has wide ranging interests which include studies of the cultures and personality of Negroes, of the adaptation of medical students, of psychosomatic illnesses, of out-patient and social psychiatry, as well as the specific concern with violence illustrated in his essay, "Contemporary Forms of Violence."

Dr. Lief first differentiates violence from aggression and then considers three types of violence, only one of which seems to have the "social" aspect identified by Beck. (You will wish to think carefully about the "detached" kinds of violence that Lief identifies.) In addition, Lief, unlike Beck, becomes somewhat involved in the source problem: "Why are human beings violent?" This question is examined more fully in Part II.

The primary purpose of the two selections of Part I is to identify the issues that rise from the concept of violence. You will need to develop your own definition of violence and related terms in order to think and write about the ethical questions involved.

Talking Violence Blues

BERNARD BECK

One common problem that has faced all who turn their attention to violence is that of definition. Although everyone seems to have a common-sense notion what violence is, it has been difficult to provide an explicit and useful definition. Whenever serious talk about violence begins, a long, frustrating excursion into definition is the first order of business. Participants rarely leave this stage of talk with a feeling of accomplishment. Instead, they content themselves with makeshift resolutions of the question and proceed to more satisfying topics. There are good reasons, however, for looking for a well-constructed definition of violence; if one could be generated, it would lead to a clearer understanding of substantive issues, including those raised in this book.

Many proposed definitions are unusable—those, for instance, that require us to know the intentions of the person who commits violence, a kind of information that is not routinely available. Others seem usable but are not—for example, those that refer to measurable physical damage to persons, a determination which is possible, although difficult and seldom carried out. The discussions that flow from such definitions often could not conceivably be based on the definitions themselves.

In many cases a definition seems to be constructed to satisfy two criteria: (1) that it be short enough and so phrased that it will sound technical, whether or not it is ever used technically; and (2) that the examples it generates be the same as those we select through our common-sense understanding of the word, whether or not the principle underlying that understanding is explicitly included in the definition. The second criterion pinpoints the most obvious deficiencies in most definitions of violence. Under many of them we are forced to include cases that everybody understands not to be instances of violence, such as automobile accidents; under others we find cases we understand to be examples of violence which do not fit the definition.

I suggest that these difficulties arise because formal definitions commonly do not express our tacit understandings, which remain inaccessible. Whenever there is a discrepancy between a formal definition and our common-sense understandings, the definitions will be sacrificed in substantive discussions. No one will forsake a topic he is interested in discussing merely because the formal definition has not been properly made to include it.

This consideration goes to the heart of the nature of definition itself. A definition does not merely protect us from criticism, keep us honest, certify our credentials, or enable us to touch all bases in the creation of intellectual products. The major work to be done by definitions is that of pointing us in directions that are most fruitful for investigation. By defining a term in one way or another, and using it in the way it has been defined, we will be most likely to raise the interesting questions and avoid the trivial or fruitless questions.

From a sociological viewpoint, community of agreement about the use of words is a phenomenon of great empirical interest. Paradoxically, the same underlying social arrangements that support such agreement also produce nonagreement, often in the form of bitter contention. The principle that explains both is that languages exist not as abstract media of communication but as media within particular social situations, defined among people with particular types of interests (sometimes cooperating, sometimes conflicting), for people in particular positions, and for people with particular histories, destinies, strategies, and goals.

How does language fit into a social context in this way? Language not only names and points to, it also calls forth responses from those to whom it is addressed. Both words which are commonly accepted as having a clear meaning (even if it cannot be stated) and words whose uses are bitterly contested (often the same words) can be understood as having a content not only of factual but also of directive material—a content of orders, suggestions, and maxims. The words instruct how to *act* rather than how to *understand*. Thus, when the motives and interests of people are in agreement on a given object, finding consensus on the applicability of words is not difficult, even when the words are hard to define. At the same time, in cases where the definition of words seems clear, there is conflict if the interests and motives of those invoking such language are at odds.

The word "violence" is an example of this phenomenon, and two sources of the difficulty can be named. First, because the notion of violence has tremendous power, people are led to try to apply it in a wide variety of situations. Each extension of meaning, no doubt profitable and illuminating in a particular discussion, blurs the precision and distinctiveness of the term still further, until a point is reached where almost any type of behavior or event can somehow be construed as violent. While each individual extension, allegory, or metaphor of violence can be fruitful, the total picture becomes one of confusion.

Second, the word "violence," when invoked in ordinary language, calls out a conventional set of appropriate responses that are both moral and practical. The question whether an event is violent is interesting not only to the academician but also to people in society who must decide how to respond to different classes of events. For example, the behavior of an elementary-school pupil may require a strong, negative response from the teacher if it is labeled violent, but it may be ignored or treated casually if it is not so defined.

From this point of view, violence is a very strong word. It matters greatly to the outcome of social situations whether particular types of action are labeled violent or are excused from the label. Many discussions of violence that begin as sober intellectual forays into the realm of definition and analysis soon become heated disputes over whether a certain kind of event can "legitimately" be called violent. The riots of recent years are an excellent example of this.

These considerations suggest a strong moral reason for seeking a proper, precise, and early definition of violence. In the minds of many in the world today, moral judgments are to be leveled upon persons, acts, and events if they are violent, and this moral attribution can occur in such a way that violence is judged positively, or in such a way that it is judged negatively. In either case, it becomes important to individuals who are considering how they should properly react to events in order to be able to decide if they are violent. In this light, the intellectual provocativeness which results from calling certain kinds of art, language, and attitudes "violent" raises very grave questions when the moral attributions ordinarily made to violent events may be extended into the new areas where the word "violence" is extended.

In discussion, "violence" often may be found in the company of such terms as "aggression," "hostility," "hatred," "fear," "anger," "harm," "pain," and "suffering." It is often not realized that there are differences among the terms in this set, and in particular that violence (a kind of behavior), may be quite different from aggression (a way in which behavior can be carried out) and from hostility (an internal state that can give rise to behavior). Likewise, violence differs from the terms in this set that name such consequences to individuals as suffering and pain, which are subjective experiences, and harm or damage, which express an observer's external judgments about the functioning of an organism. Finally, violence differs both from malice, a desire to see harm to another individual, and from a kind of mental suffering which reflects not actual damage to the physical organism but a disturbed state of sensibility.

There is no question, of course, that the words are related, in that where one of them applies the others may also be appropriate, and that the phenomena designated by them can stand in a cause-and-effect relationship. But it seems to me worthwhile to keep these words distinct, particularly since the term "violence" is ideally suited to be applied to a kind of phenomenon that cannot be readily subsumed under other attitudinal and behavioral terms.

"Violence," after all, is used in ordinary language at least to name objective kinds of events; that is, an event is violent because of characteristics it displays as it happens. Its violence, we ordinarily believe, is available to observation by outsiders. In fact, the requirement of many moral systems that we make judgments about the violence of acts is connected with the possibility of making them as observers. Thus, the conception of violence I offer will be free from some of the difficulties which have beset other attempts to define violence in terms of the intent, the understanding, the motivation of the person who initiates or authors the violent act. Similarly, it will to some extent alleviate the problem of having to make assessments of real psychological damage to victims before an act can be judged violent. This conception is based on the notion that violence is largely a categorization and distinction of interest to members of society rather than to students of it—in other words, that students of society become interested in the category of violence because the distinction between violence and nonviolence is an important one to the members of the societies they study. This sociological conception of violence may serve, if not actually as a definition, at least as a foundation for discussions of violence in a wide variety of contexts.

Violence is a socially defined category whose meaning depends on the content of another more basic conception, namely, that of a set of rights and obligations which I call the "person," which is culturally defined and socially negotiated, and which individuals can invoke. Members of a social system can make use of a definition of their participation, which has been called "citizenship." Thus, all people who are allowed to consider themselves members of the society can enforce against one another some basic claims which are theirs merely by virtue of that participation. Relations with those who are not members of the system are not governed by these rights and obligations, and are therefore freer. Within the category of citizenship are the various sets of rights and obligations which form the roles that differentiate members within a system.

At a more basic level, however, underlying and prior to citizenship, is the general notion of "being someone." In order to "be someone," an individual may not even have to be a member of the system. He need merely be recognized as existing, being present, and having to be contended with. I suggest that in every social system a set of primitive rights and obligations will be institutionalized and will attach to anyone who can be considered a person at all, and that this set of rights and obligations will have a high emotional loading and moral sanction. An individual involved in a social system can, in other words, be implicated in a wide variety of activities, can be extended into a social environment through a wide net of interactions and a wide variety of relationships; and each of these will imply certain kinds of claims that can be made on him and other claims that he can make on others. Within each social system, however, there will be defined some minimal set of conditions and characteristics that a person invokes in order to demonstrate to himself and others that he actually exists as an individual.

In most contexts, one necessary part of this definition of a person is an associated physical body. That is to say, one of the most basic components of the definition we are entitled to use as persons under any culture is that of inhabitors, possessors, and sole sovereign directors of a body. Correspondingly, the claim we have on others for respect to our bodies is different from, and stronger than, such rights as property, courtesy, and deference. We can imagine some circumstances, however, in which the notion of person does not include control and protection even over parts of one's own body; similarly, we can imagine situations in which "persons" can include extensive sets of objects and behaviors not physically and immediately related to one's own body.

Applying the label "person" to this set of definitions is deliberate, for in contrast to other kinds of rights and privileges that the individual can invoke in social situations, infringement of the particular set which constitutes the person amounts to negating the existence of the individual himself. While the particular set of things constituting the "person" will vary from one context to another, the fundamental implication imposed by such a system of definition is that any infringement on the person is an attack not on what is "mine" but on what is "me."

This conception takes account of the routine social fact that we deal with individuals not merely as biotic organisms, but as organisms situated in a social context, so that they carry about with them small arsenals of social definitions, cues, and location signals. They take responsibility for and assert sovereignty over some small piece of social space beyond the boundaries of the organism. Familiar examples of this extension are the inclusion in the notion of "person" of the definitions, rights, privileges, and behaviors attendant on the wearing of clothes and the preservation of appropriate distance between individuals in space (the concern of the newly named field of proxemics).

Because the person is a fundamental and highly charged object which can be invoked by any individual, whether or not he is a member of the social system, and because it establishes rights and obligations of that individual whenever and wherever he happens to be, infringement of the rights thus established is a serious act. It constitutes by definition an attack on the person and in fact a negation of the existence and social efficacy of the individual.

Thus, a violent act or event can be defined as one alleged to be (and socially accepted as) a violation of the victim's rights of person. To use this definition it is necessary to discover (1) that certain rights of person are claimed on behalf of someone, (2) that someone's actions are alleged to violate those rights, and (3) that some set of judges honors these claims. In a definition of this sort, the role of the objective observer is to determine what ideas and decisions are invoked by the actors in the situation. Nonobjective observers can assert a judgment of violence about an event, but the assertion is meaningful only when it includes a theory of the person which is the observer's own, and which is used instead of the institutionalized definition prevailing in the situation under study. This judgment is called nonobjective because no theory of the person is possible which does not have moral and practical implications. In other words, the judgment of violence is a value judgment, and a theory of the person that makes it possible is also value-laden.

From this viewpoint, then, questions of malice or other kinds of intent do not arise, for in order to violate this kind of personal right, the violator must be negligent, ignorant, or uncaring of the existence of the person to an extent that constitutes a denial of the claims of the person. Finally, we see that the problem of violence, both in definition and in discussion, comes not in directly characterizing the different kinds of acts that are violent, but rather in paying attention to the characteristics of the socially invokable rights whose infringement will constitute violence.

Since the judgment that an event is violent rests on a stipulation of a set of rights and obligations, people who make that judgment by applying the word take on themselves obligations insofar as they are connected to the system in which these rights and obligations are defined. Thus, the issue of violence inevitably implies a problem of legitimacy. If you see that an event is violent, it may impose on you an obligation to react to the event in appropriate ways—for instance, by resisting, punishing, or publicly condemning the perpetrator of violence, or by aiding the victim. Likewise, it imposes a burden on anyone who sees that an act is violent but condones the act. In this case, the burden is the required work of rationalization and justification. The moral and practical implications of the label "violence" under this definition account both for the vehemence of arguments over the meaning of violence and for the sense of accord and impatience with such arguments to be found among people whose hearts are in the same place.

This way of looking at violence permits us to understand some otherwise puzzling phenomena with regard to the social use of the label "violent." For example, specifically self-avowed nonviolent demonstrations call forth violence from residents of the communities in which they occur. This violence is defended, justified, and legitimized by those perpetrating it on the grounds that the presence of the "nonviolent" demonstrations is a violent provocation. Similarly, outside observers will on occasion be heard to comment that because the nonviolent demonstrator goes into a situation where he knows violence will be the outcome, he is a knowing participant in a violent event, and therefore his action itself is violent. Proponents of violent rebellion by subordinated and oppressed groups often say that the social and psychological exploitation and oppression imposed upon such groups is far more damaging, and therefore more violent, than the rebellion which is a response to it. Certain ways of talking, thinking, and believing, and even certain ways of expressing in the arts, are sometimes called violent, and may be more violent than physical assault. There are even those who argue that recreation and sports that involve body contact are violent, even though they are socially legitimate; they are violence disguised as good fun.

In each of these examples, some aspect of the person, differently defined in each case, has been infringed upon by outsiders, and on the basis of this infringement a claim is made on the alleged rights involved in the definition of person. The cases are anomalous, paradoxical, or funny because the components of person involved are not the ordinary physical components with which we are most familiar.

The first example, that of violent reactions to nonviolent demonstrations, indicates that the claimed rights of person may include a territorial element, namely the neighborhood. It further suggests that a cultural object like the person may be defined for collective entities such as communities, as well as for individuals, with a corresponding extension in the use of the notion of violence. In the second example, violence as a reaction to psychological oppression, we can look to security of an individual's self-esteem and social reputation as a basic right of the person. In the third example, disguised violence in legitimate activities, we are warned that we are viewing events which would ordinarily be grounds for someone to claim that his basic rights had been infringed. In the context of sports, however, participants specifically waive those claims in advance; presumably they accept certain assurances of intent from other participants and take steps to minimize possible physical damage.

Each of the examples shows the usefulness of examining each allegation of violence not in order to decide whether it is violent, but in order to explicate what rights are being asserted as part of the person. Rather than engaging in futile exchanges of "is-isn't," we are then led to a profitable investigation of the component rights and obligations of the person, and are involved in an empirical question rather than a definitional one.

The examples also indicate that allegations of violence lead directly to the socially defined conditions which are held to justify violence. The general form of such justification is that the victim has waived his rights of person by a prior act, so that what would otherwise be a violent act is no longer violent because it no longer infringes on rights which the victim can have supported by judges. This justification, like the allegation of violence itself, is subject to the ratification of surrounding society in the person of relevant judges.

Having indicated the empirical implications of an assertion that some event or act is violent, we can get an idea of what is at stake in accepting extensions of the meaning of violence through analogy and metaphor. Given the political implications of such extensions, we can see such attempts as political proposals whose object is a reevaluation, not merely a reconceptualization. The answer must lie either in the empirical study of the society and its institutionalized beliefs, or in the thrilling regions of moral discourse.

The kind of words we use, the understandings that we have about those words, and the shared experiences which form the base of those understandings all have practical moral consequences. Whether or not an act is violent, to label it so has serious consequences, and until we can develop better definitional understandings of the topics we speak about, we will be responsible for arbitrary judgments which may lack real content.

Contemporary Forms of Violence

HAROLD I. LIEF

Violence and Force

Violence is a generic term, encompassing a number of connotations—such as the "exertion of any physical force so as to injure and abuse . . . intense, turbulent, or furious action, force, or feeling often destructive." Other words used in connection with violence are "unnatural," "undue," "extreme," and "vehement."[1]

Violence is not necessarily identical with *force*. The latter may signify restraint via the threat of violence. When we arrange for four or five attendants to approach an assaultive patient, we use the threat of violence in order to prevent violence. The patient recognizes that resistance is futile and submits in the face of overwhelming force. This is an instance of successful deterrence. Violence differs from force in that it sooner or later gets out of bounds even if, at the outset, it had been appropriate to a given goal. It becomes behavior exercised for its own sake, and thus seems capricious, arbitrary, or "needless." Violence is often quite unexpected in its onset and unpredictable in its course, whereas *force* may be controlled, delimited, and appropriately directed toward a goal.

Violence and Aggression

There are many psychoanalysts who use the term aggression mistakenly, in a general sense, covering everything from the exploratory drive of the infant and child to the sadistic brutality of the rapist-murderer; in between they include drives such as mastery of self and the environment, self-assertion, and dominance. Aggression used in this sweeping way results in endless confusion. Murphy[2] puts it this way:

---

[1] *Webster's Third New International Dictionary of the English Language*, unabridged. Springfield, Mass.: G. & C. Merriam Co., 1964, p. 2554.

[2] L. B. Murphy, *et al., The Widening World of Childhood* (New York: Basic Books, 1962), pp. 350–351.

. . . If we use the term "aggression" to describe both the capacity to move into the environment in an active, discovering, creating, and stimulating way which produces welcome results for other people, small or large, and activity aimed to destroy, depreciate, demote, or which in other ways bring discomfort for others, small or large, we create enormous difficulties for our thinking . . . "Aggression" can mean almost anything from hostility to the vigor with which either constructive or destructive acts are carried out.

I will use the word aggression to mean behavior motivated by the wish to injure, remove, or destroy a threatening object. In this sense, aggression is a mode of emergency behavior called into play by the blocking of any drive, the inhibition of any function, or the perception of any threat, and it can be utilized by a group as well as by an individual. From this, it follows that aggression and violence are *motivationally* the same even though there are many different degrees of aggression—violence, ranging from kicking the cat or slamming the door to nuclear warfare. In the words of Scott:[3]

. . . The word aggression is widely used and misused in a variety of contexts. It may describe either an act of war by a nation or the behavior of an overenthusiastic salesman. Used precisely, "aggression" refers to fighting and means the act of initiating an attack.

Buss[4] has defined aggression in similar terms:

. . . The term aggression subsumes a large number of responses that vary in topography, energy expenditure, and consequences. All aggressive responses share two characteristics: (1) the delivery of noxious stimuli, and (2) an interpersonal context. Thus aggression is defined as a *response that delivers noxious stimuli to another organism;* the term *attack* will be used as a synonym.

Although Buss defines aggression as an attack, he paradoxically

---

[3] J. P. Scott, *Aggression* (Chicago: University of Chicago Press, 1958), p. 1.
[4] A. H. Buss, *The Psychology of Aggression* (New York: John Wiley, 1961), p. 1.

(as do many other experimental psychologists) refuses to define it in motivational terms, because "intent . . . implies teleology, a purposive act directed toward a future goal" and because "intent is a private event that may or may not be capable of verbalization, may or may not be accurately reflected in a verbal statement."

Psychoanalysts think and observe in a motivational context; if they did not they could not make use of introspective methods. Indeed, even the analysis of introspective behavioral data usually depends on the interpretation of motivation.

Violence is thus an end-point on a continuum of aggressive behavior. It is characterized by extreme force, often physical, as well as by its irrational nature, so that its original goal-orientation may be lost as it becomes an end-in-itself.

The origins of aggression are considered to be either instinctive or reactive. I believe aggression to be reactive, but in any case, the *capacity* for violence is innate in man. The emotion that usually fuels this behavior pattern is rage, and this affect seems to be widespread in the animal kingdom. Fighting occurs from the arthropods on up.

> Fighting occurs so widely in the animal kingdom that it cannot be dismissed as accidental or abnormal in occurrence. In reality, aggressive behavior is a common and apparently useful part of the daily lives of many animals, and only exceptionally does it become destructive or harmful.[5]

Most individual acts of human violence are rage-driven, as are most group-centered violent actions, such as race riots or political revolutions.

On the other hand, there are violent acts which appear to be carried out without any anger behind them. An example was the 1957 "senseless" gang killing of a fifteen-year-old boy, partially crippled by polio—the so-called "Egyptian King" homicide. In the same attack, another boy was critically injured, being stabbed a number of times with a bread knife. As Yablonsky[6] puts it:

---

[5] Scott, *op. cit.,* p. 6.

[6] L. Yablonsky, *The Violent Gang* (New York: Macmillan, 1962), p. 9.

> The motives for this crime fit no simple category. No money was taken. No direct personal revenge was involved. According to all reports, the victims did not personally know their assailants, nor did the youths who committed the homicide know their victims.

This is almost a "pure culture" example of violence for the sake of violence. Indeed, the more unconcerned, the more unfeeling, the more "cool" the killer acts, the greater are the plaudits of his fellow gang members. It is the violent act itself which is prized as an "easy, quick, almost magical way of achieving power and prestige. In a single act of unpremeditated intensity he establishes a sense of his own existence and impresses this existence on others."

Another type of violence without rage is a detached, depersonalized, goal-oriented act, namely, that of electronically controlled, push-button nuclear war. The emotions of the men pushing the buttons are irrelevant unless the act is impulsive or accidental. Rage would not be instrumental but in fact would be an obstacle in contemporary scientific warfare.

I am able to discern at least three types of violence: (1) the type driven by rage, (2) a detached type in which the significant aspect is the violent act rather than the object of the attack, and (3) a detached type in which the destruction of the object is the significant aspect, and the violence is an instrumental act required for the attainment of the goal.

I will examine these three types of violence in relation to some of the violent types and types of violence familiar to twentieth-century man: the gangster, the Western gunman, the youth who is a member of a violent gang, genocide, and nuclear war.

Some General Aspects

Anthropologists, historians, and political scientists tell us that violence has been present in every society and in every age. With the coming of the nation-state in the seventeenth century, violence came into the hands of national leaders with increasing power. Yet that power was limited, both technically and politically. Technically, the gas chamber and the atom bomb had not been invented, and politically the wielders of power were usually held accountable despite the lip service given to the doctrine of the Divine Right of Kings. In contemporary life, accountability for violence has been generally a post-mortem affair, with the trials and judgments of Hitler and Stalin occurring after their deaths. Even the culpability and accountability of their lieutenants necessitated unusual charges as exemplified in the Nuremburg and Eichmann trials. Few people raise the question of accountability for the Hiroshima and Nagasaki bombings, for we were the victors. If the United States and her allies had lost the war, we might have witnessed a trial similar to the Nuremburg trials, in which the guilt of our national leaders would have been adjudged. I am not suggesting the equal culpability of these acts of violence—genocide and atom bombing—but I am suggesting that accountability for violent acts causing mass deaths does not follow automatically; it is rather a question of who has won and who has lost.

Our modern world has witnessed technological changes permitting mass murder to be carried out on an unprecedented scale. At the very same time, as Wolin[7] has stated, we have developed increasing concern for the poor, weak, and sick members of society, developing institutions and financial assistance for their care also on a huge scale. This is a *paradoxical* social attitude in which people can actually analyze detachedly whether the United States can tolerate sixty million or 100 million dead, but become intensely aroused over the multiple postponements of the death of Caryl Chessman. Seemingly, we must have increasing concern for individual life as a necessary *defense against the total detachment* involved in contemplating millions of dead. The mind cannot grasp the enormity, the immensity of the casualties in a nuclear war. Szent-Gyorgyi[8] graphically points

---

[7] S. S. Wolin, "The Theme of Violence in Western Political Thought," paper delivered at the 39th Annual Meeting of the American Orthopsychiatric Association, Los Angeles, March 21–24, 1962.

[8] A. Szent-Gyorgyi, "The Persistence of the Cave Man," *Saturday Review,* July 7, 1962, p. 11.

out that the concept of nuclear disaster is intellectual and detached because it is outside immediate experience:

> Here we stand in the middle of this new world with our primitive brain attuned to the simple cave life, terrific forces at our disposal, which we are clever enough to release, but whose consequences we cannot comprehend. Their dimensions are too far beyond our human dimensions. When my wife tells me, "the water is hot," I am careful. . . . But if I hear that an atomic explosion has fifteen million degrees of heat, it means nothing to me. I am deeply moved if I see a man suffering and would even risk my life for him. But then I talk impersonally about the possible pulverization of our big cities, with a hundred million dead. I am unable to multiply one man's suffering by a hundred million.

As a consequence of this social split, have we become inured to mass violence? It appears as if we can contemplate non-nuclear war, such as the Korean, Indo-Chinese, or Algerian conflicts, with greater equanimity than did past generations. The very term we use to describe some of these conflicts, "brush-fire warfare," indicates the enlarging scale of violence to which we have grown accustomed.

Other aspects of modern life, such as automation and the growth of huge corporations which may house thirty thousand employees in one building, contribute to the dehumanization growing more prevalent day by day, which we desperately try to counter by our search for the meaning of individual existence. But it is the fact that the "world annihilation" fantasies of the schizophrenic have now become a reality that increases the pace of this emotional detachment while the detachment, in turn, becomes an obstacle to more energetic efforts to find nonviolent solutions to international conflicts.

Special Types of Violence—Cannibalism

Cannibalism reflects the three categories of violence to which I referred earlier. Often motivated by revenge and "consumed" with anger against neighboring tribes who trespassed on their land, stole property, particularly wives, and exerted magical influence against them, cannibals also used aggression as an instrumental act, for capture of their neighbors added to their food supply. Yet, raids against their enemies designed for revenge as well as to increase their protein intake were often a sort of tribal gamesmanship and were carried out as ritualistic exercises, as part of puberty or other religious rites. In the latter instance, the violent act becomes all important, rather than the emotions behind it or the object of its execution. In one of our "refined" civilizations, an impersonal and gigantic mouth, the crematorium, replaced the inefficient mechanisms of the savage.

Although there are certainly gangsters and, in the past, there were Western gunmen, one can truthfully say that most Americans have never seen either. Why, then, do they appear so significant in our consciousness? Robert Warshow,[9] in an illuminating essay on American movies, says, "What matters is that the experience of the gangster" (and of the Western gunman) "*as an experience of art* is universal to Americans." Since violence plays a dominant and central theme in these art forms, it stands to reason that gangster and Western movies and TV shows have had an important bearing on our concept of and attitude toward violence.

The gangster has to be viewed against the background of the dominant values in American life, equality and achievement. Lipset[10] has traced the development of these two values since the beginning of the nineteenth century, and in his view these values have had a great deal to do with the extreme emphasis on success found in our society. To paraphrase Lipset, Americans are led to feel that the game must be won no matter what methods are

---

[9] R. Warshow, *The Immediate Experience* (Garden City, N.Y.: Doubleday, 1962), quotations from "The Gangster as Tragic Hero" and "Movie Chronicle: The Westerner."

[10] a. S. M. Lipset, "Equal or Better in America," Columbia University Forum, No. 4 (1961), pp. 17–21.
b. ———, "A Changing American Character?" in *Culture and Social Character,* S. M. Lipset and Leo Lowenthal, eds. (Glencoe, Ill.: Free Press, 1961).

employed to win it. The worst thing that can happen is to lose, and to be perceived as being a failure. This places a great deal of stress on the ends rather than on the means of attaining those ends. In contrast to the ethos of the more rigidly stratified societies, where the stress falls on the value of playing the game well, rather than on its result, in America there is a constant push to achieve, to get on, to get ahead; and with the emphasis on equality comes the feeling that one is as good as anyone else, and that one has the right to success no matter how it is achieved.

Sociologists have suggested that the much greater prevalence of organized vice and racketeering in America as compared with England and other affluent countries in northern Europe reflects the greater pressure on those with deprived social backgrounds to find illegal ways of succeeding when the more legitimate fields are closed to them. It has been suggested that the rackets must be seen as one of the principal ladders of social mobility among members of minority ethnic groups.

In the case of the film gangster the path to success, irrational brutality, becomes itself the mark or symbol of success. The more sadistic he is, the more successful, thus providing one more example of violence becoming an end in itself. As Warshow states the case, "Thus brutality itself becomes at once the means to success and the content of success—a success that is defined in its most general terms, not as accomplishment or specific gain, but simply as the unlimited possibility of aggression."

Warshow demonstrates how the gangster portrays the competitive dilemma of our society in which failure is the worst thing that can happen and success becomes impossible because of the guilty fear it evokes. "Failure is a kind of death and success is evil and dangerous, is—ultimately—impossible." Our enormous attraction to the gangster film is not based alone on the vicarious acting out of our violent aggressive impulses, but because the dilemma is resolved by the death of the gangster—it is his failure, not ours, his guilt is punished, not ours. Wertham may be right in his contention that the cultural emphasis on violence has a deleterious influence on our youth, but I submit that it is not violence in a total, abstract, or generic sense that is deleterious (for violence is a fact of life, some say even more of human than of animal life, and we had better find ways of facing and controlling it before it is too late) but it is the confusion of means and ends, the extolling of the violent act as a value in itself, or as a passionless instrument of gain, that is false, misleading, and perhaps ultimately disastrous.

The differences between this type of senseless or depersonalized violence and an act of passion is sharply etched by a comparison of the gangster film and the Western. In contrast to the gangster, the Westerner is a man of honor, with a code and a style of life that is inner-directed. The Westerner's autonomy dictates the "when" and "how" of violence—it is hardly ever needless, capricious, or sadistic. While the violent act may be the high point of the drama, it is the Westerner's honor which is at stake and which is the reason for the violence in the first place. His violence is marked by control and self-restraint. In this sense it comes close to the concept of force with its use of violence or threat of violence to restrain, control, and ultimately prevent greater violence.

The Western movie has such a great hold on our imagination, says Warshow, "because it offers a serious orientation to the problem of violence such as can be found almost nowhere else in our culture." We train ourselves to deny the possibilities of violence (a recent survey I made of the reactions to the Cuban crisis found among the patients of sixty New Orleans psychiatrists amply confirms this) or to be shocked or bored by actual or by symbolic images of violence, leading to our viewing violence quite unrealistically. Through hypocrisy or fear we tend to delegate our responsibilities for the control of violence to others—generally the more irresponsible or morally vulnerable. The Western movie gives us an example, which we still cherish, of a hero whose violence makes sense, in a world where senseless violence is a daily occurrence.

Gang Violence

As indicated earlier, teen-age gang violence is characterized by the value attached to the violent act itself, "coolly" carried out with little regard to the victim or to the purpose of the act. It is the violence itself that gives the gang member a sense of his own existence, as well as a sense of belonging to a group. A conformist whose greatest fear is to be left alone, ignored, or rejected by his gang, he has no sense of autonomy, of being able to influence or manipulate his environment in any constructive fashion.

The relationship of the rewarding effects of environmental feedback to the growth of such ego functions as exploration, attention and perception, language and thinking, manipulating the surroundings, and producing effective changes in his environment, have been extremely well described by White.[11] He has chosen the word "competence" to signify those processes by which the animal or child learns to interact effectively with its environment. This occurs through a continuous chain of transactional events which include stimulation, cognition, action, effect on the environment, new stimulation, etc., in a series of spiraling processes. As I see it, the basic defect in the member of a violent gang is the failure to achieve this sense of competence. He is unable to change his environment effectively, and he gradually loses his desire to attempt constructive changes. Although White does not talk about the delinquent youth, his words are, nonetheless, appropriate in this context:

> . . . Interest wanes when action begins to have less effect; effectance motivation [here White is referring to the motivation to effect meaningful changes in one's environment] subsides when a situation has been explored to the point that it no longer presents new possibilities.

Unable to believe in the generally held values of happiness and achievement, the gang member turns to violence as an existential

[11] R. W. White, "Motivation Reconsidered: The Concept of Competence," *Psychological Review* (1959), pp. 297–333.

act. In an interesting essay, the playwright Arthur Miller[12] presents a similar thesis—that the mainspring of action in the juvenile delinquent is boredom:

> The delinquent is stuck with his boredom, stuck inside it, stuck to it, until for two or three minutes he "lives"; he goes on a raid around the corner and feels the thrill of risking his skin or his life as he smashes a bottle filled with gasoline on some other kid's head. In a sense, it is his trip to Miami. It makes his day. It is his shopping tour. It gives him something to talk about for a week. It is *life*. Standing around with nothing coming up is as close to dying as you can get. Unless one grasps the power of boredom, the threat of it to one's existence, it is impossible to "place" the delinquent as a member of the human race.

If an act of violence can give the youth a feeling of existing, it can also, if carried to its ultimate limits, symbolize, par excellence, the purposelessness of life. Miller illustrates this by referring to a story of Andre Gide's:

> Gide wrote a story about a man who wanted to get on a train and shoot a passenger. Any train, any passenger. It would be a totally gratuitous act, an act devoid of any purpose whatever, an act of "freedom" from love, without love at all, with nothing in his heart but the sheerly physical contemplation of the gun barrel and the target. In doing this one would partake of death's irreproachable identity and commit an act in revolt against meaning itself, just as death is, in the last analysis, beyond analysis.

In similar fashion the "New Wave" movies of France and Italy often depict senseless, brutal acts of cruelty, in which the violence gives the perpetrator a measure of meaningfulness, while simultaneously revealing the alleged utter futility of life.

The aggressive play of a normal child is quite different from the sadistic "play" of the adolescent gang member. In the child, the emphasis is not on the violent act itself but on its meaning for the identity of the child. He is the hero, sometimes the victim, or

---

[12] A. Miller, "The Bored and the Violent," *Harper's* (1962), pp. 50–56.

even the villain—but the act has meaning, because it is the role-playing of a child experimenting with different identities. The gang member has foreclosed on his future role identifications; the future is closed to him except in terms of the consequences of violence directed against society or (as in drug addiction) against himself.

Genocide

The ultimate in dehumanized violence was the extermination of millions of Jews and other prisoners of the Nazis in the gas chambers of Auschwitz and the other concentration camps. The efficiency with which Eichmann ran the transportation system bringing the victims to the camps, the business methods used to make a profit of the prisoners' bodies and personal effects, "including dental gold, and the utilization of his body after his death—hair sold to make cloth, fat for soap, bones and ashes for glue and fertilizer (less 2 marks for the cost of cremation)" denote the nadir in the history of human degradation.

Alvarez[13] has recently described what Bettelheim[14] described earlier—the process of regression and personality disintegration until all spontaneity and will cease—until the prisoners become indifferent to all stimuli except food, and even that response disappeared before the end.

The inability to influence the environment developed into the inability to perceive stimuli because of the extreme danger of doing so. The SS deliberately fostered this complete loss of autonomy by calculated, passionless acts of violence. When the prisoners became walking corpses, or entered the "moslem stage," they would walk indifferently to the gas chamber. At first people's identities were replaced by numbers, but in the last stages the crowds on the way to the concentration camps were never even registered, "and oblivion took over."

If we were certain that the people who ran these chambers of

---

[13] A. Alvarez, "The Concentration Camps," *Atlantic* (1962), pp. 69–72.
[14] B. Bettelheim, *The Informed Heart* (Glencoe, Ill.: Free Press, 1960).

death so efficiently were sadists, who in another society would have been placed in institutions, we would be able to discuss this sickening chapter of history as proving only that our most sadistic fantasies can be acted out. But, in fact, it is quite certain that they were not sadists, but that they were efficient, dispassionate destroyers of personality and will. Given a certain combination of societal factors, especially those which promote automatic obedience, it "could happen here" or anywhere. If the process of dehumanization continues unchecked, given man's inventiveness, it is only a matter of which type of mass violence he will decide to use. At this point in time, the odds are in favor of nuclear extermination.

Nuclear Warfare

The process of detached, depersonalized violence which I have traced through some contemporary forms of violent activity—the gangster, the juvenile gang member, and the violence of the concentration camp—reaches its apogee in nuclear warfare. Even in the concentration camp where malevolence was at its greatest, even though the prisoner was deprived of his autonomy, his will, and his personality under the impact of the violent acts of his guards, there was still *personal* contact with his oppressors. Not so in nuclear war, where a button pushed will explode a missile thousands of miles away, killing millions of people who are faceless and completely unknown to the man pushing the button. What act of violence could be more dehumanized than that, except, perhaps, blowing up one's own countrymen? Rage or any other passion plays no part at all in such a process. In this act the executive functions of the ego—the action self if you prefer—are completely separated from the emotions. A form of *dissociation,* it is an act which could be, and in a special sense is, performed by a mechanical robot—a computer.

It is this view of human beings as numbers, statistics, interchangeable pieces in a vast numbers game, that brings with it a sense of noninvolvement and indifference to the actual or potential suffering of others and permits people to tolerate the implications of mass destruction in a nuclear war. Slowly and imperceptibly this attitude grows and permits us to view an irrational world situation as if it were rational, and permits us to make decisions based on an inner logic which seems sensible, just the way the paranoid's inner logic seems airtight once one accepts the original delusional premise.

While violence is universal, not all types of violence are. War is not. There is no evidence that there is anything in the nature of man which needs warfare as its outlet—and certainly not nuclear war, a type of violence which is completely irrelevant to man's emotional life. (This is not true of irrational, rageful, or guilt-laden acts which may trigger a nuclear detonation, which in turn may accidentally touch off a world-wide holocaust—hence the need for the Human Reliability Program[15] of our nuclear forces, currently in operation.) In William James's[16] day, there may have been a need for the moral equivalent of war, but what is the moral equivalent of nuclear war?

Psychological factors, however, do play an important role in all aspects of international relations, and are intimately involved in the processes which may lead to war. Aside from the probabilities of human error, and irrational reactions by subordinates with nuclear command decisions, there are ethnocentric misperceptions leading to mistrust, while mistrust leads to further perceptual distortions in a vicious circle, increasing the difficulties of an already difficult political situation. Tension further increases the rigidity and stereotypy of responses. As Van Atta[17] has stated:

> . . . Control of the arms race is not a problem of hardware design nor of technical schemes for carefully balanced disarmament,

---

[15] Department of the Air Force, *Guidance for Implementing the Human Reliability Program* (AFM 160–55, U.S. Government Printing Office, Washington, D.C.).

[16] W. James, "The Moral Equivalent of War," in *Memoirs and Studies* (New York: Longmans, Green, 1911), pp. 267–296.

[17] L. C. Van Atta, "Arms Control: Human Control," *American Psychologist.*

detection of weapons tests, or evaluation of war-making capabilities. . . . It is a problem of human understanding and human control.

Yes, man's basic emotions, rage and pride, are certainly at the root of international conflict, but nuclear war is not a sane solution for mankind's perennial struggle for possessions, power, or belief systems. We have paradoxically reached a point in our development as a species where the act of nuclear global devastation, the most violent act of all, is best done by computers, machines which cannot feel the brute emotions which have led us to the brink of disaster.

But I will make the assumption that there will always be something in the nature of man (at least for many generations to come) that requires violent solution. Every society has need of "hate satisfaction." I think, however, that if we can find ways of preventing the dissociation of emotions from the act of violence, we can probably prevent mass violence such as genocide and nuclear annihilation, while we find better ways of sublimating aggression, not only through international games, but through nonviolent international competition.

There are two possible programs we can initiate to deal with the threat of detached violence. We can no longer return to the violence of Medea or even of the Borgias, but we can and must find societal controls which prevent detached, dehumanized violence from being carried out. As one possibility, deterrence is most effective, not in the two-group situation, as between the U.S. and U.S.S.R., but when there is a third party wielding the power of deterrence. Certainly, this is the function of the police and judicial systems in civilized countries. Beatrice Whiting pointed out many years ago that those preliterate societies having superordinate institutions had recourse to much less magic and supernatural means of violent retaliation than did those societies lacking such institutions. By analogy, a superordinate institution, such as a greatly strengthened UN, should have the power of deterrence. This demands a sweeping change in political attitude in all the countries of the world, not only in ours. But the need is urgent and the times demand it.

A second program, ultimately more far-reaching in its consequences, is a revolutionary approach to education in which the realities of emotional life are taught to our children from the nursery on, in terms appropriate to each age group. Among others, Rado and Bettelheim have been advocates of such a program. It is only through such an intense educational effort over many generations that our cave-man emotions can be modified and brought into appropriate resonance with our technical genius.

PROJECTS

1. (a) Define "violence" as Beck sees the term.
   (b) Define "violence" as Lief sees the term.
   (c) Are these definitions compatible?

2. Beck notes that a football player implicitly surrenders, for the duration of the game, some of his rights as a person. Are there other individuals or groups who also implicitly surrender such rights? Consider: bank robbers, volunteer soldiers, revolutionaries, civil disobedients. What conditions do you suppose they have in mind, analogous to the rules controlling violence on the football field?

3. Lief identifies two kinds of "detached" violence, in which rage is not a factor, but the act of violence itself provides its own meaning. Can you add examples from recent events? Is military violence (non-nuclear) detached in the sense Lief means here?

4. Albert Camus writes in *The Rebel* that rebellion and communication are the opposites of violence and silence. Monologue, he states, precedes death. Arrange to see the film *Billy Budd* (123 min., $50.00 rental; write to Audio-Film Center, 34 MacQuesten Parkway So., Mount Vernon, New York, 10550) for a cinematic experience of this belief. Discuss the relationship of Billy Budd's dilemma to Camus' statements:

   (a) "If injustice is bad for the rebel, it is not because it contradicts an eternal idea of justice, but because it perpetuates the silent hostility that separates the oppressor from the oppressed. It kills the small part of existence that can be realized on this earth through the mutual understanding of men. In the same way, since the man who lies shuts himself off from other men, falsehood is therefore proscribed and, on a slightly lower level, murder and violence, which impose definitive silence. The mutual understanding and communication discovered by rebellion can survive only in the free exchange of conversation. Every ambiguity, every misunderstanding, leads to death; clear language and simple words are the only salvation from this death."[1]

(b) "Every rebel, solely by the movement that sets him in opposition to the oppressor, therefore pleads for life, undertakes to struggle against servitude, falsehood, and terror, and affirms, in a flash, that these three afflictions are the cause of silence between men, that they obscure them from one another and prevent them from rediscovering themselves in the only value that can save them from nihilism—the long complicity of men at grips with their destiny."[2]

5. Other film suggestions which relate to man's refusal to communicate with other men, and his lack of understanding of the meaning of violence are:

(a) *The Angry Breed* (100 mins., $30.00 rental)
(b) *The Angry Silence* (95 mins., $25.00 rental)
(c) *Cool Hand Luke* (129 mins., $65.00 rental)
(d) *King Rat* (134 mins., $35.00 rental)

(Inquire of Audio-Film Center, 34 MacQuesten Parkway So., Mount Vernon, New York, 10550.)

---

[1] Camus, Albert, *The Rebel: An Essay on Man in Revolt* (New York: A Vintage Book, 1956), p. 283.
[2] Camus, p. 284.

PART II
Polemics of Violence

The contradiction of rebellion,
then, is reflected in an apparently
insoluble contradiction, of which
the two counterparts in politics
are on the one hand the opposition
between violence and non-violence,
and on the other hand the opposition
between justice and freedom.

ALBERT CAMUS
The Rebel

During the course of your reading about human violence there may appear to be as many reasons for violence as there are acts of violence. In this part, Polemics of Violence, *you will find a number of explanations for human violence based on research in biology, psychology, religion, political science, and sociology. All of these explanations require careful evaluation so that you will be able to distinguish not only types of violence but also rationalizations for acts of violence. This kind of discernment provides a critical foundation for deciding whether a particular act of violence and an ethics for action can be entertained compatibly.*

The Biological Polemic

Introduction

Man's biological history is a fascinating source for explaining human acts of violence. The fact that man has an animal as well as human history prompts such individuals as Dr. Paul MacLean from the National Institute of Mental Health; Dr. Vernon Mark, director of neurosurgical services at Boston City Hospital; and Dr. Frank Ervin, director of the Stanley Cobb Laboratories of Psychiatric Research at Massachusetts General Hospital to examine the structure of the human brain for sources of violence.

To describe his findings, Dr. MacLean coined a new word, "schizophysiology," which indicates the disorderly state of affairs in the human central nervous system. There is a dichotomy, he explains, in the functioning of our human brain. Dr. MacLean compares the evolutionary development of the brain to the construction of a house to which wings and a superstructure are added. The three prototypes which make up this "house" are the reptilian, the old mammalian, and the new mammalian elements of the human brain.[1] "While our intellectual functions are carried on in the newest and most highly developed part of the brain (the new mammalian or neo-cortex), our affective behavior continues to be dominated by a relatively crude and primitive system, by archaic structures (reptilian) in the brain whose fundamental pattern has undergone but little change in the whole course of evolution, from mouse to man."[2] The consequences of this built-in schizophysiology range from so-called normal be-

---

[1] Dr. Paul MacLean, "Alternative Neural Pathways to Violence," in *Alternatives to Violence,* ed. Larry Ng (New York: Time-Life Books, 1968), pp. 24–34.

[2] As quoted by Arthur Koestler, "The Predicament of Man," from *Alternatives to Violence,* p. 23.

havior to behavior labelled "violent," "insane," "mentally deranged."

Taking their clue from this mixture of biological inheritance which constitutes the human brain, Dr. Mark and Dr. Ervin attempt to eliminate the "reptilian" influence by the use of anticonvulsive drugs or delicate brain surgery on patients who suffer from epileptic seizures and uncontrollable acts of violence. They describe in their book, *Violence and the Brain,* how they chart the cerebral geography of the brain of the patient by recording his subjective responses to little jolts of electric current. After locating the source of the difficulty on the patient's brain map, the doctors perform a type of brain surgery—if therapy and drugs have failed—whereby small clusters of cells are destroyed by heat from strong electrical stimulation delivered through implanted electrodes. The results of this operation on the isolated cases related by Ervin and Mark are encouraging. However, they are not advocating massive implantation of electrodes in human brains as the cure for man's violence. If we could be stopped in our tracks from an act of violence (as was Dr. José Delgado's bull[3]) by the sending of a radio signal to an electrode planted in our brain, we would be something less than human, perhaps bull. Both Dr. Ervin and Dr. Mark agree that the study of the biology of violence is only one approach to eliminating random violence in human life. In the sociology of violence poverty and social deprivation can combine forces to produce greater risks of brain damage. Malnutrition, disease, and the brutality of daily life in an urban slum are ample proof of the risks. All the specialists in this field—including MacLean, Ervin, and Mark—indicate the importance of the study of the chemistry and geography of the human brain but not in isolation from or in disregard of the human social environment.

[3] Dr. Delgado of Yale University has performed two radio-controlled experiments on animals. He has stopped a bull in mid-charge and turned a monkey into a peace-maker in spite of the aggressive acts of its cagemate by the sending of radio signals to electrodes implanted in the animals' brains.

It is at this juncture—the relationship between the evolution of the human brain and the evolution of human social behavior—that a new scientific study, ethology, involves itself in the examination of human violence. Ethology, the scientific study of animal behavior, relates the patterns of instinctual animal behavior to human behavior. Its conclusions reach the best-seller lists through such books as Konrad Lorenz's *On Aggression*, Desmond Morris' *The Naked Ape*, Robert Ardrey's *The Territorial Imperative*. Man, the ethologists assert, possesses genetic endowments (inborn instincts) which are products of his evolutionary development. These endowments make up man's basic nature, expressing themselves in acts of selfishness, suspicion, acquisitiveness, and violence. According to the ethologists, the correlation between this innate endowment and the instinctual behavior of animals provides the type of insight essential for an understanding of human violence.

The three articles in this section are concerned with this ethological position, which sees both the human brain and human behavior in relationship to man's evolutionary history. The first article, "The Violent Way," is an excerpt from Robert Ardrey's latest book, *The Social Contract*. Born in Chicago, Ardrey developed his interest in the sciences of man at the University of Chicago. After graduation, he enjoyed a successful career as a playwright, before returning to the scientific study of man. A visit to Africa culminated in the writing of his book *African Genesis* (1961), the forerunner of his two other popular books, *The Territorial Imperative* (1966) and *The Social Contract* (1970).

The second article, "Is Man a Gorilla with a Gun?," is a direct reaction against Ardrey's *African Genesis* and the ethologist's premise regarding man's nature. Written by the late Thomas Merton, it reflects the criticism of a man whose interests ranged from contemplation in the style of eastern and western mysticism to social reform in the spirit of absolute pacifism. Merton was born in France, taught English at Columbia University, and then, in 1941, entered the Abbey of Gethsemani in Kentucky to become a Trappist (Cistercian) Monk. He is well known for his books of poetry, essays and religious thought, the most famous being his autobiography, *The Seven Storey Mountain.*

The final essay, "Man and Beast," is by Morton Hunt, a professional journalist and free-lance writer. His critical interest in ethology may have a direct correlation to his latest book, *The Affair: A Portrait of Extra-Marital Love in Contemporary America,* as well as to his other best-known books: *The Natural History of Love* and *Her Infinite Variety: The American Woman as Lover, Mate and Rival.*

The Violent Way

ROBERT ARDREY

In 1958 John Calhoun at Washington's National Institute of Mental Health decided to see what would happen to a rat population if he forced overcrowding. An experiment was conducted indoors, under controlled conditions, and its chief ingenuity was an arrangement of four interconnecting pens. The two end pens each had but one entrance which could be guarded by a strong male rat. But the middle pens, each with two entrances, could not be so guarded and so became the center of free social action. As the population rose, the action in these middle pens became such an animal nightmare that Calhoun was to describe it as a "behavioral sink."

In each pen was an abundance of food, water and nesting materials, along with artificial burrows for nesting mothers. And each was large enough to accommodate comfortably a group of 12 adult rats, the number that Calhoun had earlier learned was a normal size in a natural population. But as numbers rose and crowding took place, nothing like an even distribution of numbers occurred in the pens, just as nothing like equivalent behavior developed.

At the beginning of the experiment a natural status struggle took place among the males. The most powerful alphas—those individuals that rise to dominant roles in any animal population—each took possession of an end pen. Since there was but one entrance, each had only to take his position beside it to guard the pen and keep order within it. Here his harem of females made their nests undisturbed. Calhoun wrote, "In essence the dominant male established his territorial dominion and his control over a harem of females not by driving the other males out but by preventing their return." He slept by the entrance, paying no attention to the comings and goings of his females. If a male appeared, he was instantly alert, but he would tolerate the entrance of one who accepted his dominance. Such subordinates frequently slept in the pen. They never interfered with the females or attempted copulation. In general the harem females made good mothers, built proper nests, nursed and protected their young, and raised about half to weaning. But if there was order in the end pens, there was chaos in the middle.

As population rose, its weight fell on the unprotected middle pens. Here there was a class of dominant males, but they could hold no territories and fighting was frequent. Rank order shifted with victories and defeats. There emerged also a middle class frequently attacked by the alphas but rarely contending. They were sexually active but seemed unable to discriminate between estrous and nonestrous females, or even between females and juveniles. And then there were the inevitable losers, the last-in-line, the totally subordinated omegas who "moved through the community like somnambulists," who ignored all others and were ignored by all. To look at them, they seemed sometimes the fattest and sleekest, and they remained unscarred by combat. These were the dropouts.

So far, such a class structure in a crowded population might be expected. But with further crowding a class quite beyond prediction emerged. Calhoun called them "the probers." They were subordinate but active, and it was an essentially criminal class. They moved sometimes in gangs. Attacked by a dominant, they never contended yet were never discouraged. They took no part at all in the status struggle, but they were the most active males in the colony. Hypersexual, they were also bisexual, and frequently cannibalistic too. Most astonishing was their tendency toward an action which can only be called rat rape. The normal male rat has a courtship ritual. If he pursues a female to her burrow he waits outside for her to emerge and accept. He never enters. But the probers dispensed with all courtship, chased females into burrows, sometimes trampling and killing the young with abandon. Following their sexual activity, if dead babies lay about, they ate them.

The disorder of the middle pens disrupted female life more

than male. Nest-building suffered first, and throughout the last half of the experiment no nests were built at all. Infants were scattered, abandoned, eaten. Whereas infant mortality in the protected end pens was held to 50%, in the middle pens it rose to 96%. Half of the females themselves died of pregnancy disturbances or sexual assault.

Calhoun's experiment, with all its horrifying human implications, caused wide comment. Yet one observation has been little recorded. The rats enjoyed the behavioral sink. The females in particular seemed incapable of resisting the social excitement of the middle pens. Protected harem females sought the middle pens when in estrus, without interference from their overlords. Although food and water were available in the protected pens, almost all sought the middle-pen hoppers. Their behavior in the rat mob was no different from that of the nonharem females. The one advantage protecting their young was the peace and the order of the end pens, to which they could retreat. But while the end-pen alphas never left their estates, only a very small percentage of their females could resist the crowd.

Few will quarrel with the proposition that overcrowding has profound effects on human behavior. As we consider the effect on animals, however, we may properly wonder whether Calhoun's behavioral sink presents a fair analogy. His subjects were domesticated rats responding to the artificial conditions of a laboratory. Could the same drastic consequences come about among wild animals, living in a state of nature? By good fortune we may turn to three independent studies of the langur, a member of our own primate family, living under varying conditions of population density in its native India and Ceylon.

The earliest observations of the langur were made by Phyllis Jay Dolhinow in certain forests of central India where the monkeys are fairly scarce. Each troop has a range of about two square miles and rarely comes into contact with another. While troops tend to avoid or ignore each other, there is no conflict if contact occurs. There are no defended territories, and no evident boundaries between groups. Within each troop's little society males have a rigid rank order in which every individual knows his place. They almost never quarrel.

The langurs of India's central forests seemed the ideal, sunny, nonaggressive creatures of legend, and Dolhinow's study, completed in 1959, did much to reinforce the arguments of those primate students that monkeys never fight, never defend territory, never do anything but behave themselves in a fashion rarely glimpsed in human schoolyards.

Then, however, Suzanne Ripley made her equally careful study of langurs in Ceylon. Her troops were of about the same size as those Dolhinow observed. But nowhere did there exist those infinite distances for the happy, wandering life. Instead of two square miles in India's central forests, a troop in Ceylon occupied only a half to as little as an eighth of a square mile. And here there were not only territories, with actively defended, unchanging borders, but groups sought combat.

It is important to note that for these leaf-eating monkeys no shortage of food inspired conflict. Even the most arid zones of forest could carry numbers well beyond the actual population. Neither was any great damage inflicted by the continual conflict. Despite what must be described as violent behavior, still in the best territorial tradition a maximum of excitement was generated with a minimum of physical harm. And finally, the aggression directed outward infected not at all relations within the group. Although all groups studied by Ripley contained at least two adult males, and one contained six, harmony and cooperation were near-perfect. Even females joined with their males in the territorial battles. This record of inner harmony was not to be duplicated in the third study.

Yukimaru Sugiyama of Kyoto University encountered in the Dharwar forest of western India the most extreme population density of langurs yet recorded. Dolhinow's had been less than 20 per square mile, Ripley's in Ceylon about 150. Sugiyama's was over 250. Whether density was the only factor contributing to social breakdown Sugiyama could not know, but disorder approached perfection. There were territories but borders were obscure and ill-defended. When troops met, leaders fought unassisted. Neither were there the rigid rank orders of dominance so characteristic of Dolhinow's widely separated groups. Perhaps as a consequence almost all troops had only one adult male, though there might be six or 10 adult females. Sugiyama speculated that without a hierarchy regulating the relationships of males, quarrels were so disruptive that only one male usually remained. The expelled males formed their own groups in the forest.

When the sexual season approached its peak an all-male gang, with no more inhibition than Calhoun's prober rats, would descend on a troop containing females, kill or drive off the leader and any subadult males, and fight among themselves for sexual sovereignty. Far from mourning their departed overlord, the females would respond to the action with enhanced sexual stimulation and copulate with the conqueror. The episode would reach its climax when the conqueror bit to death all the infants.

Here is violent behavior on a scale unprecedented in primate observation, and it seems a direct consequence of overcrowding. Of Sugiyama's nine troops under direct observation, such scenes of riot overwhelmed four troops in a season. It is true that the slaughter of the innocents provided a form of population control. But I doubt that this is more than a by-product of social breakdown, of the triumph of disorder over order, of aggression no longer subject to social channels spilling over without inhibition into monkey immorality.

Organized society, contrary to both common and academic assumption since the days of Jean Jacques Rousseau, is not a human invention. Whether we observe the langur or rat, the lion or elephant we observe species that are no different from us in the inability of the individual to survive alone. As we face a common fact of life with these animal species, we accept with them the common necessity of group existence. Without the group we should all perish.

In such groups, animal and human, there is always a problem: to construct sufficient order so that the group may act as one in behalf of the individual, yet preserve sufficient disorder—what men would call freedom—so that diverse social partners may each fulfill their varying potentials. The problem is solved by an organizing principle which I term the social contract. This contract, which animals under normal conditions accept instinctively, provides a delicate balance between the necessary order and the necessary disorder without which vulnerable beings could not survive.

Like the territorial imperative, the social contract is a biological mechanism of selective value, restraining yet enhancing individual capacities. Territory defends the individual through control of exclusive space; the social contract defends him through concert of numbers. But it is a fragile mechanism. As the social order contains and channels our innate aggressiveness, so with environmental change it may be an object itself of aggression until new balances are restored. Any rapid change in the circumstance of species may leave order and disorder grotesquely out of balance. Such has been the change throughout the last half century in man's relation to space.

What we are just beginning to learn about the human significance of space stems almost entirely from the observations of Heini Hediger, who first established the concept of individual distance. On a March day in 1938, in Zurich's Bellevue Square, he noticed black-headed gulls sitting on the lakeside parapet. The gulls had arranged themselves evenly, just two railings apart. His curiosity caught, Hediger began watching other species. Flamingos demand twice the distance, about two feet, whereas swallows will settle for six inches. All these and many others are "distance species," but there are also "contact/togetherness species" with quite opposite inclinations. Tortoises, some monkeys and lemurs, even owls and spiny hedgehogs will crowd together in an animal pile. But such species are a minority.

The master zoo keeper extended his observations to animal training. The distance an animal demands between himself and an enemy is of a special sort, a "flight distance." Small animals tend to demand less, large animals more. But flight distance will vary according to accustomed conditions. In a protected African reserve baboons normally may not move away until you have come within 20 yards, whereas in unprotected areas they will take flight at a hundred. It is the reduction of flight distance that is known as taming. When it reaches zero, the animal is a pet.

So new is scientific concern with the spacing of animals that discussion has not yet evolved reliable terminology with definitions agreed by all. Hediger's "individual distance" has become "personal space," and as we have seen may vary with individuals in its dimension. Likewise it is widely accepted that personal space may vary with seasons. The lapwing or chaffinch may gather in quite tight little flocks in winter, but with the first sexual stirrings of the breeding season disperse to scattered, strenuously defended territories in which the demand for space is maximum. In our examination of the human crowd we have at least a language for individual contacts. But for the contacts of groups we have few such terms.

Besides individual distance Hediger gave us the term "social distance," to describe the farthest point that an animal will go as it strays from its group. The social distance of a group, in other words, may be expressed as a measure of its scatter. A baboon troop, scattering widely as it feeds, exhibits its maximum of social distance. But as dusk draws on, distance will rapidly shrink until all go to sleep in a few close trees. Social distance, then, is a measure of animal need for the familiar, and this too is a term we can agree on. But for the opposite and probably more powerful social force, the rejection of strangers, I can find no term in the literature.

I dislike and regard as an arrogance the contribution of terms to established sciences. But since this discussion cannot proceed without such terms, I shall refer to this social rejection of strangers as animal xenophobia.

Animal xenophobia is as widespread a trait among social species as any single trait we can study. A limited group of familiars, many of them perhaps with kinship relation, know each other as individuals. Each has learned what to expect of his neighbor, and in such groups sufficient order comes easily. But the stranger presents a problem. Infrequently—most infrequently—his admission will be tolerated. If it occurs, however, normal procedure will probably condemn him to the bottom of the social rank where his potential for social disruption will be minimum. Xenophobia guarantees the integrity of the group, and the least possible chance of disorder.

Until the spectacular rise of the city, human social life in many ways bore reasonable resemblance to the life of normal animal species. Space sheltered us. Xenophobia between villages might be as marked as between animal groups, and as satisfying, but social space was abundant. Personal space was ample too, and if we did not like each other nothing compelled us to look at each other too closely. We competed, of course, as men will always compete for the conventional prizes of territory, wealth, alpha position. But as long as space was our abundant asset, the territory with a fence around it was a goal that all could seek.

For every territory there is a proprietor, an alpha who has won his conventional prize. Not even, of course, in the rural society of orchard and garden, small-town grocery store or dry-goods shop do all men become proprietors. Still, the alphas are many and the prizes remain real. But as urban concentration grows and competition shifts from dominance over a piece of space to dominance over fellow men, not only do we encounter the hierarchy of despotism from which territorial man was largely protected but we encounter a vanishment of alphas. Prizes grow fewer. And as we press farther into the ever-condensing mass we find ever-enlarging human organizations, be they corporations or labor unions, political groupings or taxpayers' protest meetings. And as organizations become larger alpha ranks become fewer.

In the United States of America the normal curve of genetic endowment would suggest that at least 10 million people are potential alphas competing as they must for a diminishing number of alpha slots. Their aggressive potentiality is uncontainable within a society of diminishing prizes. Equally stark, however, is the problem of the condemned omega. When men turned earth with a spade, moved coal with a shovel, cut hay with a scythe, carried hods on their backs, the body could support human dignity though the brain be inadequate. Such work in a highly organized, highly technological society is all but gone. As opportunity for the demanding alpha is withdrawn, so refuge for the condemned omega ceases to exist. The frustrations of urban society reveal in nakedness what our earlier rural societies modestly clothed: the innate, random inequality of men.

The city is a cultural invention enforcing on the citizen knowledge of his own nature. And this we do not like. That we are aggressive beings easily given to violence; that we get along together more because we must than because we want to, and that the brotherhood of man is about as far from reality today as it was two thousand years ago; that reason's realm is small; that we never have been and never shall be created equal; that if the human being is perfectible, he has so far exhibited few symptoms—all are considerations of man from which space tends to protect us.

And yet the city is not a concentration camp. Most of us go there not as slaves or prisoners, but as volunteers. Just as Calhoun's rats freely chose to eat in the middle pens, we freely enter the city. Overcrowding is a voluntary condition.

But overcrowding, as we saw in the langur studies, can lead to a breakdown in the social structure, which in turn calls forth urban disaster. No example is more illuminating than the violence and the regime of fear that invest American urban life. That regime is as perfect in a relatively uncrowded Kansas City as in the massed densities of a Chicago or New York. Were overcrowding the cause, then this could not be so. What we witness is the drunken tottering of a social structure supported by an inadequate philosophy. Tremors first may become evident where numbers are densest. But while overcrowding may test, advance and display a social weakness, it cannot be the ultimate cause.

Aggressiveness, by definition, is the determined pursuit of one's interests. Violence is the pursuit of such interests through force, or the threat of force. They are not the same.

Without aggression as an inborn force, survival throughout all the natural world would be impossible. But likewise survival dictates aggression's limits. Without traffic laws, aggression is a drunken driver in a lethal midnight. As no population could survive without sufficient numbers sufficiently aggressive, so no population could survive were competitions customarily carried to deadly conclusion. And so has evolved throughout the species that body of rules and regulations of infinite variety which while encouraging the aggressive discourages the violent. The problem of man is not that we are aggressive but that we break our own rules.

Any species must risk extinction when aggressiveness finds its fences in ruin and violence an ever-available entertainment. But the social species risk most. For beings who are biologically dependent on the group, whose existence is impossible without the cooperation of one's fellows, the violent solution of natural disagreement becomes a form of suicide.

There are two quite different expressions of human violence: the struggles within groups of social partners and the struggles between organized societies. The second is war, and I regard it as the lesser threat to our future. War today is either unwinnable or inconclusive, as the present stalemates in Vietnam and the Near East would indicate, or it is nuclear catastrophe. Neither kind is very satisfactory. So, human violence, once expressed on the battlefield, is today being transferred to the city's streets.

There is a paradox involved. Organized warfare, although an exercise exclusively human in the vertebrate world, received reinforcement from natural law, whereas civil violence breaks every rule of social species. Intolerable though the damage of warfare might be, still it united societies, strengthened social contracts and gave outlet for animal xenophobia. But war is technologically obsolete, and its civil substitute biologically unendurable. If we are to prepare ourselves for any profound understanding of sabotage, riot, political kidnappings and assassination, then we should first inspect carefully the concept of the stranger.

I have referred to the universality of animal xenophobia. The stranger is driven out of a group's social space and physically attacked if his attentions persist. The howling monkey roars, alerting his fellows in the clan; the spider monkey barks; the lion without ceremony attacks. However the animosity for strangers is expressed, whether through attack or avoidance, xenophobia is there, and it is as if throughout the animal world invisible curtains hang between the familiar and the strange.

We have in our genetic endowment the tendency to reject strangers and, if we are to read objectively the history of civilized man, a probable propensity for violence. War may be nearly abolished, but these tendencies are not. All that is vanishing from the human scene is the cultural institution that once provided satisfaction for both without damage to social integrity. We are faced with the question, "How do we get along without war?" Subconsciously we transform our cultural channel. We transfer energies once directed outward to the inward expression known as social violence. But such an expression presents an intriguing problem, for now we must invent strangers.

The invention of strangers must be the prime foundation for the future of civil violence. And the prime ingredient for the invention of strangers must be noncommunication between those who speak the same language, share the same territory.

Students and faculty, for example, could never have accomplished in our universities even their tentative scuffles of violence and destruction if either group had not been richly provided with noncomprehension concerning the other. The universities present an excellent example indeed, since here presumably the same language is spoken with fluency, authority and precision. Yet on many a campus the handicap has been overcome so overwhelmingly that noncommunication flourishes and the supply of strangers becomes as bountiful as the enticements of violence may demand.

The achievement of the universities admittedly has been nourished by the achievements of the floundering home. A few old-fashioned families may still cling to a degree of affection and toleration, but as we all know understanding between parents and children has been for long on the way out. What goes on in the parent becomes as mysterious to the young as what the young are up to remains a mystery to the parent.

One of the few flaws that I can see in the crystalline future of civil disorder is the improbability of organized violence between parents and young. While mutual noncomprehension may reach the most perfect level, while the creation of strangers has already attained conspicuous success, while hostility flourishes and conditions of downright enmity sometimes prevail, still something is lacking. And I believe it is because the young, organized into a legion by the peer-group, face in that stranger, the parent, too contemptible, too pathetic, too bewildered an object for worthy attack. Old battered shipwrecks floating on new seas, parents tempt few guns. And the aggressive energies of their offspring are redirected to such satisfying targets as the universities and the police.

In America blacks and whites, parents and young, students and faculties have demonstrated the workability of noncommunication, the creation of strangers, and the transformation of acceptable aggressiveness into unaccepted civil violence.

A touch of paranoia is inevitable if members of a subgroup are to test their strength against the weight of a majority. Any sense of injustice, however real, must be aggrandized to a point where risk becomes tolerable. Yet I find myself doubtful that such social scenes should be characterized as neurotic, since we neglect a prime fact: that the youth with a paving stone in his hand is enjoying himself.

We enjoy the violent, just as Calhoun's rats sought the middle pens. We hurry to an accident not to help; we run to a fire not to put it out; we crowd about a schoolyard fight not to stop it. For all the Negro's profound and inarguable grievances, there has not been a racial outbreak in America since the days of Watts in which a degree of carnival atmosphere has not prevailed. I myself may have no great taste for Molotov cocktails; it is because I am timid, not because I am good. Gerald Suttles, in his work with juvenile gangs in the Chicago slums, found that the reliability of gang members to join in an action could be analyzed: stealing might attract a fair number, but the prospect of a fight would enlist almost all.

Action and destruction are fun. The concerned observer who will not grant it indulges in a hypocrisy which we cannot afford. He who regards a taste for violent action as a human perversion will not likely make any great contribution to the containment of our violent way. Similarly, the observer who seeks nothing but earnest motivation in riot and arson, who looks only to environmental deprivation, neglect, or injustice to explain it—who in other words seeks wholly in the action of the majority the motivations of the minority—may flatter himself one day that he was violence's most dependable ally.

As one views the vistas of violent behavior rising before contemporary man, a conclusion comes with too great ease that we are finished. Since men can live neither with each other nor without, extinction seems in the cards. But any such conclusion is superficial. The social contract is an arrangement of biological validity. Like the sexual impulse or human diversity, it acts, in its balancing of order and disorder, to preserve the species with a power far beyond human predilection. What is at stake in our times is not the survival of man, but the survival of man's most rewarding invention, democracy, and the proposition that man can achieve social order through voluntary action.

There is visible throughout all nature a bias in favor of order. It is an explicable force that commands the orbits of planets about their sun, moons about their planets. Order invests all organic and inorganic processes, and while hindsight may exaggerate it, still order is there. Evolution and natural selection are no more than names for those orderly, long-term processions which any may observe in the history of species. That animal treaties are honored; that baboons do not commit suicide in wars of troop against troop; that kittiwakes successfully defend their cliff-hung properties and raise their young; that lions and elephants restrict their numbers so that a habitat will not be exhausted by too many offspring; that when species can no longer meet the challenge of environment they must quietly expire: all such transactions of animals furnish simple testimony to the prejudices of order in natural ways. The contract will provide order within human societies, whether through voluntary or involuntary means.

Humans share with other higher animals three innate needs which demand satisfaction. The first is identity, the opposite of anonymity, and it is the highest. The second is stimulation, the opposite of boredom. The lowest is security, the opposite of anxiety.

These innate needs—identity, stimulation and security—form a dynamic triad. Achievement of security and release from anxiety present us with boredom. It is the psychological process least appreciated by our social planners. Increasing affluence, and decreasing economic anxiety, is producing the bored society described by Desmond Morris in *The Human Zoo.*

The bored society could not be a reality, however, were we other than the anonymous society stripped in large part of our opportunity to search for identity. It is the most pressing of motives—to know who we are in our own eyes but even more in the eyes of our fellows. Territory satisfies it in animals, as does social rank. Egalitarianism, that most admired of human possibilities by the unsophisticated young, joins hands with the anonymity of enlarging organizations so despised by the young to contribute in equal measure to the defeat of identity's satisfaction. And so the frustration of the search for identity from above, just as much as the achievement of security from below, forces the member of a contemporary society into the unendurable area of boredom. Imprisoned by both affluence and anonymity, no way presents itself but stimulation.

Pornography and riot are of a piece. They are means of stimulation. By no coincidence at all have waves of shock and sensation arrived simultaneously on the scene of advanced contemporary societies. The exhibitions of demonstrators raising the blood pressure of their close-packed groups and the exhibitions of fashion of the female body hopefully raising the blood pressure of the passing male—their appeal is the same. The private titillations of the *voyeur* with his photographs from Denmark and the private hallucinations of the sense-stretching trip with its weeds from Mexico—these too are the same. Sexual adventures among adolescents, casual adultery among their jaded elders, the display of nudity and intercourse on the screen or stage, the robbing of houses by affluent burglars, the sense-assaulting decibels of electronic music paralyzing the brains of its listeners, the baring of waitresses' breasts for the excitement of timid gentlemen, the public display of illegitimacy in the obstetrical arrangements of the famous, the public display in the literary content of ancient, commonplace terms of the street by authors with larger vocabularies available—all provide stimulation for shocker and shocked alike in bored societies with nowhere else to go.

And violence, too, is stimulating. It carries excitement for both violator and violated, whether through the joyful hatreds of the one or the fearful rages of the other. A riot in Chicago is worth all the circuses that old time emperors could provide. And like any other form of sensual shock, violence to retain its stimulation must proceed to stronger or more novel levels of expression. That adaptable animal, the human being, habituates himself all too easily to any present situation.

I believe that, as we refer to the triad of innate needs—identity, stimulation, security—we shall glimpse more clearly the difference in actions seemingly so much of a piece. We are pressed into stimulation by the flight from boredom which itself has been induced by both security and denial of identity. But novel sensory experiences satisfy only our need for stimulation. Violent experiences tend to satisfy not only stimulation but identity as well. The violent are applauded. Whether the applause be the praise of collaborators or the condemnation of antagonists, the little world of violence is recognized, identified, released from anonymity.

Such a cancerous world upholds its own values, defends its own territory, establishes its own rules, praises its own alphas, scorns or ignores its own omegas, punishes its own traitors. Whatever the nature of this little world of criminal or political conspirators, of the juvenile gang, or grim old dedicated members of the establishment of power, of rebellious militants whatever their sources of grievance or purpose, whatever indeed may be the long-term justification, still much the same processes of all the violent subgroups prevail: there is noncommunication, elimination of social compassion for the outsider. There is xenophobia, released by noncommunication to identify the majority of our social partners as the enemy. There is an illusion of central position, justifying one's own purposes as right and everybody else's as wrong, and providing a proper degree of paranoia. Righteous ends, thus proved, absolve of guilt the most violent means. And within this little world a new fellowship blooms, a new communication flourishes, anonymity vanishes, identity again becomes possible.

But the violent subgroup, even as it asserts itself, defeats itself. The student depends on the postman if he is to receive his check from home. The postman depends on the milkman if his infant children are to survive. The milkman depends on the dentist, unless he renounces toothaches. The dentist depends on the telephone system if the milkman is to make an appointment. The telephone system depends on God knows whom, black or white, if bells are to ring. And the black man depends on the ring of the telephone if he is to have hope of organizing any but an amateur riot. So it goes.

Violent subgroups now threaten our modern society. But at the same time the very intricacy of our social interdependence threatens the survival of these violent little worlds. The animal cannot stand alone, and least of all animals, modern man.

Long before total social disorder can take place, human foresight, combined with our biological need for order, should have taken command. The question we cannot now answer is when. Shall sufficient of us glimpse the road to disaster in time?

If we do, then with whatever pain we shall accept certain compromises, surrender certain rights which we believe sacred, provide prizes of identity which we now deny, contain our violent confrontations within such ritualized aggressions as negotiation, seek to correct those genuine injustices which lend respectability to violent arrangements and discourage social applause for the violator.

And if we do not? If we lack the will or the vision to see what waits for us?

A few years ago our eminent journalist and historian of the making of Presidents, Theodore H. White, published a play called *Caesar at the Rubicon*. While Rome sank deeply into anarchy, Julius Caesar by agreement stayed with his powerful army beyond the river. The play, of course, concerns his final reluctant decision to break the agreement, proceed to Rome and assume dictatorial power. And it closes with a simple comment worthy of being stamped on the coin of every democracy: "If men cannot agree on how to rule themselves, someone else must rule them."

If we have not the foresight, if we have not the will, then we shall discover one day who waits beyond our Rubicon.

Is Man a Gorilla with a Gun?

THOMAS MERTON

"Extrapolation," say the dictionaries, "is the method of finding by calculation, based on the known terms of a series, other terms, whether preceding or following." The method is proper to mathematics and works efficiently when dealing with number and quantity. When it is transferred to the realm of quality and of organic life, more still to that of history and of culture, it tends to lose its precisely exact scientific quality and becomes a venture in creativity, or even a work of fantasy. Imagination now takes the place of calculation. There can be no doubt that the scientist who seeks to learn the origin of man from a fossilized remnant of a skull that might have belonged to man or to a baboon must be blessed with a creative imagination as well as with a scientifically exact intelligence. I suppose that when Robert Ardrey, a playwright rather than a professional scientist, subtitles his book,[1] "A personal investigation into the animal origins and nature of man," he is serving notice that he intends to extrapolate with unrestrained imaginative abandon. At any rate, this is what he does!

There is of course a good basis of scientific evidence in *African Genesis.* The most recent discoveries of palaeontology made in Africa, especially the most notable, those of Dr. L. S. B. Leakey at Olduvai in Tanganyika, give very convincing indications that the origin of man was in Africa not in Asia. The Olduvai gorge is a deep canyon, fantastically rich in fossils and in primitive tools, which has preserved a seemingly complete and continuous record of the million year period in which man appeared. And here it must be clearly said that the conclusions of this very tendentious book differ radically from those of Dr. Leakey, who is certainly the most credible authority on the subject. Dr. Leakey says that the tools at Olduvai were the work of man in his earliest known form (*Zinjanthropus*). Mr. Ardrey's thesis is that the tools are the work not of man but of an ape. Indeed of an inferior ape, a vegetarian and pacifist ape, who was not even to be the "ancestor of man." The real ancestor of man in Ardrey's thesis was an ape who made not tools but weapons—and was a killer.

So while admitting that L. S. B. Leakey is a "great scientist," Mr. Ardrey says that on this point he has gone wrong, misled by sentimentality and romanticism. The term "romantic fallacy" occurs everywhere in the book, and is used to discredit any and every theory of man's origin which does not admit that he is a descendant, in the direct line, from a "killer ape." And therefore it must be said that the reader who picks up this book looking for precise and coherent information about the important new discoveries in Africa is himself the victim of an illusion. What information there is concerns mainly the discoveries and hypotheses of certain South Africans whom Mr. Ardrey greatly admires,

---

1 Robert Ardrey, *African Genesis* (New York: Atheneum, 1961).

and even this information is buried in autobiographical reminiscence, picaresque anecdote and pages of philosophical improvization.

On the basis of the remote possibility that there were, in Africa, perhaps a million years ago, tool-and-weapon-using hominids, or pre-human apes, Mr. Ardrey delivers a very aggressive homily in atheistic evolutionism. He attacks not only the traditional Christian world-view but also, much more radically, the world-views of Marx, Freud, Darwin and practically everyone else you can think of. One theory of man after another is tossed out the window with glorious enthusiasm as "romantic fallacy" —and all because some ape seems to have picked up the leg bone of an antelope and used it to crack the skull of one of his fellows. This is all the author needs in order to reconstruct entirely all social philosophy, all history, all anthropology, all psychology, all economics. For Mr. Ardrey, this one monumental act of violence explains everything.

Homo sapiens is therefore, he declares, the direct "legitimate" descendent of a transitional, carnivorous, erect-walking, right-handed and weapon-using anthropoid. Because this ape was no ordinary mild-mannered vegetarian, no "generalized fruit-eating ape," but a ruthless "killer ape," man emerged. Man is, according to Ardrey, the child not only of the ape but of the weapon. It was "the weapon that fathered man." Not only that, but Mr. Ardrey even goes so far as to hint that, instead of man developing weapons for himself, he was in some way developed by biology to be a user of weapons. "Whether man is in fact a biological invention to suit the purposes of the weapon must be a matter of future debate." Whatever that debate may be, to suppose that instead of weapons being developed for man, man was developed for weapons is carrying alienation pretty far! But it is quite characteristic of Mr. Ardrey's world-view and of its South African sources. The consequence follows immediately. Man is by his very nature an inventor and user of weapons and a defender of territory. The essence of human nature is therefore not so much rationality as trigger-happiness, or at least club-happiness and "territoriality." Even sex is set aside as a secondary, relatively meaningless urge compared with man's essential drive to beat up anything and anyone that threatens to invade his "territory." Yes, "territory" is very important here, crucially important. Man is not really interested in woman, in love, in the warmth of satisfied libido (as Freud may have thought). Man is not so deeply engaged in making a living that his very existence is shaped and dominated by the system of production (according to Marxist ideas). Man is an ape that goes berserk when he thinks he is running out of *Lebensraum,* and I must admit that Mr. Ardrey's description of two rival teams of howling monkeys trying to jam each others' broadcasts is very suggestive of modern political life.

The chief contention of Robert Ardrey's high-powered social message is that any philosophy, religious or otherwise, which takes an optimistic view of man, regards him as basically rational and progressive, and postulates that he can better himself by using his intelligence to improve his social system, is basically a "romantic illusion." It is absurd, says Mr. Ardrey, to hope that man can settle his differences over "territory" by means of arbitration rather than by bombs. "Man is a predator whose natural instinct is to kill with a weapon." It is fortunate that some members of the human race are still capable of thinking otherwise (for instance Pope John XXIII in his encyclical *Pacem in Terris*).

Quite apart from religious faith and Christian hope, it seems to me that Mr. Ardrey's thesis negates any real hope there may be for man in evolutionism. After all, the theory of natural selection postulates that a species is able to survive by progressive adaptation to new and more difficult conditions. We armed gorillas have now reached a rather crucial point in our evolutionary development in which "killing with a weapon" is about the least effective way of settling our problems and guaranteeing our survival. It would seem that if we cannot get beyond the stage where we seem to have been a million years ago, in other words, if we cannot adapt to a new situation and settle our problems by reason instead of with clubs, we are soon going to be as extinct as any dinosaur. The amusing thing about all that is that we are a species that has been given the choice of survival or non-survival. We have very large skulls and, presuming there is still a proportionate content inside them, it is up to us to make use of it for something besides inventing ways to blow ourselves up. This is so obvious that even Mr. Ardrey, after ignoring and skirting it for over three hundred pages, finally has to face it in his last chapter ("Cain's Children") with conclusions that we shall presently see.

The author of *African Genesis* is totally and slavishly committed to a philosophy of ironbound determinism which is dominated by one inexorable obsession: the "killer ape" armed with the leg bone of an antelope. Because man "descended in a direct line" from an ape with a weapon, then he is predetermined to be a killer, he is before all else a killer, and it is folly to even consider him being anything else, at least until his "lucky genes" have had a few hundred thousand more years. Mr. Ardrey confesses himself to be firmly convinced of "man's pristine depravity." Thus he is committed to a world-view in which aggression, barbarism, murder, and every form of violence are bound to prevail.

Yet the whole picture is not all of unrelieved darkness—otherwise the book would hardly have been a best seller in America. What about freedom? Man is predetermined to be a killer, but fortunately (says Mr. Ardrey) his killing habits are the basis of his freedom—freedom from vegetarianism, freedom to leave the jungle and roam around the world living on high-calorie foods and having a wonderful time. Man is a gorilla with a gun—and a credit card! "Freedom was the first gift of the predatory way," and doubtless, as man exists for the weapon, so does freedom! In any case, he says, the progress of the weapon is mankind's "most significant cultural endowment!" and to many American readers this has evidently seemed quite reasonable.

However, the idea that man is capable of destroying all life with his weapons is dismissed by Mr. Ardrey as "neo-romantic." It presumes too much of man's capacities. "While a giant effort on the part of man could conceivably bring extinction to all land vertebrates, it is impossible to believe that a world of insects would not survive." Though a nuclear disaster is, according to him, very likely, it cannot be more than a "partial disaster" as a result of which "overpopulation will cease to be a problem in India" and instead there will be plague and anarchy everywhere. A depleted population of radiated mutants may end up being devoured by rats, says our author cheerfully, but even then evolution will doubtless come out on top. This is not explained, since it is an article of faith.

Nevertheless, he has another "optimistic" alternative which is a surprising variant of the new "red or dead" realism. Man has indeed reached his peak, he has developed the absolute weapon—but now he must learn to live without it. At this point we begin to wonder if Mr. Ardrey is suddenly going to say something useful. What he says is this: if man has to live without war, he is heading for a decline. Society and culture will disintegrate without armed conflict to keep them going. Moral order "sheltered throughout all history by the judgment of arms" will collapse. But perhaps evolution will finally develop out of our race a new breed that really has and uses reason! This may take another million years. However, Mr. Ardrey would not have us be romantics, putting our trust in conscience to preserve sanity and life, for conscience is "irrational," is in league with our illusions, entirely subjective and "provincial." It is consequently a-moral. It operates with symbols and emotions, not with ideas and principles. It is animal, not rational. In fact, he regards conscience as "an anti-rational power." It has created a "chamber of dull horrors" called civilization, and neither conscience nor civilization can save us. Our only hope is the presence of Cain, our unpredictable ancestor living in our "wild genes." Cain will take care of everything, whether it be firing the weapon or avoiding a general disaster because he prefers to fight in the back streets with a switchblade knife. It is old daddy Cain who alone knows the answers and makes the choices. "We are children of Cain and were it not so, then for humanity there would be small hope."

I am prompted to reflect that this is where you end up when you lose your grasp on the real import of the higher religions. No man can really exist completely without a religion and a philosophy. If he gets rid of good ones, he will unconsciously exchange them for bad ones. If he is impatient of "myth" in higher religion then he will end up fabricating a myth of his own, and organizing his own crude fantasies into another homemade "system" which pleases him better—with consequences that are only too well known.

Now Mr. Ardrey's exploits in myth-making are not hard to observe. They are evident on every page of his book. To take just one example: on page twenty-one, he wants to give a brief description of Lake Victoria, as the spot near which man came into existence. There are innumerable ways in which one could describe Lake Victoria. Out of a hundred possible qualifiers Mr. Ardrey, characteristically, selects the following: "A hundred miles to the east spreads sprawling and enormous the cynically smiling face of Lake Victoria, poisonous with disease, crawling with crocodiles, the probable focus of our earliest human experience." I submit that people who read books like this need a little elementary training in semantics, in the interests of their basic mental and spiritual hygiene. Such a sentence (and there are hundreds like it in the book) has one function above all others: it attempts to predispose the reader a suitable feeling of disillusionment, an awareness of the general dominion of evil and violence as the basic law of all existence. Once one "feels" this, one will resist the "romantic fallacy," and will experience less compunction in reaching for a gun or firing an ICBM.

This kind of thinking is all too common in the twentieth century. Theories which substituted genes for intelligence and conscience abounded in the Europe of Mussolini, of Hitler, of Goebbels. The Second World War was the direct consequence of mental conditioning by pseudo-scientific myth. The Nazi dogma of race, blood and land developed an ideology of war and conquest out of just this kind of emotionally loaded anthropology. Everyone is aware that Hitler's racism was, in part, simply a crudely misunderstood mish-mash of popular evolutionism. Hitler's attempts to help the processes of natural selection with his gas chamber are mentioned in this book with no particular expression of romantic disapproval.

Once when the quiet and distinguished Spanish philosopher Miguel de Unamuno was lecturing at Salamanca in the early thirties, a one-armed Falangist general leaped up and expressed his impatience with all forms of humanism by shouting "Viva la Muerte!" The heroes of *African Genesis* are the killer gorilla and daddy Cain. The "God" (if we can call it that) which has watched over the gorilla's fortune and destiny is no other than Death. Mr. Ardrey is cool toward all other gods, particularly to the ones that favor non-violence and compassion. About Death he waxes lyrical. "Death is the evaluator . . . Death chooses . . . Death disposes. . . . We should all be lost in a wilderness of chance had not Death through a billion choosings erected the values of the world I know." If this last sentence had a meaning (and I am not able to find much meaning in it myself) it would be that Death is a kind of free and personal Absolute and Mr. Ardrey turns out to be no atheist after all.

Nothing can better dispose us for a third world war than the conviction that we are doomed to fight anyway, that our enemies are all well-armed gorillas too, and the only smart thing to do is to let them have it before they ambush us. In the chaotic atmosphere of a nation torn by race riots, deafened by the stridency of hate groups and of fanatics, it is understandable that readers may derive a kind of perverse comfort from this mythology—made to order for the "radical right." They will do so all the more readily because there is an unquestionably important basis of scientific data mixed in with the theatrical rhetoric and sermonizing of *African Genesis.*

Romanticism has more forms than one. The sentimentally optimistic kind that served the purposes of nineteenth-century laissez faire and the liberal myth of perpetual easy progress has obviously had its day. But it has yielded to the tough and callous romanticism of the street gang or of the fascist storm troop—a romanticism no less fallacious and deceptive for the fact that it also on occasion covers itself with a veneer of "realism" and pseudo-science. This second kind of romantic fallacy is that which we find developed and indeed monstrously over-developed in *African Genesis*. It is all the more regrettable because it is rooted in an intuition—one which in our day has become completely inescapable—of the desperateness of the human situation.

This is the greatest and most urgent truth of our time: we live in the presence of the meaningless and absurdity to which we have been inexorably reduced by our own more or less dishonest attempts to convince ourselves that we were progressing toward a definite and even a noble goal. The pessimism of the existentialists may indeed be dour and frustrated, but it has at least a certain stoic dignity about it. But this fraudulent attempt to organize the negativity and desperation of modern man around a stupidly melodramatic killer image, assembled from the less responsible surmises of popular anthropology, can do nothing whatever to help modern man in his quest for identity and for meaning. It is one thing to admit our violence and face it humbly and realistically: quite another to turn that "acceptance" into the shouting and posturing of racist self-congratulation. I do not know if this book is being read in Europe where—surely—people have had enough opportunities to grow tired of the formula. But it is still all too acceptable in America.

Man and Beast

MORTON HUNT

It would hardly seem likely that a man who spends every day watching ringdoves building their nests or bees gathering honey or mother rats nursing their newborn pups would be particularly well qualified to analyze the human psyche, prescribe ways to better mental health or advise mankind how to minimize the likelihood of nuclear war. Such, however, is apparently the case. In the past few years, the scientific study of animal behavior has emerged from relative obscurity into the glare of worldwide attention, and its practitioners, once viewed as harmless bird watchers, are now regarded as scientist prophets at whose feet modern man sits all atremble, waiting for the word. The reason is that in studying doves, bees and rats, along with hundreds of other species, zoologists and animal psychologists have recently made a number of discoveries that seem filled with profound implications for mankind. And since today we are in all sorts of trouble—personal, social and international—we are pathetically eager for any new understandings about ourselves that may hold the key to salvation. If those who study man—psychologists and sociologists—have not been able to tell us what we need to know, perhaps we can find it out from those who study animals.

But what they have been telling us is scarcely comforting. The school of animal-behavior studies that has suddenly had great impact on our thinking is known as ethology. The immensely popular books of Konrad Lorenz, Robert Ardrey and Desmond Morris are based mainly on ethological research, which holds that man is the most brutal and uninhibitedly aggressive of all animals and that these traits are genetically built into him. Ethologists believe that animal behavior is, to a great degree, chemically encoded in those long twisted chains of thousands of molecules that we call genes and that are the determiners of the biochemical processes in every cell of the body and, therefore, of the physical traits of the whole creature. Everyone agrees that it is the genes that make the fertilized ovum of, say, the mosquito grow up to be another mosquito, rather than a butterfly, swallow or rhinoceros. The ethologists, however, go much further, maintaining that the genes prescribe not just physical traits and behavioral tendencies but behavior itself, down to its finest details. The exact way a dog scratches its ear, the particular melody sung by the nightingale, the distinctive sequences of head bobbing, tail wiggling and other movements used by each species of duck during courting and the fierce but usually bloodless fights of rival male elk are all programed in advance within the genes.

So far, so good. But the ethologists argue that man, too, though he is born more helpless than any other animal and has to spend nearly the first quarter of his life acquiring the skills he needs to live the rest of it, behaves largely in accordance with genetic commands. In other words, he is largely governed by inborn instincts and, even if they don't prescribe the precise songs he sings or the exact ways he goes about courting, they do make him innately and inescapably selfish, suspicious, acquisitive—and murderous. Where other predators kill their prey but rarely their own kind, man is said to be an instinctive killer who is particularly savage toward his own species. He is not just a beast but the beastliest of all; he is, in the words of one ethological writer, "the cruelest and most ruthless species that has ever walked the earth."

Oddly enough, we seem to be fascinated by and receptive to this depressing news about ourselves. A century ago, one good Victorian lady, upon hearing the new theory that man was descended from the apes, cried out, "Let us hope it is not true—but if it is, let us pray it will not become generally known!" In contrast, not only have we accepted the theory that we are the worst of beasts, we enjoy seeing it presumably verified.

When Konrad Lorenz tells us, in *On Aggression,* that a hereditary "hypertrophy of aggression," coupled with an evolutionary lack of inhibition against killing our fellow man, makes us far more savage to our own kind than the wolf is to other wolves, we devour his every word and his book becomes a runaway best seller. When Robert Ardrey says, in *The Territorial Imperative,* that we are innate enemies of our own species and that, far from hating war, we really find it "outrageously satisfying," we all but cry amen and make his book a household word. When Desmond Morris writes of man as *The Naked Ape,* whose intelligence will never be able to rule his "raw animal nature" nor control his biological urge to aggression, we make his charges the stuff of cocktail conversation, smiling bitterly and dolefully, as if to say, "How true."

But a large number of those engaged in animal-behavior research disagree with the hard-line ethological view. Many zoologists, biochemists and animal psychologists reject the theory that most behavior is preprogramed and stored in the genes. They agree that, for biochemical reasons, animals have built-in "tendencies" to behave in certain ways but that these are specific and automatic only in lower animals; the higher the animal on the evolutionary scale, the more its tendencies are shaped, developed and organized into behavior by its interactions with its environment. A cricket will chirp, given the right conditions, without ever having heard it done; a human being, despite his tendency to use language, has to learn every word of the language he speaks. The most vigorous opponents of the ethological view of man—including anthropologists Ashley Montagu and Margaret Mead, philosopher Susanne Langer and a number of distinguished zoologists and animal psychologists—insist that even if insects and lower animals are largely guided by instincts, man himself is almost instinctless and, in any case, has no instinct to kill his own kind.

Each side in this quarrel accuses the other of spouting scientific humbug; each asserts that the other's views are dangerous to the human race; and each accuses the other of political bias in its science. Some ethologists charge their opponents with rigid adherence to a liberal and egalitarian ideology that makes them refuse to admit man's nastiness and the inherent differences among races. And some anti-ethologists see their opponents as Neo-Calvinists and social reactionaries whose views on man lend support to racist and fascist ideologies.

Great issues are thus at stake. If man is largely controlled by his instincts and if his behavior is encoded in his genes, man and his future can only be regarded with pessimism; man must then be viewed as innately dangerous and brutal and dealt with accordingly. If the poor, the indolent, the criminal, the greedy and the sadistic are acting according to their hereditary inclinations, there is little point in trying to change them: We might as well forget about compensatory education, welfare, equal job opportunities, rehabilitation of convicts and preventive mental-health programs. And if mankind is innately aggressive and warlike, it is absurd to suppose that he can ever become peaceful and loving toward his fellow man—or even that he would like to be.

But if man is not instinct-controlled, or if his instincts are amorphous and do not result in specific behavior patterns—if, in other words, he has a highly educable and modifiable nature —then it is possible to be hopeful about him and his future, despite his wretched history. One can believe that poverty is rarely the fault of the poor and that with better opportunities, they might become productive and useful; that crime is largely a product of social and psychological conditions that can be modified and perhaps eliminated; that sadism, greed, ignorance and psychosis are not inevitable expressions of our nature but forms into which that nature has been forced by circumstances. And, finally, one can even believe that it is still possible, if unlikely, that man may find ways to live in peace and to realize his ancient dream of loving and being loved by his fellow man.

Great issues, indeed. But neither the ethologists nor the other students of animal behavior seem, in their daily work, to be dealing with such matters. Their research generally looks scientifically pure, aloof and sometimes even pastoral. Some researchers, for instance, are basically naturalists, albeit with a modern touch. They observe animals under field conditions, recording and analyzing their sounds, tabulating their actions, their behavior in groups and as individuals, and making computer analyses of the data to discover meaningful patterns. One dedicated young zoologist lives alone for months at a time in the savannas of south-central Kenya, watching various members of a troop of vervet monkeys and noting their every act of eating, defecating, grooming, fighting and copulating, until he begins to perceive the social structure of the troop. Other scientists observe and virtually live with particular species of insect, fish, bird or mammal, until they recognize every gesture, every nuance of sound and behavior—until, indeed, they could advise the young stickleback, pigeon, gorillas or gerbil how best to fight off its rival and woo its mate.

While observing animals in their native habitat, some researchers tinker with one or more of the natural conditions, hoping to find a cause-and-effect relationship to behavior. A team in Antarctica captured penguins at Cape Crozier, took them 180 miles away to the middle of the perfectly flat, featureless Ross Shelf Ice and released them, to see if the birds could find their way home and, if so, how. They could and did, apparently by using the sun; under cloudy skies, they blundered around, but under clear skies, they would look up, seem to think a bit and then waddle off toward Cape Crozier. One mystery was thus solved, but another and larger one appeared: How do the penguins know about the use of solar guidance? Two contrasting theories exist: (1) Something in their genes makes them automatically use the sun as a directional guide; and (2) Some conditioning that occurs during their growing up has made them associate the sunward direction with water and food. Thus, penguin navigation, itself a trivial matter, touches upon the central issue in animal psychology—the meaning of instinct and the mechanisms through which instinctive behavior is manifested.

Some researchers have removed animals from the field and studied them in the laboratory, introducing unnatural conditions to try out the hypothesized mechanisms underlying behavior. Among ducks and many other birds, the young follow the mother faithfully about within a few hours after hatching. Lorenz was curious as to why this happens; he therefore divided the eggs laid by a goose into two batches and had one batch hatched by the mother and the other by an incubator. The goslings hatched by the mother saw her first and followed her wherever she went; the others saw Lorenz first and followed him, even when they saw their mother nearby. In popular terms, they "thought" Lorenz was their mother; in scientific terms, they had been "imprinted" with his image. (Ducklings have been imprinted to follow wooden decoys, a football and a green box containing an alarm clock, any of which looks good to them if it is the first thing they see.) Imprinting in animals seems to be the fixing in the memory of an image at a time when the nervous system is undergoing a special stage of maturation. By studying it, ethologists learn something about nature's invention of devices for survival: If ducklings don't follow the mother shortly after birth, they will be abandoned and die. More importantly, ethologists learn something about the critical periods of maturation in the nervous system—a subject that has meaning for human parents as well.

In another experiment, an American animal psychologist built a community for Norway rats, complete with unlimited supplies of food, water and nesting materials, and allowed the rat population to grow until it was far denser than ever occurs in normal circumstances. The results were startling: Some of the males became bullies, others became homosexuals and cannibals and yet others became withdrawn neurotics; the females began to abort or take poor care of their young; and infant mortality rose as high as 96 percent. Since all the physical wants of the rats were satisfied, this pathology could only mean that excessive social interaction was to blame. Rats are not men and from this study one cannot lean to conclusions about our own urban life, but at least it suggests that the interaction needed by social animals has its limits and that beyond those limits it produces a variety of behavioral disorders.

Some researchers have castrated cocks to see what becomes of their sex drive and their aggressiveness (not surprisingly, both markedly diminish); some have transfused the blood of a mother rat into the veins of a virgin rat to see if the hormones and other substances in it would stimulate the virgin's responses to young rat pups and make her behave like a mother (they did); some have raised monkeys in isolation, apart from their mothers and friends, and later introduced them, as adults, to normal monkey society to see how they fared (very badly; they were fearful, hostile, unable to mate—and never got better).

Such studies are, for the first time, yielding down-to-earth explanations of some of life's great, enduring mysteries—mother love, sexual attraction, the homemaking urge, competition and cooperation, intelligence, kindness, aggression, et al. These are obviously matters of immense intellectual interest—and of self-interest, as well, for if we understood them thoroughly in lower animals, we might understand them somewhat better in man. We are faced with self-extinction from many sources, all of our own making: overpopulation, the selfish despoiling of our air and water, the potential incineration of man in a nuclear war. It might be—and any hope is worth pursuing—that we could learn something from animals that would enable us to save us from ourselves.

In fact, however, most of the animal-behavior researchers are not seeking insights into the larger mysteries of human nature. Most of them, like other scientists, are so fascinated by some small mystifying phenomenon they've noticed that they are willing to spend years exploring it just for the pleasure of discovering what makes it so.

"I got into ethology because it was intellectually intriguing," says Dr. William Dilger of Cornell University. "I've spent ten years studying nest building in one species of bird because I was fascinated by the fact that all females of that species prepare and carry their nesting materials in the same peculiar way, even if they've never seen it done by others. I wanted to find out how that works and I think I have. But today people want ethologists to come up with answers to the big questions troubling mankind; they think we have the answers up our sleeves. I'm not at all sure we do. And I rather resent it—it's disturbing to have such responsibility thrust on one. Ethology used to be fun but not very important; now it's become important but not nearly so much fun." For better or for worse, that's the way it's going to be. The study of animal behavior will never again be a quiet backwater of zoology. Men now fervently hope, and almost demand, that animal-behavior researchers help them understand themselves and one another; and, given the present human condition, who can blame them?

Before drawing any conclusions about man, however, the first order of business is to find out how things really work among other animals, resolutely avoiding the tendency to read human feelings and motives into what they do. Anthropomorphism is a classic error: From primitive man to Pliny, from Shakespeare to the modern dog fancier, men have ascribed human sentiments and aims to their animal friends and foes. If the brown thrasher sings a long and melodious song at the close of a glorious summer afternoon, he must be rejoicing at being alive on such a day; if the stag and his rival lock horns and struggle until exhausted, it's because even peaceful beasts are willing to kill each other under the influence of jealousy; if the female cat painstakingly washes her kittens, it's because, brimming with mother love, she is taking good care of her babies; if baboons live in primitive oligarchies, it's because they, like us, need family life and friendship and are willing to pay the price of submitting to wise leadership and social regulation.

But all schools of contemporary animal-behavior study try to avoid the anthropomorphic fallacy. They start with the fact that the animals are incapable of symbolic—that is, linguistic—thinking or of emotions based in large part on cultural values. Instead of speculating as to what they might be feeling, the scientists stick to what is empirical and provable; the actual actions of the animals, the measurable changes in their bodies associated with those actions and their demonstrable survival value for both the individual and the species.

When one objectively studies the singing of birds under natural conditions, for instance, it becomes clear that one major function of bird song is species recognition; through distinctive songs and calls, the males and females of each species are able to locate one another easily and reliably. An even more important function is the male's use of song to establish his own territory. In many species, male birds attack or avoid one another during the nesting phase, using their characteristic song as the way of warning one another to stay at a distance; the result is a useful spacing out of nesting sites, giving each mating pair a chance to raise its young without interference. It is not as romantic an interpretation of bird song as that of the poets, but it is verifiable—and verified.

Territorial warnings are valuable and common throughout the animal kingdom. Many kinds of male fish wear bright colors that warn their fellows away from their chosen feeding ground; free-roaming dogs and cats urinate in many places to mark their own domain; antelopes rub their faces against branches, releasing scent from facial glands and advertising their ownership of the area. None of the animals has this purpose in mind, as far as anyone knows; the animal may mark in one way or another simply because it feels good, but the survival value of such behavior for the species makes it an evolution-chosen trait.

Animals who intrude upon one another's territory are in for a fight, but it is a fiction that such fights are motivated by fraternal blood lust, like that of Cain. A species that had a tendency to kill its own kind would be at a serious disadvantage in the struggle for survival. A male animal fights an intruding rival of the same species not with murderous intent but merely to drive him away, so that the defender will not have to coexist with him in an area too small for the two of them. Not that the territorial defender thinks this through; as far as ethologists can tell, he fights simply because the rival's size, shape, smell and behavior arouse alarm and anger—some say instinctively, others say partly due to learning in the form of youthful mock combat. In any case, the defender seeks first only to frighten the intruder off by making hostile gestures and noises; if this fails, the two do fight—usually in a ritualized fashion that means neither death nor even harm to the loser. Male cichlid fish seize each other by the lips and push and pull for hours, until one gives up, folds his fins and swims away. Stags, wild goats and male mountain sheep engage in ferocious combat, but neither combatant uses its sharp horns to pierce the other; instead, they smash their horns against each other and push, butt, strain and struggle, until one is exhausted and gives up, the victor making no effort to inflict a wound when the loser turns to leave.

So it is throughout most of the animal world: The same animals that will fight other species to the death will engage each other in fierce but primarily ceremonial and harmless struggles ending either in flight, with the victor not pursuing, or in surrender, with the beaten one giving some sign of appeasement

—a cringing posture, the turning away of the head, a rolling over on the back or some other form of exposing himself to the mortal blow. But it is never delivered; the act of appeasement ends the fight.

The appeasement gesture itself is a particularly important evolutionary development among animals that live in groups, where the loser cannot run away except at the cost of isolation. Among baboons, for instance, a defeated male will "present"—that is, offer his rump, like a female, to the victor; the latter may choose not to use the proffered rear, but the gesture alters his mood and ensures peace. The sending out of a sexual signal is, in fact, the most effective of all neutralizers of the aggressive impulse. If the female of the species looks much like the male, then she must offer stimuli that bring about changes in the emotional status of the male territorial defender, so that he does not attack her but mates with her. Whether the female does so by means of a sound, an odor or a series of movements, one need not assume conscious intent on her part—most certainly not at the lower levels of evolution and probably not even at the higher ones.

An example: A small tidal-zone fish known as the goby stoutly defends his territory against intruding males by turning dark, opening his mouth threateningly and puffing out his throat; these failing, he attacks and bites the interloper. But if a gravid female comes near, her condition provides him with various stimuli that modify his behavior, the most important being a chemical she exudes due to her gravid state. The scent of it radically changes his reactions: He turns light, rather than dark, and instead of attacking, he fans the water with his tail, makes grunting noises and leads her to a shelter he has built, where she lays her eggs and he then releases sperm over them. Without her chemical signal and his response to it, the species would perish, but neither the signal nor the response is intentional or deliberate. Both are purely automatic, as Dr. William Tavolga, a zoologist at the American Museum of Natural History in New York, proved by plugging up the noses of male gobies—who thereupon attacked gravid females just as if they were rival males. But let no one sneer at the dim-witted goby; do we not continually read in advertisements that such and such a perfume will inspire passion, or even love and marriage, in the gentleman of one's choice?

Even territorialism and courtship seem commonplace before the miracle of animal mother love. As we said earlier, which of us has not marveled at the mother cat, who knows without training that she should wash her newborn kittens and also knows when they are old enough to be on their own and therefore cuffs them away as if to help them get started? But those who have analytically studied mothering in cats have less romantic explanations of their behavior. The mothers lick their newborn young not because they know it's a good and healthful thing to do but because the young are drenched in placental fluids containing chemicals the mother has just lost and needs to replace and that, therefore, probably taste good to her. Nor does she "know" when her young are ready to be on their own; the young simply get so large that their suckling and playing are uncomfortable to her and she reacts naturally to pain and irritation.

Similarly, the group life of baboons superficially resembles life in primitive human societies; moreover, watching baboons tend their young, fight, play, fornicate and defend themselves, it is difficult not to attribute human feelings and ideas to them. But dispassionate scientific observation dispels the anthropomorphic fallacy. Baboon mothers do care for their young, but baboon society ignores sick or wounded adults; they are simply abandoned as the troop moves on. Dominant males pair off briefly with females in heat, but there are no long-lasting alliances and nothing like family life, not even of the polygamous variety. Communication is largely a matter of gestures, and deals only with immediate situations (there is no passing on of ideas or history); and the major social activity is not work, play nor sexual behavior but grooming—the picking of insects and dirt out of one another's hair. And this is probably an instinctive impulse based on biological need. Observers have noted that a baboon who is away from his group even for a day or two will return heavily infested with ticks and other parasites he cannot remove and that would soon seriously affect his health.

On the importance of studying animal behavior functionally and without anthropomorphism, all sides agree. They disagree sharply, however, about the actual mechanics underlying the behavior they see and about the implications of that behavior for mankind. At one pole, as we have already seen, are the ethologists. The word ethology has caught on with the public (almost as much as ecology) and has come to mean almost all kinds of animal-behavior studies; but among professionals, it still signifies, in Lorenz' own words, "the study of innate behavior; the study of species-specific drive activities." Lorenz, codirector of the Max Planck Institute for Behavioral Physiology in Seewiesen, Bavaria, virtually founded the specialty of ethology two generations ago and remains its principal figure.

The basic tenet of ethology is that by far the largest part of what animals—including man—do is instinctive. For each bit of behavior, there is a blueprint stored away in the nervous system and passed on within the genes of that species. External stimuli and experiences do play a part—but mostly as releasers, or actuators, of the fixed action patterns genetically programed within the animal.

In the years between the two World Wars, Lorenz and his students, reacting against the limitations and artificiality of laboratory experiments in rat psychology, turned to the study of many other species under natural conditions, where each has a repertoire of complicated acts specific to its own kind—acts that seem to appear automatically when the animal needs them and without having learned them in any sense comparable with that of behaviorist psychology.

The female digger wasp of the species *Pepsis marginata,* for example, when ready to lay an egg, goes in search of a host for it and unerringly picks out a tarantula of the species *Cyrtopholis portoricae* (no other species of insect, not even any other species of tarantula, will do) and digs a hole in front of it, attacks it and finds a chink in its armor through which she stings it into immobility, then drags it into the hole and lays her egg in its abdomen, finally covering the hole over—all without ever having seen any of this done.

A complicated procedure such as this is made up of many small separate acts, and the ethologists think it is the separate acts that are specifically gene-produced and inheritable. As proof, they point out that in hybrids, these small acts are recombined, even as are colors, markings and other hereditary traits. Lorenz' own favorite subjects of study have been ducks and geese, each species of which goes through a courtship procedure involving a whole series of gestures and signs (the bill shake, the head flick, the tail shake, the grunt whistle and others). In each species, the sequence of acts is specific and invariable; but in hybrids, the sequence is altered, some acts appearing earlier or later, some disappearing, some changing form, all in predictable ways—presumably corresponding to the altered configuration of gene loci in the chromosomes.

Each species, therefore, has a complete set of genetic blueprints for behavior that serves to satisfy its four great drives—hunger, fear, sex and aggression. Circumstances may modify somewhat the precise behavior of the creature, but they cannot change its essential nature; the deer will never be a tiger, the hawk will never be a cow.

The aggression of animals toward their own kind, however, is held in check by inhibiting mechanisms such as the ritualization of fighting, appeasement gestures and the like. In man, unhappily, the brain has outstripped the rest of his biology; appeasement is no safeguard when killing is too quick, too easy and too impersonal to be stopped by the animal gesture. The beast within us is incompetent to handle the tools of murder the man within us has invented.

From such evidence and theorizing, ethologists are almost bound to draw gloomy and misanthropic conclusions, for the dismal record of history and the sorry state of the present world must be direct reflections of man's innate nature. Here, for instance, are the acerbic comments of Eckhard H. Hess, a distinguished animal psychologist at the University of Chicago. "As an ethologist," he says, "I believe that man is an animal—not a better kind of animal but merely a more complicated one. A lot of liberals and intellectuals—even in the biological sciences—try to deny this evidence, because it contradicts their ideological notions about the equality and the perfectibility of all men. In the do-gooder way of thinking, any discussion of the genic constitution of human beings and their behavior is supposed to smack of racism, and that's very bad, while anything that blames environment is very good. But to deny the biological basis of man's behavior, you have to overlook or deny 99 percent of what we know about biology today."

At the pole opposite the ethologists are those students of animal behavior who take their direction from the late Dr. T. C. Schneirla of the American Museum of Natural History. His disciples, who can be found at Rutgers, Johns Hopkins, the University of North Carolina and other institutions, espouse the developmental view. They disagree with Lorenzian instinct theory almost *in toto*; they regard the idea that the genes incorporate fixed action patterns as primitive and simplistic. Even in low-level creatures, they claim, behavior patterns arise out of a continuing dialectic between biological tendencies and experience; they develop out of the interaction between genotype and environment and do not exist preprogramed within the genotype, awaiting only the signal of the right releasers to turn them on. Schneirla studied tropical army ants at close range and noticed that even though the ant's behavior is largely metabolic and automatic, the newly hatched workers stay close to the colony for a few days and seem to flounder around; it takes a while before they become proficient at following trails and performing tasks. Even for them, therefore, behavior is not totally instinctive.

Everyone knows, moreover, that cats "instinctively" kill mice, but one researcher observed the behavior of growing kittens and concluded that this so-called instinct is the complex end product of an almost inevitable series of learning experiences based on biological tendencies. The kitten automatically pays attention to moving objects; this leads to playful chasing, which leads to seizing and biting, which leads, in turn, to tasting blood—each experience providing new gratifications and building toward the mouse-killing pattern. If, however, a kitten is carefully conditioned not to chase or bite mice, or misses the crucial steps at the critical period of its development, it may never become a mouser but remain indifferent toward mice all its life.

Much the same is true of mother love. In several laboratories, researchers have been studying mothering in rats and cats and find it to be a complicated phenomenon assembled out of earlier experiences, physical needs and elemental gratifications yielded by the mothering acts themselves. The mother cat, for instance, licks her own nipples and genitals during pregnancy, because they are swollen and feel uncomfortable. This not only helps the mammary glands develop but prepares her to lick her newborn young, who taste the same as her genitals and are, as we saw earlier, wet with the fluids she needs to restore her own chemical balance. The initial licking is an essential first step that leads to others: It stimulates movement and internal functions in the young and conditions them positively to her, and vice versa. The young, now aroused and hungry, begin random and reflexive nuzzling and sucking of the mother and only accidentally come upon her teats; they learn, however, and day by day get better at it. Their suckling relieves the mother's own congestion and continues to make them pleasing to her; she, too, learns, grows perceptibly more adept at caring for her young as time goes by and is distinctly more skillful with a second litter than with the first.

Summing up these and other experiments by developmentalists, Dr. William Tavolga—the zoologist who played tricks on the male goby fish—says, "The whole concept of instinct is superfluous. Certainly, we see plenty of stereotyped behavior in every species, typical of that species, that seems to appear automatically as the creature grows up in its normal environment. But is it instinctive? Not in the way Lorenz means; for at every level of organization, from the amoeba to man, behavior develops out of the interaction between the cytoplasm and the environment. You cannot go directly from the DNA molecule to a specific piece of behavior, and there is no special or separate category of behavior that can be called instinctive."

On the basis of such evidence and theorizing, the developmentalists draw radically different conclusions from the ethologists about the grand design of animal behavior and especially about the nature of man. In a review of Ardrey's *The Territorial Imperative,* the distinguished psychologist J. P. Scott wrote that it presents a "simple-minded," "uncritical," "adolescent," "oversimplified" and "largely erroneous" picture of human nature. In another book review, Schneirla wrote that Lorenz' *On Aggression* is based on "dubious assumptions" and presents a "naïve" and "outdated" view of human nature. Ashley Montagu, editing a volume of rebuttals of ethology, goes furthest of all: "Man is man because he has no instincts," he writes; "everything he is and has become he has learned, acquired, from his culture." This view is shared by some very unlikely bedfellows: anti-Communist liberals and anti-liberal Communists, pacifist intellectuals and violence-addicted Maoists, pot-smoking hippies and bespectacled scholars, all of whom believe that man is not inherently aggressive or selfish and that his present character is wholly a product of a bad system; to change him, one need only change it. They disagree only about what changes to make. Some "only"!

Most of the people working today in the field of animal behavior take positions somewhere between these two poles of thought. The emerging view of animal-behavior researchers is that the entire nature-nurture, innate-learned, instinct-experience issue is outmoded, if not meaningless; some behavior is purely innate, some entirely learned, but by far the largest part of it results from interactions between genotypic tendencies and environmental influences.

Young squirrels, for example, begin to handle, gnaw and crack nuts by way of natural response to their feel and smell but have to learn by trial and error how to put these several activities together in a useful sequence. Many birds make the right nest-building movements without seeming to require a period of experiment, but they use the wrong materials at first, the right ones later. Songbirds, as they reach maturity, will sing their characteristic song, but inaccurately and incompletely, unless they hear others of their species singing. Monkeys reared in isolation climb and swing like other monkeys but cannot socialize, play or mate, because these complex patterns require much learning. Learning is not all, however: Such monkeys cannot be socialized later on, because they have passed a critical period, during which certain maturational changes take place in the nervous system that are essential to the socialization process.

To understand how the genotype and the environment interact and, therefore, to understand the emerging answer to the ancient nature-nurture puzzle, one has to look closely at animals; even then, he may miss it unless he is lucky. Dr. William Dilger, the Cornell ethologist, regards the nature-nurture issue as a non-question but is himself a perfect example of a man who has found an answer to it in one species, partly by years of dedicated observation and partly by accident.

Long ago, in studying another problem altogether, Dilger was using as his laboratory animal a species of tiny green African parrot known as the peach-faced lovebird, which, along with the unusual "loving" behavior of mated couples, has another curious trait: The female of the species cuts out strips of leaves or thin bark with her bill, tucks the strips in among the feathers of the lower part of her back and carries them in this fashion to the place where she is building a nest. Dilger says:

> Every female lovebird does it the same way, whether or not she's ever seen other females doing it. I had a rather naïvely instinctivist view of things in those days and it looked to me like a perfect example of an innate, fixed action pattern, a part of the animal's genotype. I even used it in my lectures as a classical example of instinctive behavior.
>
> Then a kind of accident happened in the lab here about ten years ago. We were raising a bunch of females and a young

lab assistant of mine took care of them and gave them food, water, grit and whatever they needed. Lovebirds don't build nests when they're young, so he didn't bother to give them nesting materials and didn't think to mention it to me. But although young birds don't build nests with the material, they do *play* with it—they run under it, pull it around, peck at it and other things of the sort. Finally, they reached breeding age and we paired them—and, to our surprise, not one of those birds could cut out strips and tuck them into her feathers. Not one of them ever managed it. They were simply incapable of it. They showed a great deal of *interest* in the stuff, but all they managed to do was demolish it. Something hadn't happened to them, between the ages of six months and a year, that should have happened. They had missed experiences they needed to have in order to form what I had taken to be a completely innate behavior pattern. They have only a core of response to the situation—a crude, imperfect action with the nesting material that requires experience to modify. They improve their behavior a little the next time and this leads them to modify it a little more the time after that, and so on, until they have acquired the final pattern.

I did some modifying of my own—this whole experience was a key factor in my shift away from the strict ethological viewpoint. I've been studying lovebirds ever since and seeing things I had never noticed before. I've been able to break down tucking behavior into nine separate neuromuscular components—all of them innate—and do things to the birds to see which of the nine are modifiable by experience, which need experience to result in useful behavior and which are essential to other components. I've deprived them of nesting materials at different stages of their lives, I've given them materials but shaved the feathers off their back and rump, so they can't learn to tuck. I've let them learn to tuck and go through nesting and *then* shaved off their feathers. From it all, I've gotten a clearer idea of the way in which one specific piece of behavior, in one species of bird, is constructed out of crude genotypic tendencies as they are modified, perfected and pieced together by experiences gained from the environment.

Recently, I've been studying the same interplay in the case of the lovebirds' courtship procedures. Ethologists have generally considered courtship rituals of birds to be strictly instinctive, and it is true that all male lovebirds do the same things when courting females, even without having seen them done by others. The male has to give the female a lot of signals and get certain positive signs back from her before she'll accept him. We have descriptive names for the things he does—"switch sidling," "squeak twittering," "displacement scratching," "head bobbing" and so on—and every male does them, and they always work. But if you really live with the birds, you begin to see differences. I had cages of them right here in my office for years, so that I could see them all day long, no matter what else I was doing. After a long while, I began to see that the novice male makes a lot of mistakes. He does all the things he should do and they look perfect, but he doesn't know *when* to do them; his timing is no good. The female looks as if she's just sitting there; but actually, she's giving him very subtle signals that mean "Stop!" or "Not now!" or "Come on!" If she fluffs her cheek feathers slightly, she's agreeable; if she compresses them, she isn't—tiny things like that. It's very hard to recognize—hard for the male bird as well as the human observer. But he has to learn, because if he rushes in when he shouldn't, he'll get nipped. An experienced male won't make that mistake. So, once again, even in a seemingly innate and rigid pattern of behavior, there's a lot of learning, a lot of genotype-environment interaction.

Lovebirds vary their responses a little; men vary theirs a great deal. More so than any other animal, we are able to modify our reactions to the stimuli we encounter; indeed, we build entire cultures out of those modifications. Less so than any other animal are we provided with ready-made fixed action patterns to satisfy our drives or forced by metabolic processes to respond to stimuli in predictable ways. Each animal has its own diet; men have scores of them. Each animal has its own coital position; we have 10, 20, 100. Each animal preens or grooms itself in a species-specific fashion; we have innumerable ways of doing so. Each of the social animals has a relatively unvarying form of group life; we, in our brief time on earth, have created everything from the Athenian city-state to communistic dictatorships.

It is true that, like other animals, we are impelled to action by hunger, fear, anger and sexual desire. But we are not directed by instinct to take specific actions in order to satisfy those drives. The actions one might call instincts in the clam are not only simpler but different in quality from those one might call instincts in the lovebird and radically unlike those often referred to as instincts in man. This is not to say that the study of animal behavior can teach us nothing about ourselves. It can and will, even as the study of animal physiology can and does contribute much to human medicine. But even if one thoroughly studies the skeleton, nervous system, blood and tissues of the rabbit, he is not qualified to diagnose and heal the ills of man; their similarities are instructive, but their differences are crucial.

Above all else, we have learned from animal-behavior studies that the more complicated an animal is, the less its behavior is rigidly programed by the genotype, the more its behavior is developed through experience. The conclusion that man's instincts are very much like those of lower animals is unjustified and misleading. What the evidence justifies instead is the conclusion that man's instincts operate on a level very different from those of most other animals and do not result in specific, predictable, stereotyped behavior patterns.

The clinical experience of every psychotherapist and psychoanalyst since Freud indicates that human beings have only the most amorphous and undifferentiated kinds of instincts and that our training within the family and outside it is what makes us either heterosexual or homosexual, monogamous or polygamous, sybaritic or ascetic, convivial or reclusive, combative or passive. We do not automatically become any of these things; we express our sexual "instinct"—one wishes there were another word for it when referring to man—in whatever way we are taught. And without teaching, we can do almost nothing: In some orphanages, where children get almost no individual attention other than feeding and changing, many of them are unable even to *walk* by the age of three or four. So much for man's instincts.

Yet for want of a better word, let us agree to call man's genotypic tendencies instincts—while insisting that this means something very different from instincts in lower animals. Man may be innately and instinctively aggressive in the sense that he is chronically restless and irritable; in need of change and excitement, challenge and difficulties; quick to anger when frustrated, and to strike out—or feel the desire to do so—at whatever limits him, threatens him or presses in upon him. But man is not programed and his aggressive drive can be directed in many ways and serve many different ends. One man uses it to become Nero but another to become Marcus Aurelius; one man's aggressive instinct makes him Hitler, another's makes him Gandhi.

The record of man's inhumanity to man is horrifying, when one compiles it—enslavement, castration, torture, rape, mass slaughter in war after war. But who has compiled the record of man's kindness to man—the trillions of acts of gentleness and goodness, the helping hands, smiles, shared meals, kisses, gifts, healings, rescues? If we were no more than murderous predators, with a freakish lack of inhibition against slaughtering our own species, we would have been at a terrible competitive disadvantage compared with other animals; if this were the central truth of our nature, we would scarcely have survived, multiplied and become the dominant species on earth. Man does have an aggressive instinct, but it is not naturally or inevitably directed to killing his own kind. He is a beast and perhaps at times the cruelest beast of all—but sometimes he is also the kindest beast of all. He is not all good and not perfectible, but he is not all bad and not wholly unchangeable or unimprovable. That is the only basis on which one can have hope for him; but it is enough.

PROJECTS

1. In "The Violent Way," Ardrey writes: "We have in our genetic endowment the tendency to reject strangers and, if we are to read objectively the history of civilized man, a probable propensity for violence."

(a) Do you think that Ardrey gives a concise definition for and ample evidence of this "genetic endowment" and "probable propensity" for violence?

(b) What responses would Thomas Merton and Morton Hunt give to this statement in "The Violent Way"?

(c) What critical response would you give to such a statement?

2. "Aggressiveness, by definition, is the determined pursuit of one's interests. Violence is the pursuit of such interests through force, or the threat of force. They are not the same." Referring back to Part I, *Definitions of Violence,* has Ardrey made a clear distinction between aggression and violence in his article? Has he used these explicit and/or implicit definitions consistently throughout his essay?

3. Is violence a source for human enjoyment and stimulation? Write an essay responding to Ardrey's statement that (a) "He who regards a taste for violent action as a human perversion will not likely make any great contribution to the containment of our violent way," or (b) "And violence, too, is stimulating. It carries excitement for both violator and violated, whether through the joyful hatreds of the one or the fearful rages of the other. A riot in Chicago is worth all the circuses that old-time emperors could provide."

4. Debate the following. "Resolved: A riot stemming from the slum conditions of the United States is a type of violence originating from a bored society."

5. "If we have not the foresight, if we have not the will, then we shall discover one day who waits beyond our Rubicon." Does Ardrey's essay give any evidence for the source of this foresight which is so greatly needed by humanity, or does humanity's genetic endowment and probable propensity for violence doom both foresight and will to the level of wishful thinking?

6. Thomas Merton writes about a type of romanticism which gives us a perverse comfort in knowing that man is indeed a well-armed gorilla. Morton Hunt confirms this notion by referring to the Victorian lady's response to the theory that man was descended from the apes, "Let us hope it is not true—but if it is, let us pray it will not become generally known!"

(a) Do you consider this type of opinion regarding the nature of man as a source of "perverse romanticism"?

(b) Is there evidence that this type of "perverse romanticism" is gaining in popularity among college students as the proper perspective to have regarding the nature of man?

(c) Is such "romanticism" a positive or negative factor for the educational scene?

7. "It is one thing to admit our violence and face it humbly and realistically: quite another to turn that acceptance into the shouting and posturing of racist self-congratulation."

(a) What does Thomas Merton mean by the terms "humbly" and "realistically"?

(b) How would Ardrey define these terms?

(c) How would you define such terms, especially in relationship to your response to the position of the ethologists?

8. Write an essay evaluating: "Ethology as a science is an anthropomorphic fallacy."

9. Arrange to see the film *Lord of the Flies*—a British film production based on William Golding's novel. (90 minutes, black-and-white, released by Continental Distributing, 241 East 34th St., N.Y., N.Y. 10016)

(a) What reaction would Ardrey, Merton, and Hunt have to this film?

(b) Evaluate your own reaction in view of these readings regarding the biology of violence.

Bibliography

ARDREY, ROBERT. *African Genesis*. New York: Atheneum, 1961.
———. *The Social Contract*. New York: Atheneum, 1970.
———. *The Territorial Imperative*. New York: Atheneum, 1966.
LORENZ, KONRAD. *On Aggression*. London: Methuen, 1966.
MACLEAN, PAUL D. "Alternative Neural Pathways to Violence." In

Alternatives to Violence, edited by Larry Ng. New York: Time-Life Books, 1968.

MacLean, Paul D. "Man and his Animal Brains," *Modern Medicine.* February 3, 1964.

Mark, Vernon, and Ervin, Frank. *Violence and the Brain.* New York: Harper & Row, 1970.

Merton, Thomas. *Faith and Violence.* Notre Dame, Indiana: University of Notre Dame Press, 1968.

Morris, Desmond. *The Human Zoo.* New York: McGraw-Hill, 1969.

———. *The Naked Ape.* New York: McGraw-Hill, 1967.

Ng, Larry. *Alternatives to Violence.* New York: Time-Life Books, 1968.

Ochberg, Frank, and others. *Violence and the Struggle for Existence.* Boston: Little, Brown & Co., 1970.

The Psychological Polemic

Introduction

The psychological study of violence as a mode of human behavior originated with the father of psychoanalysis, Sigmund Freud. His concepts of id, ego, and superego are almost as familiar to us as our own names. Freud used these terms to illustrate the nature of the human psyche which confronts within its instinctual life the forces of *Eros* (constructive, love force) and *Thanatos* (destructive, death force). Both *Eros* and *Thanatos* as instinctual drives are deadly forces since they seek immediate gratification of needs without any reference to "reasonable" means or ends for the fulfillment of those needs.

Civilization began, Freud believed, when man renounced these instinctual drives as absolute necessities in his life and chose to repress them for his own survival and the preservation of communal life. This "civilization" of instinctual drives does not eliminate them in any way from the human organism. The term "repression" indicates this fact—as do other psychological terms such as "sublimation," "projection," and "introjection." Man transforms his animal life into human life by exchanging the "pleasure principle" (full, immediate, painless gratification of his needs) for the "reality principle" (delaying, restraining, modifying immediate needs for other "assured" needs). This transformation may be described as the shifting from immediate satisfaction to delayed satisfaction, from pleasure to restraint of pleasure, from joy (play) to toil (work), from receptiveness to productiveness, from absence of repression to security.[1]

The reality principle, Freud asserted, functions on the conscious level of human life—reasoning, judging, remembering. The pleasure principle, on the other hand, operates on the

[1] Herbert Marcuse, *Eros and Civilization,* Vintage Books Edition, 1962, p. 12. (Helpful resource for an analysis of Freudian themes.)

unconscious level of human life, and as phantasy or dream is free from the rule of the reality principle. Both principles, however, demand our psychic energy, creating a basic duality within human experience similar to the "schizophysiology" of the human brain described by Dr. MacLean. This duality is not apparent on the surface of life since man is willing to repress immediate gratification of his needs for the life of reason and community. Society, the cultural expression of man's willingness to be repressed, assumes the major responsibility for proper repression. Freud was convinced that between the social mores of his culture and the forceful demands of his own father, man is properly "repressed" for human life.

The gift of this repression is civilization. Yet civilization is not static. It is dynamic in its birth, rebellions, counter-rebellions, and death. This dynamic quality results from the confrontation in all societies between the pleasure principle and the reality principle. Proof of this is seen in the history of civilization. No culture, past, present or future, controls the pleasure principle in an absolute sense. Freud discovered from his study of disturbed patients that a conscious, forceful repression of a need reappears in a forceful expression of this need in the unconscious. And so it is with civilization. What it represses and masters consciously, it still retains unconsciously. The implication of this psychological theory fascinates many contemporary writers including R. D. Laing and Herbert Marcuse.

> What civilization masters and represses—the claim of the pleasure principle—continues to exist in civilization itself. The unconscious retains the objectives of the defeated pleasure principle. Turned back by the external reality or even unable to reach it, the full force of the pleasure principle not only survives in the unconscious but also affects in manifold ways the very reality which has superseded the pleasure principle. The *return of the repressed* makes up the tabooed and subterranean history of civilization.[2]

---

[2] Herbert Marcuse, *Eros and Civilization,* p. 15.

The history of the individual parallels the history of civilization. As individuals, we repress the immediate need for gratification only to find it later in a phantasy or dream. Yet in good faith, we allow the "violence of love," as Laing describes it in his book, *The Politics of Experience,* to be performed on us by our parents, our educators, and our politicians. If "love" of and for our culture is not strong enough in our lives (when immediate needs are more essential than "assured" needs), aggression and violence erupt. Freud was certain that this type of eruption is always present both in the life of the individual and in the history of civilization. It is the eternal battle between freedom and necessity—freedom to be happy on our own terms and necessity to conform for the sake of security. The unconscious, both within the cultural and individual experience, will not let us rest from this conflict. It has some archaic dream, Freud believed, which sees freedom and necessity as integral partners in human life. Aggression and violence are the conscious costs we pay for not realizing this dream.

As you know from your reading in psychology, Freudian theories have been modified by such writers as Carl Jung, Anna Freud, Alfred Adler, Harry Stack Sullivan, and Rollo May. The three articles in this section are examples of such modifications although all three indicate a dependence on Freud's concept of repression and its relationship to aggression (the "nice" psychological term, as Bruno Bettelheim points out, for violence). But see, in Part I, the distinction between these two terms.

The first selection, "Violence: A Neglected Mode of Behavior," is by Dr. Bruno Bettelheim. He is director of the Orthogenic School at the University of Chicago, where he is also Rowley Professor of Education and a professor in the departments of psychology and psychiatry.[3] Author of many books in his field, including *Children of the Dream* (a study of communal

[3] D. Dempsey, "Bruno Bettelheim is Dr. No," *New York Times Magazine,* January 11, 1970.

child-rearing in Israel and American education), *Love Is Not Enough,* and *Truants from Life,* he is one of the most influential thinkers involved in the study of child psychology today.

"Violence and the Masculine Mystique" is by Lucy Komisar, a New York free-lance writer who has published articles in the *New Yorker, Saturday Review* and the *Village Voice.* In her article, the "masculine mystique" has an interesting parallel to the "feminine mystique" as a current repressing factor in our American civilized order. In order to unmask these "mystiques," both sexes need consciousness-raising experiences (group experiences that discover and examine all types of repression among the participants).[4]

The final article, "The Mystification of Experience," comes from R. D. Laing's book, *The Politics of Experience.* Laing studied medicine at Glasgow University, was a psychiatrist in the British Army, a physician at Glasgow Royal Mental Hospital, and a faculty member at the University of Glasgow. In addition he was associated with the Tavistock Clinic and later in his career was appointed the Director of the Langham Clinic in London. Now he has a private practice as a psychoanalyst. His wide interests as a psychoanalyst and psychiatrist in the human experience of sanity, love, violence, communication are reflected in the titles of some of his books: *Reason and Violence* (with David Cooper), *Sanity, Madness and the Family, Vol. 1: The Families of Schizophrenics* (with Aaron Esterson), *The Divided Self.*

---

[4] Vivian Gornick, "Consciousness ♀," *The New York Times Magazine,* January 10, 1971, pp. 22 ff. (An account of ten women from New York City in a consciousness-raising session.)

Violence: A Neglected Mode of Behavior

BRUNO BETTELHEIM

These violent delights have violent ends.—
Romeo and Juliet

Aggression is by now a respectable object of study among students of human behavior. But in this paper I should like to refer to violence, which the same scholars tend to ignore or else treat with contempt. I may even share their contempt. But simply agreeing that violence is bad resolves nothing. To study aggression in detail while we close our eyes to its source is like wishing to clean out all filth without soiling our hands. If we are serious about understanding aggression and its role in society, we have to start with a good look at the desire to do violence. Robert Ardrey, whose *African Genesis* found deservedly widespread attention,[1] makes the important point that Cain, and not Abel, is the father of man. If we are children of Cain, it behooves us to know Cain well, to examine carefully his behavior and what causes it, and not to look away in disgust. The good friar of Verona knew that violent delights have violent ends. But if they were not delights, would we not shun them, since we all know they lead to disaster?

Man and society were born out of both: violence and gentle cooperation. To neglect either wellspring of life in our efforts to better human relations will be fruitless. In this paper I use aggression and violence as terms so closely related as to be interchangeable. I intend it as an invitation to study violence seriously, and not to stop short as its milder form, aggression.

---

[1] Robert Ardrey, *African Genesis* (New York: Atheneum, 1961).

Violence and Heroes

One of our best literary critics, Robert Warshow, wrote a defense of the Western movie, in particular of the gunfighter as moral hero.[2] This assertion is startling, since few of us would accept the cowboy in the Western as our moral hero, or gunfighting as an ideal way to solve moral problems. But let us remember that the sword-bearing Achilles stands as *the* moral hero at the beginning of Western civilization. Because of distance in time, the vast difference in settings, and our veneration of *The Iliad,* it is often difficult to recognize what Simone Weil was the first to point out—that *The Iliad* is a poem of violence.[3] Violence there was before Homer. But with him appears the new civilizing Greek spirit, and this he casts into his poems. The new attitude he represents is that violence is the central problem to be dealt with in a world striving to be civilized, and that nothing good ever comes of violent means. Paris, who broke violently the peace of Menelaus' home, has to perish. So does the greatest hero, Achilles, who tried to join the avenging party, not to speak of the fate of Agamemnon.

The human race, in *The Iliad,* is not divided into victorious heroes and victims. If there were conquering heroes, violence might even seem justified, at least to the victors. But in the course of *The Iliad,* if the Greeks win one day, the Trojans do the next, and in the end all of them perish. In this poem there is not a single man who does not, at one time or another, have to bow his neck to force. That the use of violence leads to retribution, with almost geometric rigor—this was a main subject of Greek thought; it is the soul of *The Iliad*. Therefore, our first great epic impresses on us that we have to think seriously of what our inner and outer attitudes to violence should be. It

---

[2] Robert Warshow, *The Immediate Experience* (Garden City, N.Y.: Doubleday, 1962).

[3] Simone Weil, "The Iliad, or the Poem of Force," *Politics* (November 1945).

may also explain the gunfighter of the Western film as a moral hero—why he has taken such hold of our imagination, and not only among youngsters but also among grownups.

This condition exists, Warshow thinks, chiefly because the Western

> offers a serious orientation to the problem of violence such as can be found almost nowhere else in our culture. One of the well-known peculiarities of modern civilized opinion is its refusal to acknowledge the value of violence. . . . We train ourselves to be shocked or bored by cultural images of violence, and our very concept of heroism tends to be a passive one: we are less drawn to the brave young men who kill large numbers of our enemies than to the heroic prisoners who endure torture without capitulating.

What we do seek in the Western is

> the image of a single man who wears a gun on his thigh. The gun tells us that he lives in a world of violence, and even that he "believes in violence." But the drama is one of self-restraint: the moment of violence must come in its own time and according to its special laws, or else it is valueless. There is little cruelty in Western movies, and little sentimentality; our eyes are not focused on the sufferings of the defeated but on the deportment of the hero.
>
> Really, it is not violence at all which is the "point" of the Western movie, but a certain image of man, a style, which expresses itself most clearly in violence.

He is there to "suggest that even in killing or being killed we are not freed from the necessity of establishing satisfactory modes of behavior."

This, then, is our problem: to establish "satisfactory modes of behavior" though we live in a society where violence is rampant. The gunfighter in the Western has found his solution to the problem. Obviously, it cannot be ours, but he at least, as Warshow has shown, takes the problem seriously, and we ought to do the same.

Violence and Child-rearing

Nowadays, parents receive a great deal of help in accepting their children's instinctual desires, as far as intake and elimination are concerned. Even about sexual behavior we tend to be more understanding, more accepting in our emotional attitudes. But as far as violence is concerned, Freud might never have written *Civilization and its Discontents,* or have concluded it by saying:

> The fateful question for the human species seems to me to be whether and to what extent their cultural development will succeed in mastering the disturbance of their communal life by the human instinct of aggression and self-destruction.

If this is the fateful question, and I certainly agree that it is, what measures are we taking to help our children do a better job of mastering the disturbance of their communal life that comes from the instinct of aggression? Freud certainly did not mean denial or suppression to be the answer, any more than he meant it for our sexual instincts. About these drives we have followed his teaching and try to be reasonable. We try to satisfy them within acceptable limits, so that they do not generate so much pressure as to cause explosive outbreaks or a crippling of the total personality. In regard to violence I find no such reasonable efforts.

Children are supposed neither to hit nor to swear at their playmates. They are supposed to refrain from destroying their toys or other property—so far, so good. But what outlets for violence *do* we provide for them? As a matter of fact, in regard to violence, we are so unreasonable that here is where the parent is apt to resort to violence himself. Few children of the educated middle class are slapped for masturbating any more, though they are not exactly raised in sexual freedom. But let the same parent meet with violence in his youngster, and as likely as not he will slap the child or thunder at him, thus demonstrating that violence is all right if one is older and stronger, and makes use of it under the guise of suppressing it.

So we end by using violence to suppress violence, and in doing so teach our children that, in our opinion, there is just no other reasonable or intelligent way to deal with it. Yet the same parents, at another moment, would agree that suppression is the worst way to deal with the instincts.

Unlike Wertham, who pleads for the suppression of vicious comics, I am convinced that neither comics nor television seduce the innocent.[4] It is high time that both the myth of original sin and its opposite—that of original innocence—be dispatched to the land of the unicorns. Innocence is neither an inborn characteristic nor a useful weapon; most of the time it is little more than an anxious clinging to ignorance.

Particularly in matters of violence, there is no protection in ignorance. Elsewhere I have tried to point out that one's ignorance of the nature of violence, as during the Nazi regime, did not lead to bliss but to death.[5] Those under Hitler who wished to believe that all men are good, and that violence exists only in a few perverted men, took no realistic steps to protect themselves and soon perished. Violence exists, surely, and each of us is born with his potential for it. But we are also born with opposite tendencies, and these must be carefully nurtured if they are to counterbalance the violence. To nurture them, however, one must know the nature of the enemy, and this is not achieved by denying its existence.

What concerns me here is that, contrary to good therapy, Wertham attacks the symptom instead of the underlying disease. This error he did not make in *The Show of Violence*,[6] where he made exactly the opposite case: namely, that in the treatment of criminals it will not do to legislate against crime; that the only intelligent way to do away with crime is to do away with what breeds it. Comic books are apt to reinforce delinquent tendencies

---

[4] F. Wertham, *Seduction of the Innocent* (New York: Rinehart, 1953).

[5] Bruno Bettelheim, *The Informed Heart* (New York: Free Press, 1960).

[6] F. Wertham, *The Show of Violence* (Garden City, N.Y.: Doubleday, 1949).

and to teach new and better ways of being delinquent. But then the basic issue is the delinquent tendencies, not the comics. And the case of the children merely reflects the pattern among adults.

Violence as Normal Behavior

We have abolished the red-light districts and outlawed prostitution. I am all for such progress, mainly because it offers the girls more protection from being exploited. But for those who cannot afford the call girl, we have closed off an easy way to discharge both sexual and violent tendencies. Worse, by asserting that there is no place for sex outside of marriage, and none for violence in our society, we force each individual to suppress his violent tendencies till they build up to a pitch where he can no longer deny them or control them. Then they suddenly erupt in isolated acts of explosive violence.

These outbursts are conspicuous. By their spectacular nature they even give the impression that ours is an age of violence. So we clamor for still greater suppression of even small eruptions of violence that could act as safety valves, draining off small amounts and leaving a balance that the individual could assimilate. Even among psychoanalysts, Freud's death instinct is not quite respectable, because we decree that what is supposed not to exist cannot and does not exist; all evidence to the contrary is simply disregarded as nonexistent.

What I believe is needed, instead, is an intelligent recognition of "the nature of the beast." We shall not be able to deal intelligently with violence unless we are first ready to see it as part of human nature, until we have gotten so well acquainted with it, by learning to live with it, that through a slow and tenuous process we may one day domesticate it successfully. In short, we cannot say that because violence *should* not exist, we might as well proceed as if it did not.

Violence is, of course, a short cut toward gaining an objective. It is so primitive in nature that it is generically unsuitable to get for us those more subtle satisfactions we want. That is why it stands at the very beginning of man's becoming a socialized human being. It is not only the heroic sagas, marking man's entry into the modern world, that are so dominated by themes of love and violence; it is true of our own entrance to life. The temper tantrum, so characteristic of the child about to become a complex human being, shows how the violent and destructive outburst heralds our coming ability to master inner drives and the external world.

Though we do not wish to acknowledge how normal this really is, many a birthday party of happy, normal children should teach us better. The birthday child, in his natural eagerness to get at the enticing present, will tear off the wrappings to get at the toy. And if the box he is ripping should be part of the game, so much the worse for the game. Thus desire begets violence, and violence may destroy the object desired. In this sense, as in many others, violence is both natural and ineffective. It rarely reaches its goal or else, in getting at it, destroys it. True, discharge itself is a goal. But then we discharge the anger, and there is no further need to find out what caused it; it does nothing to prevent what enraged us from happening again.

To recount the evils of violence here is unnecessary. Having shown in my simple example that violence is a normal mode of human behavior, I shall say no more of its nature. Instead I shall consider whether our attitudes toward violence are reasonable, given our goal to contain it, and what ways might better serve our ends.

Gang Warfare

Let me begin with the obvious, which is too often neglected when we think about violence. Whether or not it will be used or avoided depends entirely on what alternative solutions are known to a person facing a problem. Thus, violence is the behavior of someone who cannot visualize any other solution to a problem that besets him. It shows up most clearly in gang warfare.

Today we are constantly bombarded by images of a life of ownership and consumption, but for a great number of people the means to consumership are slim. This is particularly true of many young people before they find a sure place in our economic system, and even more so for those from marginal or submarginal backgrounds. Yet they are told that without such things they cannot have a satisfying life. They feel helpless to provide themselves with what they feel is even a minimal satisfaction of the demands we create in them. But they see no alternative to reaching their goals except through violence, while the pressures of frustration only tempt them more to use it. Nothing in their education—and I shall return to this later—has equipped them to deal with violence, because in their whole educational life we have denied its existence.

Lewis Yablonsky, in an excellent analysis of what makes for the violent gang,[7] remarks with irony that their views and outlook, as in a nightmarish mirror, merely reflect back the official ethos. The purpose of violence for the gang member is to achieve precisely what are the major values of respectable society: success and prestige in the eyes of one's peers. He quotes one homicidal youngster who explains his actions as follows: "I'm not going to let anybody be better than me and steal my 'rep' [reputation]. . . . When I go to a gangfight I punch, stomp and stab harder than anyone."

Yablonsky has correctly described what the violent act does for the doer. He says that the very fact that senseless, not premeditated, violence is most respected by the gang shows the function that violence has for them. Despairing of alternative solutions, or, perhaps more correctly, convinced that for them no alternatives exist, they seek a quick, almost magical way to power and prestige. In a single act of unpremeditated intensity, they at once establish a sense of their own existence and forcefully impress this now valid existence on others.

---

[7] Lewis Yablonsky, "The Violent Gang," *Commentary* (August 1960), pp. 125–130.

Frustration and Anxiety

Unfortunately, gang youth is merely one extreme of a situation that breeds violence, not only among gangs but among normal, decent human beings. While similar situations exist all over the United States, I found the best account of it in Oscar Lewis' *Children of Sánchez,* the scene of which is laid in highly urban Mexico City. To understand fully what I mean, it will have to be read.[8]

Suffice it here to say that Jesús Sánchez, tied deep within himself to the communal ways of his old village life but wishing desperately to make a go of life in twentieth-century industrial society, is defeated again and again in his aspirations. Yet he is kept going, even driving himself beyond endurance, to see, at least, his children succeed in this world that is so alluring while it frustrates at every turn. Bewildering frustration and the fact that he can see no way out lead both him and his children to be violent, simply because they know of no alternative solution.

Nor is it only the lower-class world of the gang or the children of Sánchez who share the feeling that no alternatives exist, no ways out. The whole of our society seems caught in a spirit of believing that we lack alternatives. "Red or dead" seems to be the slogan—either preparing for violence by creating weapons that are ever more destructive, or turning violence against the self: being ready to surrender without resistance to communism if it should knock at our door. And this anxiety about world affairs trickles down to college boards and grades and so on through the fabric of our lives.

In the face of such persistent anxieties about success and survival, and by denying that violence is one way out, we fail to provide any safe or constructive channels for draining it off. Ours is by no means an age of greater violence than others—on the contrary. But the chances for discharging violent tendencies are now so severely curtailed that their regular and safe draining

---

[8] Oscar Lewis, *The Children of Sánchez* (New York: Random House, 1961).

off is not possible any more. So the essential questions then are: How can violence be husbanded? How can it be discharged in ways that are socially useful? Rural life before farming was mechanized offered the child at least a chance for vicarious discharge of violence. In my native Austria, slaughtering the pig was a distinct highlight in the lives of peasant children. But so were chopping wood and other forms of aggressive manipulation of nature which at least provided outlets that were socially useful and contributed to the well-being of the family. Moreover, such a discharge was safe; it aroused no counteraggression in the target.

Our competitive or spectator sports are no real substitute, because, in the first place, they raise the aggressive feelings of competition to the boiling point. And, secondly, for every time that one wins, one is likely to lose, and every lost game builds up more aggression than the player may have discharged in playing.

Violence and Education

Having said this much, I must admit that I am at a loss to suggest what we should do. Maybe we should not go so far in suppressing violence in our children. Maybe we should let them experience—within safe limits—how damaging violence is, thus not denying them acquaintance with a tendency they must learn to control. But it is not the only way. If our experience at the Orthogenic School may serve as an example, children seem to want to learn *about* aggression, and not just to discharge it, though they want that too. Right now, the stories we teach them in class never contain any incidents of aggression. No child ever hits, becomes angry, or destroys things in an outburst. The worst they do is to tease or to pout. All of them live on Pleasant Street, in Friendly Town.

Maybe if our educational procedures were to acknowledge aggression, our children would not have to be glued to the television screen to see a bit of violence. Maybe there was some psychological wisdom to those old-fashioned readers where the child was told over and over what cruel fate befalls the evil-doer.

While these stories scared the children, they allowed for some vicarious discharge of hostility, and, having discharged it, the children's positive tendencies could be freed for the learning process. We can do even better. We can tell children through stories that people are sometimes angry at each other and quarrel, but that they can make up, and that if they do they will have a better life together.

It is peculiar to our culture that, in pushing the competitive spirit to a pitch, we stress those aggressive emotions that power competition, though aggression itself is tabooed. In a way we commit a parallel folly in our schools. But certainly one way to deal with anger is not to arouse it in the first place. Yet for quite a few children, our nice teaching materials do exactly that. Seeing pictures of the nice houses that other children have, when they themselves are living in slums, makes them angry.

How angry this makes some unfortunate children, so angry that they cannot learn, is taught us over and over by our children. One such child, who grew up in a variety of foster homes, was unable to learn and repeated first grade three times. While at the Orthogenic School, he finally was able to learn to read and print words as complicated as *soldier, submarine, fireman,* and *fighting*—all terms that were in line with his dominant feelings of hostility. But he still could not learn to read simple words like "come here," because no one had ever wanted him to come or had lovingly called out to him.

Considering the number of adopted children who feel strongly about their natural parents having given them up, and considering also the number of children who have severe emotional difficulties with their parents, I wonder if the time has not come to add neutral stories to our primers. I mean stories where family relations are not touched upon, so that children who find them upsetting can learn to read more enjoyably without anger being aroused.

Once we do offer our children a chance to learn what is foremost in their minds, or I should say what is most deeply buried there, then they learn fast and furiously,[9] like the Maori children in Sylvia Ashton-Warner's novel *Spinster*.[10] The heroine, a teacher, realized that these children wrote exciting stories of their own, only the titles of their stories were less apt to be "Fun with Dick and Jane" than "I Want You" or "I'm scared." One of these Maori children, Tame, wrote:

I ran away from my
mother and I hid
away from my mother
I hid in the Shed and
I went home and
got a hiding.

Having just read this, the teacher goes to the standard primer and turns curiously to the page from which this child was supposed to learn to read. There she finds the following story:

Mother went to a shop.
I want a cap, she said.
I want a cap for John.
She saw a brown cap.
She saw a blue cap.
I like the blue cap, she said.

Irini, a six-year-old, asks the teacher to spell several words, and then writes with concentration. Finally she brings the teacher what she has written:

Mummie said to Daddy
give me that money else
I will give you a hiding.
Daddy swear ta Mummie
Daddy gave the money

---

[9] This familiar construction, "learning fast and furiously," tells how well-known (though neglected) is the fact that we learn fast and well if, through the act of learning, we can also discharge fury, or "attack the problem," as we say.

[10] Sylvia Ashton-Warner, *Spinster, A Novel* (London: Secker & Warburg, 1958).

to Mummie. We had
a party. My father
drank all the beer by
hisself. He was drunk.

The teacher turns again to the primer and finds a story about parents:

Look at the green house.
Father is in it.
It is father's home too.

There is Mother.
She is in the green house.
She can see us.
Let us run to mother.

Compare the matter-of-fact acquaintance with aggression in these Maori tales with those in primers of the British dominions or our own up-to-date efforts.

Mrs. Ashton-Warner describes how she had to find what she calls "key words" in order to get her Maori children interested in reading and writing. Long before her, our children at the Orthogenic School forced us to similar conclusions. If we wanted them to learn, we too had to convince them that reading, writing, and spelling would help them with what concerned them most deeply. When we did that, children who for years had resisted learning even the simplest words, had been unable to learn to read from primers that pictured life in a single color—as all sweetness and light when their world was just as often drab and unhappy—these children were suddenly eager to read. Some of them who for years had not learned to read a single word then learned to recognize, read, and spell a hundred words or more in a couple of weeks' time.

When we felt they were ready for it—that is, when we felt that the resentment of learning built up through previous school experience had waned—we introduced to them certain ideas, in a short talk, in language they could understand. We told them that what is hardest to do—and the biggest problem in learning and living, but at the same time the most important one—is to master one's own scary ideas; that to learn words that help us separate the event of which we are afraid from what we only think about this event is greatly helpful. Because, while scary events that really happen are overpowering, our only thinking about them, or talking and reading about them, need not be. And in this way we come to understand them and learn to deal with them.

After such an explanation, three of our children picked as the first words they wanted to learn, *scary, fire,* and *hit.* To me it seems that in these three words our children, without knowing it, outlined a course on how to deal with aggression, at least in the classroom-learning situation. One word, *hit,* deals with animate aggression; the second, *fire,* with inanimate destruction; and the third, *scary,* with the outcome of aggression and destruction. If we permit them to state their aggressive tendencies, they can also come to recognize their scary character, and only this kind of recognition can lead to something better than denial and suppression. It can bring the conviction that in self-protection, and to avoid scary experiences, one must deal in constructive ways with the tendency to violence, both one's own and that of others.

A small sample of the emotionally charged words our children usually learn to read after seeing them once, and learn to spell and write after a few repetitions, are the following: *fire, knife, cut, crash, shoot, kill, hit, bite, teeth, cry, fight, jail, scream, yell.* Consider how much aggression they reveal, and the desire to learn about it. And compare these with what are generally considered easy words to learn.

It is just as enlightening to see how closely the words selected by our emotionally disturbed children compare with what Mrs. Ashton-Warner tells of her normal Maori children who were learning to read:

Rangi, who lives on love and kisses and thrashings and fights

> and fear of the police and who took four months to learn "come," "look," and "and," takes four minutes to learn: butcher-knife; goal; police; sing; cry; kiss; Daddy; Mummie; Rangi; haka (a native word); fight.

Each of our children selected different words because what was emotionally significant to one was not so to the others. The interesting thing is that all children learned emotionally charged words, even ones not too meaningful to them, when they saw that they were charged words for another child. They shared not only learning but each other's emotions.

As we developed our method we realized that charged or scary words sometimes aroused too much emotion. We then devised many categories, only five of which I shall mention: scary words, not-nice words, nice words, warm words, and cold words. Maybe I should mention some of the nice words the children selected. They include things like *orange juice, milk, play,* and *hot dog.* And they tell us what experiences the children think are needed to counterbalance violence. In view of the fact that most primers concentrate on what we would call nice words, it might also be of interest that the children learn the not-nice and scary words much faster and more permanently than the nice words.

To make some comparison with "normal" learning: though our children do not, like Rangi in *The Spinster,* learn eleven words in four minutes, one of our boys who learned four nice words in one day, learned ten angry ones on the same day, including ones as difficult as *witch, tornado,* and *fighting.* Which shows how the wish to master what is important to us is a powerful motivating force for learning to read, whether important things happen to be pleasant or not. And that learning about violence makes for learning in general. Because learning what the world is really like means learning about emotions—and that includes violence and what it is really like. Mastery through understanding is still the best way to equip our children for dealing with their own tendencies to violence.

For this reason the recent heated discussions about Viet Nam and related issues, pro and con, in public and at the dinner table, are a heartening sign. First, it brings into the open the ineffectiveness of violence as a way of ending our anxiety about nuclear war. And, second, it brings widespread attention to possible positive alternatives. In place of "red or dead," either one a defeat, it offers peace through compromise. And it documents how self-defeating a solution is force, since it can only bring a war in which nobody wins. "Thought," said a living British physicist,

> is born of failure. Only when action fails to satisfy human needs is there ground for thought. To devote attention to any problem is to confess a lack of adjustment which we must stop to consider. And the greater the failure the more searching is the kind of thought which is necessary.[11]

It is good that we are thinking of alternatives to violence where our children can hear us.

---

[11] L. L. Whyte, *The Next Development in Man* (New York: New American Library, 1950).

Violence and the Masculine Mystique

". . . there are worse things than war; and all of them come with defeat. The more you hate war, the more you know that once you are forced into it, for whatever reason it may be, you have to win it."

ERNEST HEMINGWAY
—from *Men at War*

"You must perform the act for them, Charlie. You know your function. Kill the enemy. So they will give you recognition of your manhood *Charlie. Never your humanity."*

MYRNA LAMB
—from the feminist play *Mod Donna*

LUCY KOMISAR

"We will not be humiliated," President Nixon declared in his speech to the country after the invasion of Cambodia. "It is not our power but our will and character that is being tested tonight." Agonizing over the specter of an America that acted like "a pitiful, helpless giant," he vowed that he would not see the nation become "a second-rate power" and "accept the first defeat in its proud 190-year history."

Nixon's resolve stiffens (masculine) and he sends troops into Cambodia so that we are not forced to submit (feminine) to a peace of humiliation. The big stick hasn't changed much since Teddy Roosevelt, only now it's a stockpile of missiles and bayonets on rifles and bombs that plow gracelessly into a womb that burns with napalm.

The United States of America is "the clear leader among modern, stable, democratic nations in its rates of homicide, assault, rape, and robbery, and it is at least among the highest in incidence of group violence and assassination," declared the National Commission on the Causes and Prevention of Violence. Most of those violent crimes are committed by males between the ages of 15 and 24; a majority of them are poor and a disproportionate percentage are black.

"Violence is actually often used to enable a young man to become a successful member of ghetto society," reported the Commission. "Proving masculinity may require frequent rehearsal of the toughness, the exploitation of women, and the quick aggressive responses that are characteristic of the lower-class adult male." The report called ghetto life a "subculture within dominant American middle-class culture in which aggressive violence tends to be accepted as normal in everyday life. . . . An altercation with overtones threatening a young man's masculinity, a misunderstanding between husband and wife, competition for a sexual partner, the need to get hold of a few dollars—these trivial events can readily elicit violent response."

The only thing wrong with that is the Commission's assumption that its observations apply only to the lower classes. What it has described, in fact, is the "masculine mystique," a conception of manhood so central to the politics and personality of America that it institutionalizes violence and male supremacy as measures of national pride. The masculine mystique is based on toughness and domination, qualities that once may have been necessary in a time when men felled trees and slew wild animals. Now they are archaic and destructive values that have no legitimate place in our world but continue to exist as idealized standards for some lofty state of "masculinity." The mystique has characterized many nations, but it is particularly dangerous in contemporary America because of our distinctively high levels of internal violence, our "Bonnie and Clyde" tendencies toward its glorification, our enormous capacities for mechanized warfare, and our virtual obsession with being Number One.

A quote from a man I know: "When I was a little boy and

had come home crying after a beating from some local bully, my mother would push me out and lock the door, demanding that I go back to give as good as I had gotten. She said boys who didn't fight back were sissies."

Little boys learn the connection between violence and manhood very early in life. Fathers indulge in mock prize fights and wrestling matches with eight-year-olds. Boys play cowboys and Indians with guns and bows and arrows proffered by their elders. They are gangsters or soldiers interchangeably—the lack of difference between the two is more evident to them than to their parents. They are encouraged to "fight back," and bloodied noses and black eyes become trophies of their pint-sized virility.

Little Men

The differences between boys and girls are defined in terms of violence. Boys are encouraged to rough-house; girls are taught to be gentle ("ladylike"). Boys are expected to get into fights, but admonished not to hit girls. (It is not "manly" to assault females—except, of course, sexually, but that comes later.) Boys who run away from fights are "sissies," with the implication that they are queer. As little boys become big boys, their education in violence continues. The leadership in this country today consists of such little boys who attained "manhood" in the approved and heroic violence of World War II. They returned to a society in which street and motorcycle gangs, fast cars, and fraternity hazing confirmed the lessons of war—one must be tough and ready to inflict pain in order to get ahead.

The phallic/power symbol of our age is, of course, the automobile. The World Health Organization says that traffic accidents are the most common cause of death among young males in highly motorized countries. Often cars are stolen not to keep or sell, but for the joy of the ride and the sense of power and controlled violence it offers. Madison Avenue contributes its influence by selling cars as if they were magical potency potions. Chivalry's knight on horseback has become man on "horsepower" —even modern terminology substantiates the metaphor.

A young philosophy instructor at a Catholic men's college in New Jersey, who leads a "consciousness-raising" group for some of his students, says most of them have grown up with the same conception of what it takes to prove one's manhood: "You have a car and 'make' as many girls as possible. It's very important to have an impressive car; the freshmen all believe the ads that if you've got a Dodge Charger, you're going to get laid more." The system militates against tenderness, he says. "No physical display between men is acceptable except to fight, and the *only* acceptable response when someone questions your manhood is to fight. Most freshmen think there's something faggoty about being a draft dodger."

He adds, "Some guys are so obsessed with their manhood and masculinity that they can't make love: they feel it's effeminate to be sensitive or affectionate."

Boys are introduced into "manhood" through innocent pastimes like boxing, brawling, and football. And not-so-innocent pastimes like war. Consider phrases like "The manly art of self defense," "Join the army, be a man" (variation: "The army will make a man out of him"). Gene Tunney's autobiography is called simply *A Man Must Fight*. Men who have been brought up in this tradition, and whose memories of war, real or imagined, have bolstered their self-respect during years of bringing home the bacon, are traumatized by the young men (students and peace marchers) who refuse to accept pain, mutilation, and death as initiation rites into manhood.

Even at a time when the protest leader is beginning to replace the football star as campus hero, football remains a passion with a large number of American men. The game, with its crashing, smashing bodies and carefully controlled violence, deserves a closer scrutiny to see how it reflects the quest for manhood.

The Great Touchdown of Virility

For the past half dozen years, I have observed the phenomenon of the masculine mystique operating on a group of newspapermen who frequent a bar in my neighborhood. They drink heavily, rhapsodize about prize fighters and men who earn their living by physical labor, share football afternoons watching the barroom television, and treat women mostly as "dumb broads" to be taken in bed and ignored in serious conversation. There are some exceptions.

Several of them urged me to read Frederick Exley's *A Fan's Notes,* an autobiographical novel which had been nominated for the National Book Award. I read it and realized how it must have been a mirror for many of them—yet neither they nor Exley appear to have understood the significance and the logic of his story.

The book's Fred Exley is an impotent writer (impotent in his work and, in one episode, impotent in bed) who seeks fame and recognition and whose hero is Giants' football player Frank Gifford. Exley's father was a tough, athletic, working-class man whose drinking often ended in violence. The son longs for "some sunnier past" when men could prove their virility with the muscles in their arms. His book never indicates any recognition of the fact that his idolatry of football and of the hard-drinking laborer—and his exploitation of women—mask the fear that he is "unmanly," that he is "womanish"—the epithet he uses to describe a despised Hollywood publicist. His anguished search is futile, for he reaches out for a definition of manhood that can no longer exist for most men, except through the shallow medium of television. Exley's own words offer a vivid picture of the masculine mystique. First the football hero as symbol of the time when manhood was easily defined and won by power and dominance:

> Why did football bring me so to life? I can't say precisely. Part of it was my feeling that football was an island of directness in a world of circumspection. In football a man was asked to do a difficult and brutal job, and he either did it or got out. There was nothing rhetorical or vague about it. . . . It smacked of something old, something traditional, something unclouded by legerdemain and subterfuge. It had that kind of power over me, drawing me back with the force of something known,

> scarcely remembered, elusive as integrity—perhaps it was no more than the force of a forgotten childhood. Whatever it was, I gave myself up to the Giants utterly. The recompense I gained was the feeling of being alive.

Then, Exley's image of his father as the symbol of the virility he seeks to attain:

> . . . when I think of him now, I think of rough-cotton work shirts open at the collar, a broad masculine face made ruddy by exposure and a Camel cigarette dangling from the corner of his pensive mouth. There was nothing about him that did not suggest his complete awareness that he got his bread by the sweat of his brow and the power of his back. . . . Like most athletes he lived amidst the large deeds and ephemeral glories of the past, recalling a time when it must have seemed more Elevated. . . . my father drank—I was about to say too much, which would not be entirely accurate. My father could not, or so my mother recalls, drink even the most limited amounts of beer without becoming moody, argumentative, and even violent; and on one occasion he beat a man so badly that the man had to have pulled what few teeth my father left him.

Lastly, Exley's certainty that he had failed the test of masculinity in the eyes of his father. He was a small boy being introduced to Steve Owen, the coach of the Giants:

> "Are you tough?" Owen asked.
> "Pardon, sir?"
> *"Are you tough?"*
> "I don't know, sir."
> Owen looked at my father. "Is he tough, Mr. Exley?"
> Though more than anything I wanted my father to say that I was, I was not surprised at his answer.
> "It's too soon to tell."

Hunting, bullfighting, cockfighting. Is it a more "humane" sport to shoot an animal for the pure joy of watching it fall or more "virile" to torture it slowly under the guise of letting it fight back—and subjecting the killer to the threat of death himself? What thrilling, "macho" feeling overcomes spectators at the gruesome sight of two male chickens with metal spurs attached to their feet fiercely hacking each other to bits? Ernest Hemingway went to his own violent death without making all that perfectly clear.

How far is it from the glorification of man killing animals to what amounted to national admiration for the killers of the Prohibition era and the men who terrorized the country with gangland power? After all, Dutch Schultz and Al Capone were only following in the heroic, virile tradition of Billy the Kid and the James brothers. And like Hemingway's bullfighters, they did everything with flamboyant style. In 1872, a Kansas City newspaper, reporting a robbery in which a little girl was shot in the leg, called it "so diabolically daring and so utterly in contempt of fear that we are bound to admire it and revere its perpetrators." Still dripping with nobility a few days later, it said that the robbers had carried out their crime "with the halo of medieval chivalry upon their garments." The criminals were thought to be Frank and Jesse James.

If manhood is equivalent to strength and power, those attributes must be constantly tested and proven to new challengers. "I knew a guy who was very short," a friend of mine recalls. "He told me that he used to fantasize that he was Audie Murphy. He would go into a working-class bar where nobody knew him and he'd do this act. He'd sit at the bar, maybe for a half hour and growl at the bartender. After a while, someone would come over and maybe say something or poke him on the shoulder, and he'd spin around and hit the guy over the head with a beer bottle. He was always sitting there waiting for someone to provoke him, and he always had the bottle ready."

Some people say men fight in bars because they get drunk, but that has nothing to do with it. Men fight in bars because that's the only place where it's allowed. (That is probably the reason why Exley's father got into fights after only a few beers.) Society instills feelings in men that they ought to fight and then makes it illegal—except in war. Working-class bars are 'masculine' places—the football on TV, the absence of women, and the fights are all part of the effort to recapture that lost ideal.

Postscript: On May 29, a short item buried in the back pages of *The New York Times* reported that actor Audie Murphy, America's most decorated soldier in World War II, had been booked for assault with intent to commit murder after a gun went off during a fight he had with a dog trainer.

In the old West ("where men were men and women were women") gunfighters were often called on to prove themselves in duels with younger men who wagered their lives against the chance to be known as "the man who shot the fastest gun in . . . , etc." Today's shoot-em-ups in defense of manhood unfortunately tend to involve more than the principals.

The Soft Battlefield

The ultimate proof of manhood, however, is in sexual violence. Even the language of sex is a lexicon that describes the power of men over women. Men are "aggressive" as they "take" or "make" women, showing their potency ("power") in the "conquest." Women, on the other hand, "submit" and "surrender," allowing themselves to be "violated" and "possessed." Havelock Ellis declares the basic sado-masochism of such a concept to be "certainly normal." He says: "In men it is possible to trace a tendency to inflict pain on the women they love. It is still easier to trace in women a delight in experiencing physical pain when it is inflicted by a lover and an eagerness to accept subjection to his will."

Sadism *cum* virility is offered the fans who flock to James Bond films to see their hero play out their fantasies alternately in sensual embraces with women and bloody combat with men. In *Goldfinger,* for instance, Bond has his arms around a chorus girl when he sees the reflection of an assassin in her eye. He wards off the blow with her body, a consummation which seems as satisfying to his manhood as the one he originally had in mind. There is as little tenderness and as much brutality in the sexual encounters as in the fight scenes. If homosexuality were in fashion, it is likely that James Bond could make love to the men and beat up the women without changing his sentiments toward either.

Chivalry was an early example of the worship of masculine violence tied in with sexual dominance. Then and later, duels were fought to protect the honor of women and wars waged to uphold the honor of states. In the latter endeavor, the women were raped instead of honored. Both traditions have been proudly continued, and in both the women have been objects to conquer and to parade as the validation of someone's manhood: *they have no honor of their own*.

Rape on foreign battlefields has always been met on the homefront with shrugs about men having certain "needs" and the "tensions" that build up in wartime. So soldiers get penicillin along with their K-rations, and they express their "manhood" by forcing women to submit to them. Those that lie with prostitutes are participating in rape in just as real a sense—they are enjoying the bitter fruits of the rape of a country that forces its citizens to choose between death and degradation.

In 1966, an American patrol held a 19-year-old Vietnamese girl captive for several days, taking turns raping her and finally murdering her. The sergeant planned the crime in advance, telling the soldiers during the mission's briefing that the girl would improve their "morale." When one soldier refused to take part in the rape, the sergeant called him "queer" and "chicken;" another testified later that he joined in the assault to avoid such insults. When one *country* ravages another to avoid being called "chicken," how unusual is it that soldiers follow suit? Both in the name of that elusive "manhood."

According to Seymour Hersh, some of the GIs who conducted the My Lai massacre raped women before they shot them. The day after that "mission," an entire platoon raped a woman caught fleeing a burning hut. And a couple of days later a helicopter door gunner spotted the body of a woman in a field. She was spread-eagled, with an Eleventh Brigade patch between her legs. Like a "badge of honor," reported the gunner. "It was obviously there so people would know the Eleventh Brigade had been there."

Machismo and the Don Juan cult, modern versions of chivalry, are brushed off as Latin oddities. Spaniards and Italians defend their honor with "passion killings"—and everyone winks. But they are not the only men who regard women as trophies in rape or seduction or who think wife-beating is a joke (literally, as in "When did you stop beating your wife?"). How different are those passion killings from Southern lynchings conducted in the name of white womanhood and against the imagined sexual onslaughts of black men? It is not a coincidence that white supremacy in the South organized the "Knights" of the Ku Klux Klan. That was an assertion of masculinity in the face of humiliation by other men; it was as much male supremacy as white supremacy.

The writing of Eldridge Cleaver epitomizes the way in which many black men, too, hold violence equivalent to masculinity, fully in the American tradition. "The boxing ring is the ultimate focus of masculinity in America," says Cleaver in *Soul on Ice;* "the two-fisted testing ground of manhood, and the heavyweight champion, as a symbol, is the real Mr. America." Cleaver recognizes the historical significance of violence in our culture:

> Whether we quench our thirst from the sight of a bleeding Jesus on the Cross, from the ritualized sacrifice in the elevation of the Host and the consecration of the Blood of the Son, or from bullfighting, cockfighting, dogfighting, wrestling or boxing, spiced with our Occidental memory and heritage of the gladiators of Rome and the mass spectator sport of the time of feeding Christians and other enemies of society to the lions in the Coliseum—whatever the mask assumed by the impulse, the persistent beat of the drum over the years intones the chant.

However, his own cry is not a protest against that definition of masculinity but anguish that black men cannot live up to it:

In back rooms, in dark stinking corners of the ghettos, self-conscious black men curse their own cowardice and stare at their rifles and pistols and shotguns laid out on tables before them, trembling as they wish for a manly impulse to course through their bodies and send them screaming mad into the streets shooting from the hip. Black women look at their men as if they are bugs. . . .

Hemingway and Mailer: The Bulls of Literature

Alan Sillitoe, author of "Saturday Night and Sunday Morning," writes: "An intellectual obsession with violence is a sign of fear. A physical obsession with it is a sign of sexual impotence." Interesting, then, that Ernest Hemingway, who composed hosannas to manly brutality, took his own life with a gun and that Norman Mailer, one of America's most self-conscious "machos," once stabbed his wife and has been in more than one barroom and cocktail party brawl.

In 1927, Hemingway published *Men Without Women,* a collection of stories which I expect reflect his conception of ultimate manhood. The stories are variously written about a bullfighter, a boxer, several soldiers, some hired gunmen, etc. Women are represented as unwelcomely pregnant (in a story pointedly titled "White Elephants"); as prostitutes, as deceivers, or as fools. Ultimately, Hemingway's answer is to eschew women for more "masculine" pastimes—fishing, for example:

> I lay in the dark with my eyes open and thought of all the girls I had ever known and what kind of wives they would make. It was a very interesting thing to think about and for a while it killed off trout-fishing and interfered with my prayers. Finally, though, I went back to trout-fishing, because I found that I could remember all the streams and there was always something new about them while the girls, after I had thought about them a few times, blurred and I could not call them into my mind and finally they all blurred and all became rather the same and I gave up thinking about them almost altogether. ("Now I Lay Me")

Critic Leslie Fiedler thinks Hemingway's concern with violence reflects a pathological inability to deal with adult sexuality. If, as Sillitoe says, obsession with violence is a sign of impotence, trading women for fish is one way to avoid that embarrassing confrontation.

Mailer is more extravagant than Hemingway in his exaltation of violence: "Men who have lived a great deal with violence are usually gentler and more tolerant than men who abhor violence," he says. "Boxers, bullfighters, a lot of combat soldiers, Hemingway heroes, in short, are almost always gentle men."

What romantic drivel! My Lai, cauliflower ears and broken noses, slit throats, cement blocks splashing into Mafia cemeteries, guts spilling out of gored intestines—do the actors in such violent dramas radiate the compassion and understanding Mailer attributes to them? Not to mention the Chicago police Mailer himself has had occasion to describe without recourse to adjectives like "gentle" or "tolerant."

If Mailer's ideal man of the world is described in such incredible terms, what about his man in bed? Sex is conquest, a contest, an opportunity for domination. Mailer compares the "event" in bed to the bullfight. Sometimes he sees himself as the matador, sometimes as the bull. He calls his penis "the avenger" (For what "crime" or "insult" does he avenge himself against women?), and he recalls how he "threw her a fuck the equivalent of a 15-round fight."

In *Sexual Politics,* feminist Kate Millet devotes an entire chapter to an analysis of Mailer's obsession with violence, showing how his equation of violence and masculinity masks an overriding fear of homosexuality as well as a contempt for women. Beginning with *The Naked and the Dead,* Mailer could barely speak either of sex or violence in terms that did not include the other. Millet cites a speech by Sergeant Croft:

> All the deep dark urges of man, the sacrifices on the hilltop, the churning lusts of night and sleep, weren't all of them contained in the shattering, screaming burst of a shell . . . the

phallus-shell that rides through a shining vagina of steel . . . the curve of sexual excitement and discharge, which is after all the physical core of life.

Mailer equates the opposite of violence—pacifism—with the opposites of maleness—femaleness and homosexuality—both of which arouse his contempt. The logical outcome of this ideology, says Millet, is war and violence, the only protection against the pacifism he labels "unmanly." And the violence that Mailer venerates is the logical extension and proof of the aggressiveness this society considers an innate part of the truly masculine personality. "Men are aggressive, women are passive," says the conventional wisdom. "Men are dominant and venturesome; women are yielding and receptive." The dictionary definition of passive is "inactive, but acted upon; offering no resistance, submissive; taking no part, inert." That sounds more like a vegetable than a human being of *any* sex.

The truth of the matter is that neither men nor women are born "aggressive" or "passive"; the values of masculinity and femininity (as this society sees them) are drummed into them by parents, teachers, the media, and other agents of social education. The California Gender Identity Center, for one, has discovered that it is easier to use surgery to change the sex of an adolescent male who has been erroneously brought up as a female than to undo the cultural conditioning that has made him act like a woman. The report of the Center concludes that masculine and feminine roles are determined by *social forces,* not by the nature of a person's genitals.

In other words, this society has inculcated values of aggression and dominance in males and those values have led logically to violence and destruction in the name of good old, unadulterated manhood. Behavioral scientists back up this assertion with their own investigations and analyses. Sometimes teenage delinquents play the same games adults do—they hope to preserve their honor through "cold wars" without resorting to actual battle. Anthropologist Walter Miller, who studied gangs in the 1950's, observed a number of groups in full-scale war preparations 15 times; only once did they escalate into conflict. "A major objective of the gang members was to put themselves in the position of fighting without actually having to fight." They often avoided warfare by tipping off the police or "reluctantly" accepting mediation from social workers.

The similarity between saber-rattling by teenage delinquents and modern nation-states is obvious. "Gang members fight to secure and defend their honor as males; to secure and defend the reputation of their local areas and the honor of their women; to show that an affront to their pride and dignity demands retaliation," says Miller, adding almost unnecessarily that "great nations engage in national wars for almost identical reasons." (The "theatre of war" is a fit appellation for the locus of this kind of masculine play-acting.) Miller concludes that teenage violence and international warfare stem from the same pathological root.

An End to the Game

Violence and male supremacy have been companions in the course of civilization. The domination of women by men has been the prototype of the control men have tried to exercise over other men—in slavery, in war, and in the marketplace. Bernard Clark, professor of government at the London School of Economics, speaks glowingly of "the fierce masculine joy of striving for possession according to some more or less acknowledged rules of a game." That is the game that President Nixon plays, the game that wins acclaim from Hemingway and Mailer, the game that enshrined Jesse James as a national hero, and the game that spills buckets of human blood and guts on battlefields at home and abroad.

That game says that to be a man one must possess, control, dominate—and that domination must be assured by force and violence. Masculinity is interpreted to *demand* male supremacy. Ironically, now in the black community, men are calling on women to step back so that they can "assert their manhood."

The "masculinity game" can't have a winner unless it also has a loser. The rules of the game require that the losers be reduced to humiliation and powerlessness—to the classic status of women. Such was the "emasculation" of black men under slavery and segregation. And consequently, they know that the reassertion of that kind of "manhood" requires the suppression of their women.

John Wayne is the quintessential player in The Game. His role in "The Green Berets" would be an embarrassing parody if patriotic zeal were not immune to wit. Wayne is tough-fisted, hard-talking, and never walks away from a fight; thanks to providence, righteousness, and his rugged, muscular frame, he never loses. But it never happens in real life like in the movies. They probably wouldn't like the metaphor, but the "hard hats" constitute a Greek chorus to masculinity—they extol it through physical labor, vulgar comments at passing women, and patriotic fervor for "our brave fighting men in Vietnam." Sometimes the defense of their manhood, otherwise largely expressed through applauding someone else's violence, forces them to beat up people who disagree with them.

The enemies of national "virility" are called "effete," a word that means "sterile, spent, worn-out" and conjures up the picture of an effeminate pantywaist—the inveterate 90-pound weakling who is always getting sand kicked in his face, probably by a burly construction worker. More to the point, effete comes from "out" plus "fetus"—exhausted by bearing.

Perhaps we *are* "exhausted by bearing"—tired to death of bearing up under the super-masculine mystique that is a national neurosis and that sets a country to counting bodies the way it counts touchdowns—and cataloguing both as a measure of its manhood.

Is it only coincidental that in the early morning hours of the last demonstration of outrage at the invasion of Cambodia and the deaths of American college students, President Nixon was compelled to talk about football—or that he repeated that theme in May at a Billy Graham rally in Knoxville, Tennessee?

"As one who warmed the bench for four years, it's finally good to get out on the football field here at Volunteer Stadium," he said. "And even if we're on the 20-yard line, we're going to be over that goal line before we're through." Nixon talks about "our-brave-fighting-men-in-Vietnam" as if they were Fred Exley's Giants—the essence of manhood wrapped up in hard hats and shoulder pads. All America has to suffer because young Richard Nixon never made the team.

Ironically, the "he-men" who occupy the ringside seats at prize fights, football games, and wars don't recognize the significant difference between their "masculinity" and that of the athlete and frontiersman they adulate. They generally enjoy their violence *vicariously*; there is no call for personal courage. Richard Nixon is *still* warming the bench, and sending others to shoot Vietnamese villagers or scorch them with napalm is hardly an exercise in bravery.

The President is the symbol of a country with a castration complex—a nation that feels its manhood already wilted by the refusal of the Viet Cong to spread its legs for the gang-bang we have organized.

The beginning of a challenge to the masculine mystique of violence and domination comes now from those who were its first victims: women. Today women are demanding new definitions of masculine and feminine that do not require the dominance of one sex over the other. We have rejected all the myths about masculine aggression and feminine passivity and we seek to replace them with values that encourage human relations based on equality, compassion, and respect.

Today the masculine mystique is no longer just a matter of concern for the women who have suffered its ill effects most universally. The caveman mentality outlived its usefulness when technology made the hunter obsolete, and its extension into national and international politics now threatens to destroy everything men *and women* have built since then.

Today men need a kind of courage that is only exhibited by those who have no doubts at all about their *manhood*—and that is the courage to assert their *humanity*.

The Mystification of Experience

R. D. LAING

It is not enough to destroy one's own and other people's experience. One must overlay this devastation by a false consciousness inured, as Marcuse puts it, to its own falsity.

Exploitation must not be seen as such. It must be seen as benevolence. Persecution preferably should not need to be invalidated as the figment of a paranoid imagination; it should be experienced as kindness. Marx described mystification and showed its function in his day. Orwell's time is already with us. The colonists not only mystify the natives, in the ways that Fanon so clearly shows,[1] they have to mystify themselves. We in Europe and North America are the colonists, and in order to sustain our amazing images of ourselves as God's gift to the vast majority of the starving human species, we have to interiorize our violence upon ourselves and our children and to employ the rhetoric of morality to describe this process.

In order to rationalize our industrial-military complex, we have to destroy our capacity to see clearly any more what is in front of, and to imagine what is beyond, our noses. Long before a thermonuclear war can come about, we have had to lay waste our own sanity. We begin with the children. It is imperative to

[1] Frantz Fanon, *The Wretched of the Earth* (London: MacGibbon and Kee, 1965); also Frantz Fanon, *Studies in a Dying Colonialism* (New York: Monthly Review Press, 1965).

catch them in time. Without the most thorough and rapid brainwashing their dirty minds would see through our dirty tricks. Children are not yet fools, but we shall turn them into imbeciles like ourselves, with high I.Q.'s if possible.

From the moment of birth, when the Stone Age baby confronts the twentieth-century mother, the baby is subjected to these forces of violence, called love, as its mother and father, and their parents and their parents before them, have been. These forces are mainly concerned with destroying most of its potentialities, and on the whole this enterprise is successful. By the time the new human being is fifteen or so, we are left with a being like ourselves, a half-crazed creature more or less adjusted to a mad world. This is normality in our present age.

Love and violence, properly speaking, are polar opposites. Love lets the other be, but with affection and concern. Violence attempts to constrain the other's freedom, to force him to act in the way we desire, but with ultimate lack of concern, with indifference to the other's own existence or destiny.

We are effectively destroying ourselves by violence masquerading as love.

I am a specialist, God help me, in events in inner space and time, in experiences called thoughts, images, reveries, dreams, visions, hallucinations, dreams of memories, memories of dreams, memories of visions, dreams of hallucinations, refractions of refractions of refractions of that original Alpha and Omega of experience and reality, that Reality on whose repression, denial, splitting, projection, falsification, and general desecration and profanation our civilization as much as on anything is based.

We live equally out of our bodies and out of our minds.

Concerned as I am with this inner world, observing day in and day out its devastation, I ask why this has happened?

One component of an answer is that we can *act* on our *experience* of ourselves, others and the world, as well as take action on the world through behavior itself. Specifically this devastation is largely the work of *violence* that has been perpetrated on each of us, and by each of us on ourselves. The usual name that much of this violence goes under is *love.*

We act on our experience at the behest of the others, just as we learn how to behave in compliance with them. We are taught what to experience and what not to experience, as we are taught what movements to make and what sounds to emit. A child of two is already a moral mover and moral talker and moral experiencer. He already moves the "right" way, makes the "right" noises, and knows what he should feel and what he should not feel. His movements have become stereometric types, enabling the specialist anthropologist to identify, through his rhythm and style, his national, even his regional, characteristics. As he is taught to move in specific ways out of the whole range of possible movements, so he is taught to experience out of the whole range of possible experience.

Much current social science deepens the mystification. Violence cannot be seen through the sights of positivism.

A woman grinds stuff down a goose's neck through a funnel. Is this a description of cruelty to an animal? She disclaims any motivation or intention of cruelty. If we were to describe this scene "objectively," we would only be denuding it of what is "objectively," or better, ontologically present in the situation. Every description presupposes our ontological premises as to the nature (being) of man, of animals, and of the relationship between them.

If an animal is debased to a manufactured piece of produce, a sort of biochemical complex—so that its flesh and organs are simply material with a certain texture in the mouth (soft, tender, tough) a taste, perhaps a smell—then to describe the animal *positively* in those terms is to debase oneself by debasing being itself. A *positive* description is not "neutral" or "objective." In the case of geese-as-raw-material-for-*pâté,* one can only give a negative description if the description is to remain underpinned by a valid ontology. That is to say, the description moves in the light of what this activity is a brutalization of, a debasement of, a desecration of: namely, the true nature of human beings and of animals.

The description must be *in light of* the fact that the human beings have so brutalized themselves, have become so banal and stultified, that they are unaware of their own debasement. This is not to superimpose onto the "neutral" description certain value judgments that have lost all criteria of "objective" validity, that is to say, any validity that anyone feels needs to be taken really seriously. On "subjective" matters, anything goes. Political ideologies, on the other hand, are riddled with value judgments, unrecognized as such, that have no ontological validity. Pedants teach youth that such questions of value are unanswerable, or untestable, or unverifiable, or not really questions at all, or that what we require are metaquestions. Meanwhile Vietnam goes on.

Under the sign of alienation every single aspect of the human reality is subject to falsification, and a positive description can only perpetuate the alienation which it cannot itself describe, and succeeds only in further deepening it because it disguises and masks it the more.

We must then repudiate a positivism that achieves its "reliability" by successfully masking what is and what is not, by serializing the world of the observer, by turning the truly given into *capta* which are *taken as given,* by denuding the world of being and relegating the ghost of being to a shadow land of subjective "values."

The theoretical and descriptive idiom of much research in social science adopts a stance of apparent "objective" neutrality. But we have seen how deceptive this can be. The choice of syntax and vocabulary is a political act that defines and circumscribes the manner in which "facts" are to be experienced. Indeed, in a sense it goes further and even creates the facts that are studied.

The "data" (given) of research are not so much given as *taken* out of a constantly elusive matrix of happenings. We should speak of *capta* rather than data. The quantitatively interchangeable grist that goes into the mills of reliability studies and rating scales is the expression of a processing that we do *on* reality, not the expression of the processes *of* reality.

Natural scientific investigations are conducted on objects, or things, or the patterns of relations between things, or on systems of "events." Persons are distinguished from things in that persons experience the world, whereas things behave in the world. Thing-events do not experience. Personal events are experiential. Natural scientism is the error of turning persons into things by a process of reification that is not itself part of true natural scientific method. Results derived in this way have to be dequantified and dereified before they can be reassimilated into the realm of human discourse.

Fundamentally, the error is the failure to realize that there is an ontological discontinuity between human beings and it-beings.

Human beings relate to each other not simply externally, like two billiard balls, but by the relations of the two worlds of experience that come into play when two people meet.

If human beings are not studied as human beings, then this once more is violence and mystification.

In much contemporary writing on the individual and the family there is assumed some not-too-unhappy confluence, not to say pre-established harmony, between nature and nurture. Some adjustments may have to be made on both sides, but all things work together for good to those who want only security and identity.

Gone is any sense of possible tragedy, of passion. Gone is any language of joy, delight, passion, sex, violence. The language is that of a boardroom. No more primal scenes, but parental coalitions; no more repression of sexual ties to parents, but the child "rescinds" its Oedipal wishes. For instance:

> The mother can properly invest her energies in the care of the young child when economic support, status, and protection of the family are provided by the father. She can also better limit her

cathexis of the child to maternal feelings when her wifely needs are satisfied by her husband.[2]

Here is no nasty talk of sexual intercourse or even "primal scene." The economic metaphor is aptly employed. The mother "invests" in her child. What is most revealing is the husband's function. The provision of economic support, status and protection, in that order.

There is frequent reference to security, the esteem of others. What one is supposed to want, to live for, is "gaining pleasure from the esteem and affection of others."[3] If not, one is a psychopath.

Such statements are in a sense true. They describe the frightened, cowed, abject creature that we are admonished to be, if we are to be normal—offering each other mutual protection from our own violence. The family as a "protection racket."

Behind this language lurks the terror that is behind all this mutual back-scratching, this esteem-, status-, support-, protection-, security-giving and getting. Through its bland urbanity the cracks still show.

In our world we are "victims burning at the stake, signaling through the flames," but for some, things go blandly on. "Contemporary life requires adaptability." We require also to "utilize intellect," and we require "an emotional equilibrium that permits a person to be malleable, to adjust himself to others without fear of loss of identity with change. It requires a basic trust in others, and a confidence in the integrity of the self."[4]

Sometimes there is a glimpse of more honesty. For instance, when we "consider society rather than the individual, each society has a vital interest in the *indoctrination* of the infants who form its new *recruits*."[5]

---

[2] T. Lidz, *The Family and Human Adaptation* (London: Hogarth Press, 1964), p. 54.

[3] Ibid., p. 34.

[4] Ibid., pp. 28–9.

[5] Ibid., p. 19.

What these authors say may be written ironically, but there is no evidence that it is.

Adaptation to what? To society? To a world gone mad?

The family's function is to repress Eros; to induce a false consciousness of security; to deny death by avoiding life; to cut off transcendence; to believe in God, not to experience the Void; to create, in short, one-dimensional man; to promote respect, conformity, obedience; to con children out of play; to induce a fear of failure; to promote a respect for work; to promote a respect for "respectability."

Let me present here two alternative views of the family and human adaptation:

> Men do not become what by nature they are meant to be, but what society makes them. . . . generous feelings . . . are, as it were, shrunk up, seared, violently wrenched, and amputated to fit us for our intercourse with the world, something in the manner that beggars maim and mutilate their children to make them fit for their future situation in life.[6]

and:

> In fact, the world still seems to be inhabited by savages stupid enough to see reincarnated ancestors in their newborn children. Weapons and jewelry belonging to the dead men are waved under the infant's nose; if he makes a movement, there is a great shout—Grandfather has come back to life. This "old man" will suckle, dirty his straw and bear the ancestral name; survivors of his ancient generation will enjoy seeing their comrade of hunts and battles wave his tiny limbs and bawl; as soon as he can speak they will inculcate recollections of the deceased. A severe training will "restore" his former character, they will remind him that "he" was wrathful, cruel or magnanimous, and he will be convinced of it despite all experience to the contrary. What barbarism! Take a living child, sew him up in a dead man's skin, and he will stifle in such senile childhood with no

[6] E. Colby, ed., *The Life of Thomas Holcroft, continued by William Hazlitt* (London: Constable & Co., 1925), vol. 2, p. 82.

> occupation save to reproduce the avuncular gestures, with no hope save to poison future childhoods after his own death. No wonder, after that, if he speaks of himself with the greatest precautions, half under his breath, often in the third person; this miserable creature is well aware that he is his own grandfather.
>
> These backward aborigines can be found in the Fiji Islands, in Tahiti, in New Guinea, in Vienna, in Paris, in Rome, in New York—wherever there are men. They are called parents. Long before our birth, even before we are conceived, our parents have decided who we will be.[7]

In some quarters there is a point of view that science is neutral, and that all this is a matter of value judgements.

Lidz calls schizophrenia a failure of human adaptation. In that case, this too is a value judgement. Or is anyone going to say that it is an objective fact? Very well, let us call schizophrenia a successful attempt not to adapt to pseudo-social realities. Is this also an objective fact? Schizophrenia is a failure of ego functioning. Is this a neutralist definition? But what is, or who is, the "ego"? In order to get back to what the ego is and what actual reality it most nearly relates to, we have to desegregate it, de-depersonalize it, de-extrapolate, de-abstract, de-objectify, de-reify, and we get back to you and me, to our particular idioms or styles of relating to each other in social context. The ego is by definition an instrument of adaptation, so we are back to all the questions this apparent neutralism is begging. Is schizophrenia a successful avoidance of ego-type adaptation? Schizophrenia is a label affixed by some people to others in situations where an interpersonal disjunction of a particular kind is occurring. This is the nearest one can get at the moment to something like an "objective" statement, so called.

The family is, in the first place, the usual instrument for what is called socialization, that is, getting each new recruit to the human race to behave and experience in substantially the same

---

[7] J.-P. Sartre, Foreword to *The Traitor* by André Gorz (London: Calder, 1960), pp. 14–15.

way as those who have already got here. We are all fallen Sons of Prophecy, who have learned to die in the Spirit and be reborn in the flesh.

This is also known as selling one's birthright for a mess of pottage.

Here are some examples from Jules Henry, an American professor of anthropology and sociology, in his study of the American school system:

> The observer is just entering her fifth-grade classroom for the observation period. The teacher says, "Which one of you nice, polite boys would like to take (the observer's) coat and hang it up?" From the waving hands, it would seem that all would like to claim the honor. The teacher chooses one child, who takes the observer's coat. . . . The teacher conducted the arithmetic lessons mostly by asking, "Who would like to tell the answer to the next problem?" This question was followed by the usual large and agitated forest of hands, with apparently much competition to answer.
>
> What strikes us here are the precision with which the teacher was able to mobilize the potentialities of the boys for the proper social behavior, and the speed with which they responded. The large number of waving hands proves that most of the boys have already become absurd; but they have no choice. Suppose they sat there frozen?
>
> A skilled teacher sets up many situations in such a way that a *negative attitude can be construed only as treason.* The function of questions like, "Which one of you nice, polite boys would like to take (the observer's) coat and hang it up?" is to blind the children into absurdity—to compel them to acknowledge that it is better to exist absurd than not to exist at all. The reader will have observed that the question is not put, "Who *has* the answer to the next problem?" but *"Who would like to tell it?"* What at one time in our culture was phrased as a challenge in skill in arithmetic, becomes an invitation to group participation. The essential is *that nothing is but what it is made to be by the alchemy of the system.*
>
> In a society where competition for the basic cultural goods is

a pivot of action, people cannot be taught to love one another. It thus becomes necessary for the school to teach children how to hate, and without appearing to do so, for our culture cannot tolerate the idea that babes should hate each other. How does the school accomplish this ambiguity?[8]

Here is another example given by Henry:

> Boris had trouble reducing 12/16 to the lowest terms, and could only get as far as 6/8. The teacher asked him quietly if that was as far as he could reduce it. She suggested he "think." Much heaving up and down and waving of hands by the other children, all frantic to correct him. Boris pretty unhappy, probably mentally paralyzed. The teacher quiet, patient, ignores the others and concentrates with look and voice on Boris. After a minute or two she turns to the class and says, "Well, who can tell Boris what the number is?" A forest of hands appears, and the teacher calls Peggy. Peggy says that four may be divided into the numerator and the denominator.[9]

Henry comments:

> Boris's failure made it possible for Peggy to succeed; his misery is the occasion for her rejoicing. This is a standard condition of the contemporary American elementary school. To a Zuni, Hopi or Dakota Indian, Peggy's performance would seem cruel beyond belief, for competition, the wringing of success from somebody's failure, is a form of torture foreign to those noncompetitive cultures.
>
> Looked at from Boris's point of view, the nightmare at the blackboard was, perhaps, a lesson in controlling himself so that he would not fly shrieking from the room under enormous public pressure. Such experiences force every man reared in our culture, over and over again, night in, night out, even at the pinnacle of success, to dream not of success, but of failure. In school the external nightmare is internalized for life. Boris was not learning arithmetic only; he was learning the *essential night-*

---

[8] J. Henry, *Culture Against Man* (New York: Random House, 1963), p. 293.

[9] Ibid., p. 27.

mare also. To be successful in our culture one must learn to dream of failure.[10]

It is Henry's contention that in practice education has never been an instrument to free the mind and the spirit of man, but to bind them. We think we want creative children, but what do we want them to create?

> If all through school the young were provoked to question the Ten Commandments, the sanctity of revealed religion, the foundations of patriotism, the profit motive, the two-party system, monogamy, the laws of incest, and so on . . .[11]

. . . there would be such creativity that society would not know where to turn.

Children do not give up their innate imagination, curiosity, dreaminess easily. You have to love them to get them to do that. Love is the path through permissiveness to discipline; and through discipline, only too often, to betrayal of self.

What school must do is to induce children to want to think the way school wants them to think. "What we see," in the American kindergarten and early schooling process, says Henry, "is the pathetic surrender of babies." You will, later or sooner, in the school or in the home.

It is the most difficult thing in the world to recognize this in our own culture.

In a London class, average age ten, the girls were given a competition. They had to bake cakes and the boys were to judge them. One girl won. Then her "friend" let out that she had bought her cake instead of baking it herself. She was disgraced in front of the whole class.

Comments:

1. The school is here inducting children into sex-linked roles of a very specific kind.

---

[10] Ibid., pp. 295–6.
[11] Ibid., p. 288.

2. Personally, I find it obscene that girls should be taught that their status depends on the taste they can produce in boys' mouths.

3. Ethical values are brought into play in a situation that is at best a bad joke. If coerced into such game-playing by adults, the best a child can do is to play the system without getting caught. I most admire the girl who won and hope she will choose her "friends" more carefully in future.

What Henry describes in American schools is a strategy that I have observed frequently in British families studied by my colleagues and myself.

The double action of destroying ourselves with one hand, and calling this love with the other, is a sleight of hand one can marvel at. Human beings seem to have an almost unlimited capacity to deceive themselves, and to deceive themselves into taking their own lies for truth. By such mystification, we achieve and sustain our adjustment, adaptation, socialization. But the result of such adjustment to our society is that, having been tricked and having tricked ourselves out of our minds, that is to say, out of our own personal worlds of experience, out of that unique meaning with which potentially we may endow the external world, simultaneously we have been conned into the illusion that we are separate "skin-encapsuled egos." Having at one and the same time lost our *selves* and developed the illusion that we are autonomous *egos,* we are expected to comply by inner consent with external constraints, to an almost unbelievable extent.

We do not live in a world of unambiguous identities and definitions, needs and fears, hopes, disillusions. The tremendous social realities of our time are ghosts, specters of murdered gods and our own humanity returned to haunt and destroy us. The Negroes, the Jews, the Reds. *Them.* Only you and I dressed differently. The texture of the fabric of these socially shared hallucinations is what we call reality, and our collusive madness is what we call sanity.

Let no one suppose that this madness exists only somewhere

in the night or day sky where our birds of death hover in the stratosphere. It exists in the interstices of our most intimate and personal moments.

We have all been processed on Procrustean beds. At least some of us have managed to hate what they have made of us. Inevitably we see the other as the reflection of the occasion of our own self-division.

The others have become installed in our hearts, and we call them ourselves. Each person, not being himself either to himself or the other, just as the other is not himself to himself or to us, in being another for another neither recognizes himself in the other, nor the other in himself. Hence being at least a double absence, haunted by the ghost of his own murdered self, no wonder modern man is addicted to other persons, and the more addicted, the less satisfied, the more lonely.

Once more there is a turn of the spiral, another round of the vicious circle, another twist of the tourniquet. For now love becomes a further alienation, a further act of violence. My need is a need to be needed, my longing a longing to be longed for. I act now to install what I take to be myself in what I take to be the other person's heart. Marcel Proust wrote:

> How have we the courage to wish to live, how can we make a movement to preserve ourselves from death, in a world where love is provoked by a lie and consists solely in the need of having our sufferings appeased by whatever being has made us suffer?

But no one makes us suffer. The violence we perpetrate and have done to us, the recriminations, reconciliations, the ecstasies and the agonies of a love affair, are based on the socially conditioned illusion that two actual persons are in relationship. Under the circumstances, this is a dangerous state of hallucination and delusion, a mishmash of fantasy, exploding and imploding, of broken hearts, reparation and revenge.

Yet within all this, I do not preclude the occasions when, most lost, lovers may discover each other, moments when recognition does occur, when hell can turn to heaven and come down to earth, when this crazy distraction can become joy and celebration.

And, at the very least, it befits Babes in the Wood to be kinder to each other, to show some sympathy and compassion, if there is any pathos and passion left to spend.

But when violence masquerades as love, once the fissure into self and ego, inner and outer, good and bad occurs, all else is an infernal dance of false dualities. It has always been recognized that if you split Being down the middle, if you insist on grabbing *this* without *that,* if you cling to the good without the bad, denying the one for the other, what happens is that the dissociated evil impulse, now evil in a double sense, returns to permeate and possess the good and turn it into itself.

When the great Tao is lost, spring forth benevolence and righteousness.

When wisdom and sagacity arise, there are great hypocrites.

When family relations are no longer harmonious, we have filial children and devoted parents.

When a nation is in confusion and disorder, patriots are recognized.

We must be very careful of our selective blindness. The Germans reared children to regard it as their duty to exterminate the Jews, adore their leader, kill and die for the Fatherland. The majority of my own generation did not or do not regard it as stark raving mad to feel it better to be dead than Red. None of us, I take it, has lost too many hours' sleep over the threat of imminent annihilation of the human race and our own responsibility for this state of affairs.

In the last fifty years, we human beings have slaughtered by our own hands coming on for one hundred million of our species. We all live under constant threat of our total annihilation. We seem to seek death and destruction as much as life and happiness. We are as driven to kill and be killed as we are to let live and live. Only by the most outrageous violation of ourselves have we achieved our capacity to live in relative adjustment to a civilization apparently driven to its own destruction. Perhaps to a limited extent we can undo what has been done to us and what we have done to ourselves. Perhaps men and women were born to love one another, simply and genuinely, rather than to this travesty that we call love. If we can stop destroying ourselves we may stop destroying others. We have to begin by admitting and even accepting our violence, rather than blindly destroying ourselves with it, and therewith we have to realize that we are as deeply afraid to live and to love as we are to die.

PROJECTS

1. "If we are children of Cain, it behooves us to know Cain well, to examine carefully his behavior and what causes it, and not to look away in disgust."

Write an essay noting (a) the relationships between the theories of Bettelheim and Ardrey regarding human violence and indicating (b) whether or not, from your perspective, we are indeed "Children of Cain."

2. Discuss Bettelheim's definition of innocence: "Innocence is neither an inborn characteristic nor a useful weapon; most of the time it is little more than an anxious clinging to ignorance." Would you agree with Bettelheim that "it is high time that both the myth of original sin and its opposite—that of original innocence—be dispatched to the land of the unicorns"?

3. Is the type of education Bettelheim suggests in his article a viable alternative for preventing violence? Devise an outline for a discussion about the nature of human violence and its alternatives with elementary children, with junior-high and senior-high students.

4. Debate: Student demonstrations which end in violence on the college campus in America are the products of permissive middle-class parents who have not taught their children the value of fear and its by-product, discipline, or the value of delay and restraint in attaining their needs. (Use Bettelheim's article, "Children Must Learn to Fear," *New York Times Magazine,* April 13, 1969.)

5. Answer Bettelheim's question, "What measures are we taking

to help our children do a better job of mastering the disturbance of their communal life that comes from the instinct of aggression?" by making a list of realistic alternatives to violence which could succeed, in your opinion, in performing this task.

6. Arnold Arnold writes in his book, *Violence and Your Child*, that the TV and comic book displays of brutality can be that final burden on a child's psyche—in addition to the other social and psychological factors of violence—which destroys his mental equilibrium. For this reason these influences of violence on children should be eliminated.

(a) How does his argument compare with Bettelheim's position regarding violence on TV and in comic books?

(b) Whose position do you find most convincing? Why?

(c) How "realistically" should violence be portrayed in the media?

7. Discuss Lucy Komisar's analysis of the "masculine mystique" in relationship to (a) the "feminine mystique." (Refer to Betty Friedan's book, *The Feminine Mystique,* New York: W. W. Norton & Co., 1963.) (b) Freud's, Ardey's, and Bettelheim's theories of man's instinct of aggression, violence and death.

8. Debate: Lucy Komisar's argument regarding the masculine mystique proves that there are no grounds for a belief in man's instinctual nature of violence.

9. Arrange to see the film, *The Green Berets.* (141 mins.—color—Audio-film Center, 34 MacQuestion Parkway So., Mt. Vernon, New York, 10550.) Divide the class into groups representing the positions of Freud, Ardrey, Bettelheim, and the Woman's Liberation Movement. Representing these people, analyze the film in regard to

(a) its portrayal of the "masculine mystique."

(b) the "realism" of its insight into American life.

(c) war as an outlet for man's aggressive nature.

10. "Only by the most outrageous violation of ourselves have we achieved our capacity to live in relative adjustment to a civilization apparently driven to its own destruction."

(a) What does Laing mean by this violation of ourselves—this violence of love?

(b) In what sense would Freud and Bettelheim agree with him?

(c) Do you agree with Laing regarding this "violence of love"?

(d) How can we as citizens of a certain culture discern the violence we do to ourselves and the violence we allow others to do to us? Is Laing asking for an impossible abstraction?

Bibliography

ARNOLD, ARNOLD. *Violence and Your Child.* Chicago: Henry Regnery Company, 1969.

BETTELHEIM, BRUNO. "Children Must Learn to Fear," *New York Times Magazine.* April 13, 1969.

———. "Violence: A Neglected Mode of Behavior." In *Violence in the Streets,* edited by Shalom Endleman, Chicago: Quadrangle Books, 1968.

BONDURANT, JOAN. *Conquest of Violence.* Princeton, N.J.: Princeton University Press, 1958.

BUBER, MARTIN. *I and Thou.* New York: Charles Scribner's Sons, 1958.

DE JESUS-MARIE, BRUNO. *Love and Violence.* New York: Sheed and Ward, 1954.

DEMPSEY, D. "Bruno Bettelheim is Dr. No." *New York Times Magazine,* January 11, 1970.

ERIKSON, ERIK. *Childhood and Society.* New York: W. W. Norton & Co., 1963.

———. *Gandhi's Truth.* New York: W. W. Norton & Co., 1969.

FREUD, SIGMUND. *Sexuality and the Psychology of Love.* (Reprint) New York: Crowell-Collier Co., 1963.

FRIEDAN, BETTY. *The Feminine Mystique.* New York: W. W. Norton & Co., 1963.

FROMM, ERIC. *The Art of Loving.* New York: Harper and Row, 1956.

———. *The Sane Society.* New York: Holt, Rinehart & Winston, 1955.

Gandhi, Mohandas. *Nonviolent Resistance.* New York: Schocken Books, 1962.

Gordon, James. "Who is Mad? Who is Sane? The Radical Psychiatry of R. D. Laing," *The Atlantic*, January, 1971.

Gornick, Vivian. "Consciousness ♀," *New York Times Magazine,* January 10, 1971.

King, Martin Luther, Jr. *Strength to Love.* New York: Harper and Row, 1963.

Komisar, Lucy. "Violence and the Masculine Mystique," *The Washington Monthly.* July 1970.

Laing, R. D. *Politics of Experience.* New York: Ballantine Books, 1967.

Marcuse, Herbert. *Eros and Civilization.* Vintage Books Edition, 1962.

Maslow, Abraham. *Religions, Values and Peak Experiences.* Columbus, Ohio: Ohio State University Press, 1964.

May, Rollo. *Love and Will.* New York: W. W. Norton & Co., 1969.

Reik, Theodor. *Of Love and Lust: On the Psychoanalysis of Romantic and Sexual Emotions.* New York: Farrar, Straus and Cudahy, 1957.

Watts, Alan. *Nature, Man and Woman.* New York: Pantheon Books, 1958.

———. *Psychotherapy East and West.* New York: Mentor Books, 1963.

Additional Bibliography on Violence and Love: See *Humanitas,* Volume 2, Number 2, 1966. (Fall)

The Religious Polemic

Introduction

Violence in the name of some divine cause is as ancient as man's religions. Hinduism and Judaism in their archaic past have served the Infinite in destructive, cruel forms and actions. The offspring of Judaism, Christianity and Islam, perpetuated their own variety of divine violence by carrying on bloody crusades and conquests in the name of God. Even the contemplative religions of the east, Taoism and Buddhism, have compromised with a type of nationalistic religion in order to bring death to the enemy. And this concept of a divine command to do violence for some transcendent cause continues into the present—sometimes in more refined forms.

It is easy to condemn religion for its lack of conscience about violence; yet it is this tradition which stimulates man to have his most profound thoughts about nonviolence, universal peace, and the brotherhood of all men, and to discipline his life according to these ideals. Perhaps it is precisely in this paradox, found in the history and literature of man's religions, that we find the paradox in our own lives. All motives, including religious motives, are complicated by the fact that nonviolence and violence are intricately connected. Gandhi, one of the greatest advocates of nonviolence, wrote about the violence of his daily life in the simple acts of breathing and eating. But it is necessary, Gandhi believed, to have the courage to live with the tension of this truth and to make it a creative force in a life of nonviolence.

As long as it remained secluded in non-political communes, Christianity found it relatively easy to live with this tension. However, when it was legitimized by the Roman Emperor Constantine in the fourth century A.D., all this tension crumbled into theological rationalizations regarding "just states," "just wars," and "religious" men who could go to war to preserve the state with clear conscience. Two of its greatest theologians, Augustine and Thomas Aquinas, developed casuistic arguments indicating those conditions which make a state "just" and those by which it ceases to be "just." The next development was logical—what are the conditions for the "just war"? Christian theologians formulated seven conditions:

(1) The cause fought for must itself be just.

(2) The purpose of the warring power must remain just while hostilities go on.

(3) War must be truly the last resort, all peaceful means having been exhausted.

(4) The methods employed during the war to vanquish the foe must themselves be just.

(5) The benefits the war can reasonably be expected to bring for humanity must be greater than the evils provoked by the war itself.

(6) Victory must be assured.

(7) The peace concluded at the end of the war must be just and of such a nature as to prevent a new war.

It is not difficult to see that the rationale for these conditions rests on a definition of what is "just." Such a definition was given by two leaders of the Protestant Reformation, John Calvin and Martin Luther. What is "just" is defined in reference to the survival of the Christian State, which is a temporal institution ordained by God. If there is a revolution or if an individual violates the laws of the State, the legitimate response from the State is "force" against such a revolution or individual. "Violence" is a term that cannot be applied to the action of the Christian State, which seeks to correct the evil ways of the rebel or the heretic. The term "violence" is applicable only to the group or individual who chooses to act against the State. Therefore Calvin attacked revolutionaries as he would "ferocious beasts" and considered any tyranny (as some residents considered Calvin's city-state of Geneva to be during his "reign") better than the disorder of revolt. Luther, also, responded with a "forceful" condemnation against the peasant revolt of his day.

This revolt was violence against an institution ordained by God. The institution was obligated to respond with force.

The legacy of these religious rationalizations influences both sacred and secular interpretations of "just states," "just wars," "just revolutions," "just violence" in our contemporary scene. Men carve over the doors of their institutions "For God and Country" and willingly send their sons off to war. Other men, in the same religious tradition, pour blood over draft records at Selective Service offices and willingly go off to prisons. Still other men out of a sense of religious conscience call for a revolution which will bring a society to its knees by force, by violence, for the cause of justice. All claim they are motivated by a religious sense of duty.

The two essays included in this section are attempts by contemporary Christian thinkers to examine the implications of rationalizations for violence. "Christian Realism in the Face of Violence" comes from Jacques Ellul's book *Violence: Reflections from a Christian Perspective*. Ellul is Professor of Law and Government at the University of Bordeaux, France. His interests range from social criticism (*The Technological Society, Propaganda, The Political Society*) to theological themes (*The Presence of the Kingdom, Violence*). During World War II he played an active role in the French Resistance Movement —a possible inconsistency for the conclusion of this essay. In the first paragraph of this selection, Ellul refers to Georges Sorel, a French writer who worked out to his own satisfaction an ethics of violence in *Reflections on Violence*. These two French critics, Sorel and Ellul, stand in sharp contrast to one another regarding the morality of violence.

"The Conflict Between Individual and Social Morality" is an excerpt from the late Reinhold Niebuhr's book *Moral Man and Immoral Society*. Niebuhr was minister, author, and Professor of Christian Ethics at Union Theological Seminary in New York. His own type of religious realism grew out of his ministry in Detroit where he discovered the difference between individual morality with its ideal of unselfishness and group morality with its ideal of justice. He confronts us with this striking contrast in order to correct a sentimental reasoning which rationalizes this distinction away. Both writers, Ellul and Niebuhr, are asking us to make a penetrating analysis of violence —especially that violence done in the name of divine justice.

Christian Realism in the Face of Violence

JACQUES ELLUL

I must emphasize that, from two points of view, the order of violence cannot be brought under moral judgment. The man who practices violence cannot pretend to be acting as a moral being and in the name of some value; and the outsider cannot validly pass moral judgment on that violence—such a judgment would be meaningless. Sorel indeed attempts to work out an ethic based on violence, but obviously he fails. And our moralists who address the practitioner of violence in the name of virtue or religion or the good are indulging in meaningless behavior. The order of violence is like the order of digestion or falling bodies or gravitation. There is no sense in asking whether gravitation is a good thing or a bad one. If "nature" were not a much misunderstood term, and especially if there were not so many people (those, namely, who paved the way for the reign of violence) who actually believe that Nature is beneficent, I would say that what we have here is an expression of Nature. Gandhi said as much when he declared that violence is "the law of the brute."

I am not saying that violence is an expression of *human* nature. I am saying, for one thing, that violence is the general rule for the existence of societies—including the societies that call themselves civilized but have only camouflaged violence by explaining and justifying it and putting a good face on it. I am saying also that when a man goes the way of violence he enters a system of necessities and subjects both himself and others to it. For such is the necessity in this world. Curiously enough, those who, nowadays, justify violence almost always argue that it is necessary. Many a time I have been told: "But after all, when a poor or unemployed man has nothing, nonviolence is useless, it cannot help him; only violence can. He *has* to use violence." It is certainly true that when a man suffers severe poverty or humiliation, rage is the only expression left him. But in giving way to his rage he should realize that he is acting on the animal level and is obeying a necessity; that he is not free. Again, the champions of the oppressed tell us: "Things being what they are, can anyone believe that true civic order can be established, that there can be genuine dialogue with the enemy? Dialogue demands that both parties be in a position to speak and reason with each other. But we who side with the poor—what resources do we command?" Violence! "Some people are incorrigible"—that is, the rich, the powerful, who "have fallen so low that love does not touch them. . . . In politics, it is difficult to make an alliance with the saint, the pure-hearted, and particularly difficult for the poor, whose rightful impatience urges them on." Thus Father Marcel Cornelis.[1] So, he adds, there is only one remedy for the ills of the poor: violence. Father Maillard agrees: "It is always the violence of the oppressor that unleashes the violence of the oppressed. The time comes when violence is the *only possible* way for the poor to state their case."

All this amounts to an acknowledgment of violence as necessity. And indeed violence is not only the means the poor use to claim their rights; it is also the sole means available to those in places of power. Jesus Christ told us what the order of this world is like: "You know that the rulers of the Gentiles lord it over them, and their great men exercise authority over them" (Matthew 20:25). And Jesus did not protest against this situation. Let us be clear about this: the text from Matthew refers not only to the chiefs of a legally established government (kings, etc.) or the controllers of wealth (bankers, etc.) but to all who come into positions of leadership. And there is no way for them to keep their power except by violence. All of them are *megaloi,* obsessed with grandiose ideas, whether they be leaders of the proletariat or revolutionary movements, or notables in the field

[1] "La non-violence et les pauvres," in *Cahiers de la réconciliation*, Paris, 1967.

of economics or science. All of them are subject to the same necessity: to tyrannize over and use others; that is, they are subject to the order of violence, which is a necessity. But "necessity" means "law." There is a law of violence.

The Law of Violence

Realistic appraisal shows that violence is inevitable in all societies, whatever their form. This established, however, we must be equally realistic in examining the consequences. We grant that there is an inescapable law of violence, but we must be equally clear-sighted as to the results. It is disingenuous to say, "Violence is the only way open to us; but you'll see, the results will be excellent." Here the second aspect of Christian realism enters in: you must know what you are doing.

The first law of violence is continuity. Once you start using violence, you cannot get away from it. Violence expresses the habit of simplification of situations, political, social, or human. And a habit cannot quickly be broken. Once a man has begun to use violence he will never stop using it, for it is so much easier and more practical than any other method. It simplifies relations with the other completely by denying that the other exists. And once you have repudiated the other, you cannot adopt a new attitude—cannot, for example, start rational dialogue with him. Violence has brought so many clear and visible results; how then go back to a way of acting that certainly looks ineffectual and seems to promise only very doubtful results? So you go on using violence, even if at first you had thought that violence would be only a temporary expedient, even if you have achieved thorough change in your own or the general political situation. Mr. André Malraux, the government official, has a bodyguard of police armed with automatic pistols; the same Mr. Malraux, in the days when he was a revolutionary, carried an automatic himself. That, as we have seen, is the way with revolutions. They are born in violence and establish the reign of violence for a generation or two. Violence broke out in France in 1789, and continued, with a few interruptions, up to 1914, when it was mutated into world war. And the Marxist idealists are simply naïve when they believe that, once a reactionary government has been overthrown by violence, a just and peaceful regime will be established. Castro rules only by violence, Nasser and Boumedienne likewise; there is no difference at all between their regimes and the previous colonialist regimes that they ousted by violence. It is one of Mao's greatest merits that he has the courage frankly to repudiate socialist idealism and to see clearly that violence perpetuates itself. But he errs when he declares that a doctrine is involved here. The fact is that once violence is loosed, those who use it cannot get away from it.

The second law of violence is reciprocity. It is stated in Jesus' famous word, "*All* who take the sword will perish by the sword" (Matthew 26:52). Let me stress two points in connection with this passage. There is the insistence on "all." There is no distinction between a good and a bad use of the sword. The sheer fact of using the sword entails this result. The law of the sword is a total law. Then, Jesus is in no sense making a moral valuation or announcing a divine intervention or a coming judgment; he simply describes the reality of what is happening. He states one of the laws of violence. Violence creates violence, begets and procreates violence. The violence of the colonialists creates the violence of the anticolonialists, which in turn exceeds that of the colonialists. Nor does victory bring any kind of freedom. Always, the victorious side splits up into clans which perpetuate violence. The violence of the blacks at Newark was justified. But it prompted the violence of the forces of order, whose Commission of Inquiry declared (February 12, 1968) that the black riot was not justified. I find this commission very interesting. It stated clearly: ". . . our country cannot fulfill its promises when terror reigns in the streets and when disorder and disregard of the law tear our communities apart. . . . No group can improve its condition by revolt." Well and good. But to remedy the situation the commission recommends measures looking to centralized government control (which would only invite more federal interference and also infringe on the citizens' liberties); for example, development, on the federal level, of a plan for coping with disorder, and the creation of a special police force for suppressing riots. How can anyone fail to see that (people being what they are) this means a stronger system of repression —the normal result of violence. And as the violence of the government increases, the people, their own violence temporarily curbed, nurse their hatred. The French and the Italians were held in check by the Nazi occupation. The moment they were liberated, their violence exploded, and they perpetrated crimes and torturings that imitated the atrocities of the Germans. I am bound to say that I saw no difference at all between the Nazi concentration camps and the camps in which France confined the "collaborators" in 1944 (at Eysses or Mauzac, for example).

The man who, in whatever way, uses violence should realize that he is entering into a reciprocal kind of relation capable of being renewed indefinitely. The ethic of violence is a truly new ethic, permitting neither peace nor surcease. "Suppression" of a revolt is not intended to assure peace. In this respect, the Hitlerites were more honest than our modern socialists, anticolonialists, etc. They made no pretenses about wanting to usher in an era of peace. They said frankly that their aim was to establish a new ethic, a new norm of human relationships, namely, violence. No, they were not savage beasts; they were straight-thinking men who had made violence the supreme value in life, the thing that gave a meaning to life. What our moralists and theologians of violence take to be a new and recent discovery is simply the result, and at the same time a repercussion, of what the Hitlerites proclaimed. We have not escaped the Nazi contamination of violence; and in their ways of operating, the anticolonialist movements still echo Nazism. Violence imprisons its practitioners in a circle that cannot be broken by human means. Study of the possible results of violence shows that it will have only one certain result: the reciprocity and the reproduction of violence. Whether any other results are attained—equal rights, legitimate defense, liberation, etc.—is wholly a matter of chance, and all those results, too, are subject to the reciprocity which is one of the laws of violence.

The third law of violence is sameness. Here I shall only say that it is impossible to distinguish between justified and unjustified violence, between violence that liberates and violence that enslaves. (We shall return to this problem farther on.) Every violence is identical with every other violence. I maintain that all kinds of violence are the same. And this is true not only of physical violence—the violence of the soldier who kills, the policeman who bludgeons, the rebel who commits arson, the revolutionary who assassinates; it is true also of economic violence—the violence of the privileged proprietor against his workers, of the "haves" against the "have-nots"; the violence done in international economic relations between our own societies and those of the Third World; the violence done through powerful corporations which exploit the resources of a country that is unable to defend itself. Examples of this last are oil in the Middle East, or the agricultural specialization (cotton, sugarcane, bananas, etc.) forced on a country that is totally the victim of exploitation. Asturias has demonstrated that, even though no shot is fired, sheer violence is at work.

Psychological violence also is subject to the law of sameness. It is simply violence, whether it takes the form of propaganda, biased reports, meetings of secret societies that inflate the egos of their members, brainwashing, or intellectual terrorism. In all these cases the victim is subjected to violence and is led to do what he did not want to do, so that his capacity for further personal development is destroyed. Psychological violence, though it seems less cruel than the policeman's bludgeon, is in fact worse, because the reaction it stimulates does not take the form of pride or self-assertion.

The psychological violence all countries employ is absolutely the worst of violences, because it lays hold of the whole man, and, without his knowing it, gelds him. Violence means all these things, and to try to differentiate among them is to evade the problem. The velvet-glove violence of the powerful who maintain the regimes of injustice, exploitation, profiteering, and hatred has its exact counterpart in the iron-fist violence of the oppressed. Likewise the violence of nations, be they weak or powerful, encourages violence in their people. When a nation—as all European nations do—trains its young men in the most extreme kinds of violence in order to prepare them for battle (parachutists, etc.), the result is bound to be that the whole nation imitates this violence.

Moreover, to say that sameness is one of the laws of violence is to say that, on the one hand, violence has no limits and, on the other, that condoning violence means condoning every kind of violence. Once you choose the way of violence, it is impossible to say, "So far and no further"; for you provoke the victim of your violence to use violence in turn, and that necessarily means using greater violence. We have seen the so-called escalation of war in Vietnam. But, mind, this "escalation" is not a result of chance or of a government's wickedness; there never are limits to violence. When you begin to employ torture in order to get information, you cannot say: "This bit of torturing is legitimate and not too serious, but I'll go no further." The man who starts torturing necessarily goes to the limit; for if he decides to torture in order to get information, that information is very important; and if, having used a "reasonable" kind of torture, he does not get the information he wants, what then? He will use worse torture. The very nature of violence is such that it has no limits. We have seen that it is impossible to set up laws of warfare. Either no war happens to be going on, and then it is easy to make agreements as to the limitations that should be established; or else a war is under way, and then all agreements fall before the imperative of victory.

Violence is hubris, fury, madness. There are no such things as major and minor violence. Violence is a single thing, and it is always the same. In this respect, too, Jesus saw the reality. He declared that there is no difference between murdering a fellow man and being angry with him or insulting him (Matthew

5:21–22). This passage is no "evangelical counsel for the converted"; it is, purely and simply, a description of the nature of violence.

Now the third aspect of this sameness that characterizes violence: once we consent to use violence ourselves, we have to consent to our adversary's using it, too. We cannot demand to receive treatment different from that we mete out. We must understand that our own violence necessarily justifies the enemy's, and we cannot object to his violence. This is true in two senses. A government that maintains itself in power only by violence (economic, psychological, physical, or military violence, or just plain violence) absolutely cannot protest when guerrillas, revolutionaries, rioters, criminals attack it violently. It cannot plead that it represents justice legitimately constraining dangerous assassins. And this holds even when economic violence is met by physical violence. But the opposite also holds, namely, that the revolutionary or the rioter cannot protest when the government uses violence against him. To condone revolutionary violence is to condone the state's violence. Yet in recent years we have been hearing endless protests from the revolutionaries. They seem to think that all the "rights" are on their side, but that the state may act only in strict accordance with the law. Almost every week rioters complain about police brutality; what about their own brutality?

During the Algerian war, France's left-wing intellectuals constantly protested against the brutality of the French army and its use of torture, but pronounced legitimate the torturings and massacres committed by the National Liberation Front. "They have to do these things," we were told, "for no other way of operating is open to them." This "they have to" amounts to saying, "In the face of the increase of crime, we simply have to use torture as a preventive measure." The revolutionaries who claim for themselves the right to use violence but deny it to the state, who demand that the state act correctly, in the light of love, justice, and the common weal, are guilty of hypocrisy (such as Mr. Debray exhibited during his trial). I certainly do not condone the dictatorial government of a Barrientos. I do ask, however, that the man who uses violence at least have the courage to admit the consequences of his action, namely, violence against himself. Let him refrain from appealing to great principles—a Declaration of Rights, democracy, justice—in the hope of escaping the reaction of the power he has attacked. We must recognize, and clearly, that violence begets violence. Does anyone ask, "Who started it?" That is a false question. Since the days of Cain, there has been no beginning of violence, only a continuous process of retaliation. It is childish to suppose that today's conditions are unprecedented, to say, "There are dangerous communists about, we must be on guard against them," or, "This government is basely imperialistic and dictatorial, we must overthrow it." When a man is born, violence is already there, already present in him and around him.

Violence begets violence—*nothing else*. This is the fourth law of violence. Violence is par excellence the method of falsehood. "We have in view admirable ends and objectives. Unfortunately, to attain them we have to use a bit of violence. But once we are the government, you will see how society develops, how the living standard rises and cultural values improve. If we revolutionaries are only allowed to use a little violence (you can't make an omelet without breaking eggs), you'll see the reign of justice, liberty, and equality." That kind of thing is repeated again and again, and it sounds logical enough. But it is a lie. I am not making a moral judgment here, but a factual experimental judgment based on experience. Whenever a violent movement has seized power, it has made violence the law of power. The only thing that has changed is the person who exercises violence. No government established by violence has given the people either liberty or justice—only a show of liberty (for those who supported the movement) and a show of justice (which consists in plundering the erstwhile "haves"). And I am speaking not only of the revolutions of 1789, 1917, or 1933, or the revolutions of Mao, Nasser, Ben Bella, Castro; what I say above is true also of "liberal" or "democratic" governments (I have cited the U.S.A. as an example). Sometimes indeed such a government is captured by the very thing it fights. To combat communist propaganda by "good propaganda" is in fact to fall victim to the psychological violence of the enemy. The violent struggle against racism—at first against Hitler's racism—has caused the development of racism throughout the world. Before 1935, racism was very rare and sporadic. But the opposition to Hitler's racism, by propaganda and by arms, made the opposers familiar with his vision of man and society. In fighting racism by violence we have all become racists.[2] In the United States, the moment the struggle became violent, the blacks began to move from antiracism to racism. Exactly the same thing happened in the case of anticolonialism: its corollary, evident among all the African peoples, is nationalism. And the spirit of nationalism cannot be expressed save by violence. The French resistance to Nazism aimed to create a free and just republic. In 1945, the *same resisters* massacred 45,000 people at Sétif in Algeria, and in 1947 they massacred almost 100,000 in Madagascar.

It is a very serious matter that in spite of multiplied experiences, every one of which showed that violence begets violence, there should still be illusions on this score. Violence can never realize a noble aim, can never create liberty or justice. I repeat once more that the end does not justify the means, that, on the contrary, evil means corrupt good ends. But I repeat also: "Let the man who wants to use violence, do so; let the man who thinks there is no other way, use it; but let him know what he is doing." That is all the Christian can ask of this man—that he be aware that violence will never establish a just society. Yes, he will get

---

[2] Characteristically, Pastor Albert B. Cleage, Jr., of Detroit, one of the leading spokesmen for black power in the U.S.A., declared that violence is *redemptive.* (The idea of violence as purificatory was advanced in France to justify the violence of the liberation in 1944–45.) But after the riots Pastor Cleage said: "Now we are no longer afraid; now it is the white man who is afraid." Quite right. But this proves that violence is not redemptive and that, contrary to Pastor Cleage's opinion, violence does not open the way to negotiation but only transfers fear from one side to the other.

his revenge; yes, he will subdue his "enemy"; yes, he will consummate his hatred. But let him not confuse hate with justice. I quote from J. Lasserre's article "Révolution et non-violence":[3] "We do not believe that peace can come out of violence, that justice can issue from generalized criminality, that respect for man can emerge from contemptuousness. Hatred and crime result neither in justice nor in reconciliation, but in bitterness, cowardice, vice and crime. . . . All these attitudes are in no way propitious for the creation of a just and humane society. . . . [Those who hold them] have bent the knee to the bloody idol. And since they are swept along by the internal logic of violence, their struggle soon ceases to be a means of attaining justice and becomes an end in itself. Ultimately, the cruelest and most clamorous among them take over—the toughest, not the most just. And the revolution is aborted under the dictatorship of a new tyrant. How can you defend and build man when you begin by suppressing and destroying men?" In other words—words that apply to absolutely all cases: "Violence never attains the objectives it sets up." And, tragically, the proponents of violence always talk the same way. Here are some sentences that appeared in *Le Monde* (April 27, 1967):

"What a wonderful future we could look forward to, and soon, if only two or three or more Vietnams flourished [*sic*] on the surface of the globe, each with its countless dead, its terrible tragedies and its daily feats of heroism, each delivering blow after blow to imperialism, compelling it to spread its forces thin to meet the assault of the growing hatred of the world's peoples! . . . Where we die does not matter much. Death will be welcome, if only our war cry penetrates receptive ears, if only another hand reaches out to take our weapons, if only other men rise up to intone the funeral chants as the machine guns crackle and new battle cries and songs of victory sound out."

Who said that—Hitler or Che Guevara? No one could tell, save for the fact that Vietnam was mentioned. (Hitler too often

---

[3] *Cahiers de la réconciliation*, Paris, 1967, pp. 34–36.

attacked imperialism.) But who could imagine that a leader capable of such words would lead the way to justice and freedom?

Finally, the fifth law of violence is this: the man who uses violence always tries to justify both it and himself. Violence is so unappealing that every user of it has produced lengthy apologies to demonstrate to the people that it is just and morally warranted. Hitler, Stalin, Mao, Castro, Nasser, the guerrillas, the French "paras" of the Algerian war—all tried to vindicate themselves. The plain fact is that violence is never "pure." Always violence and hatred go together. I spoke above of the rather useless piece of advice once given Christians: that they should make war without hatred. Today it is utterly clear that violence is an expression of hatred, has its source in hatred and signifies hatred. And only a completely heartless person would be capable of simply affirming hatred, without trying to exonerate himself. Those who exalt violence—a Stokely Carmichael or a Rap Brown, for instance—connect it directly with hatred. Thus Rap Brown declared: "Hate has a role to play. I am full of hatred, and so are the other blacks. Hate, like violence, is necessary for our revolution." Carmichael has repeatedly spoken of the close relation between hate and violence. In one of his speeches[4] he declared: "As Che Guevara said, we must develop hatred in order to transform man into a machine for killing."

It is absolutely essential for us to realize that there is an unbreakable link between violence and hatred. Far too often intellectuals, especially, imagine that there is a sort of pure, bloodless violence, an abstract violence, like that of Robespierre, who dispassionately ordered executions. We must understand that, on the contrary, hatred is the motivator of violence. If I quote Brown and Carmichael it is not because they have a monopoly on hatred, but rather because they state, boldly and clearly, the truth that is universally relevant. A government, when it goes to war, can

[4] At the conference in Havana, August 2, 1967.

afford to refrain from declarations and proclamations of hatred of the enemy (unless Hitler is the enemy!), because, being in a position of power, it can put on a show of magnanimity. Nevertheless, the violence exercised by the French and American governments in Algeria and Vietnam, respectively, involves hatred, only in these cases the hatred is expressed by intermediaries. The head of the government can keep on declaring his good will, his objectivity, his freedom from hate, for he is not directly engaged in the military action. He can keep on pretending to pray and professing to love humanity. He can praise nonviolence, as President Johnson did when Martin Luther King was assassinated. But all that is façade. A ruler has to save face and show that he is a well-disposed man; he has to justify himself! But this means becoming part of the system characteristic of violence, which tries to justify itself. Brown and Carmichael also follow this pattern, and even while they justify themselves they continue to protest their blamelessness. Listen to Brown: "The white taught us violence. Violence is a part of American culture. . . . The only answer to slaughter is slaughter. . . . We hate the white because he has always hated us. . . . A black cannot love himself unless he hates the white."[5] And Carmichael: "The white exploits people, he must be crushed. . . . Violence is the only way to destroy the American capitalism that oppresses us."[6] Usually, history or the need to retaliate or the unavailability of other means is cited to justify violence. The argument runs: (1) Violence is inherent in history, history makes for violence (an argument we shall deal with further on); or (2) "We are treated with violence, and the only way to cope with that is violence" (which is a confirmation—and out of the mouth of the proponents of violence—of what I have called a law of violence, namely, continuity. But these apologists forget that their own

---

[5] In an interview published in the *Nouvel observateur*, September, 1967.

[6] *Ibid.* I certainly agree that the colonialists and the whites started the violence. But here I am stressing only one point, namely, the system of justification.

violence also creates new violence!); or (3) "Such and such a system is unjust, and only violence can change it. We are driven to violence."

Very often, purely imaginary constructs are set up to excuse, sustain, or justify hatred. Countless writings show this concern for legitimacy. But it soon becomes plain that if you are going to justify your violence, it cannot be just any kind of violence. There has to be a legitimate kind of violence! Thus, for example, Father Jarlot stated: "Unjust violence can be repelled only by just violence."[7] And he called for a theology of just violence. But how could he miss seeing that, in saying this, he was entering into the vicious circle that "just war" theologians were caught in and have never escaped from; they have emitted only platitudes and empty phrases. And to pose the problem of just violence is to start that whole thing over again. What makes violence just? Its objective? We have seen that violence corrupts the best of ends. Is it the way it is used that makes violence just? But violence has no limits. Here is sheer stupidity. Stokely Carmichael recently declared that the blacks do not want to fight in Vietnam. "We don't want to be a generation of murderers," he said (and that meant: we don't want to go to Vietnam to fight). "To escape that, we are ready to plunge the United States into chaos."[8] This means that using violence to create chaos in the United States is right, but fighting in Vietnam is murdering. This is a very common type of "reasoning." It shows up the weakness of the pro-violence position; for this position is based entirely on irrational choices and blind hatred. But there is the need to feel justified! And at that point violence can be quite as hypocritical as the conservative bourgeois system. Hitler's system is the best example in point. The violence of the Hitler party in 1932 and 1933 was fascinating to watch. Cynical in the face of bourgeois hypocrisy, it aimed to destroy the traditional moral system and to create a virile community; to repudiate paternalism, exalt

[7] At a press conference held at the Vatican, March 26, 1968, on the occasion of the anniversary of the encyclical *Populorum progressio.*

[8] Discours à la mutualité, Paris, December 6, 1967.

stern self-control and willingness to meet death, and establish equality at whatever cost in pain and suffering. All this was an ideal that, to the young athirst for absolutes, seemed far nobler than the mediocre aims proposed by those of their countrymen who frankly favored violence. But this ideal was mere verbiage, façade; this was "pure" violence. What came of it was an orthodoxy, a statism, more rigorous and coercive than the one it displaced; a morality just as hypocritical as the old one, a social conformism just as blind, and a dictatorship that fooled the people with its lies.

Violence is hypocritical. And to say that the question of legitimizing violence is a false question is also hypocritical. For to say that is to say in effect that violence can be legitimized only by "the communal action of men, which is a revolutionary action."[9] But if any action, provided it be the "communal action of men," legitimizes violence, then we shall have to put up with a great many wars fought by enthusiasts who completely disregard the authorities. And to say that revolutionary action itself legitimizes violence is to introduce a value judgment. People do not start a revolution blindly, without cause and without hope of success. First, they decide that the conditions obtaining are bad, and then . . . So, like it or not, all this leads back to a theory of just violence!

It is very important to be clear about this persistent longing for justification. I do not say that the practitioner of violence feels uneasy and that therefore he must be experiencing pangs of conscience; but in acting violently he is so unsure of himself that he has to have an ideological construct that will put him at ease intellectually and morally. That is why the person inclined to violence is necessarily the victim propaganda aims at; and, conversely, violence is the theme that above all others lends itself to propaganda. Champions of violence ought to do a little thinking about the poor moral quality of those who are led to violence, and also about the fact that there can be no political violence

---

[9] Abribat at the Bordeaux conference, February 15, 1967.

without propaganda—that is, without engineering demonstrations, without debasing man even as it professes to liberate and exalt him.[10]

These are the laws of violence, unchanging and inescapable. We must understand them clearly if we are to know what we are doing when we damn violence.

The Conflict Between Individual and Social Morality

REINHOLD NIEBUHR

A realistic analysis of the problems of human society reveals a constant and seemingly irreconcilable conflict between the needs of society and the imperatives of a sensitive conscience. This conflict, which could be most briefly defined as the conflict between ethics and politics, is made inevitable by the double focus of the moral life. One focus is in the inner life of the individual, and the other in the necessities of man's social life. From the perspective of society the highest moral ideal is justice. From the perspective of the individual the highest ideal is unselfishness. Society must strive for justice even if it is forced to use means, such as self-assertion, resistance, coercion and perhaps resentment, which cannot gain the moral sanction of the most sensitive moral spirit. The individual must strive to realise his life by losing and finding himself in something greater than himself.

These two moral perspectives are not mutually exclusive and the contradiction between them is not absolute. But neither are they easily harmonised. Efforts to harmonise them were analysed [by Reinhold Niebuhr]. It was revealed that the highest moral insights and achievements of the individual conscience are both

[10] On the relation between violence, justification, and propaganda, see my *Propaganda* (New York: Knopf, 1965).

relevant and necessary to the life of society. The most perfect justice cannot be established if the moral imagination of the individual does not seek to comprehend the needs and interests of his fellows. Nor can any non-rational instrument of justice be used without great peril to society, if it is not brought under the control of moral goodwill. Any justice which is only justice soon degenerates into something less than justice. It must be saved by something which is more than justice. The realistic wisdom of the statesman is reduced to foolishness if it is not under the influence of the foolishness of the moral seer. The latter's idealism results in political futility and sometimes in moral confusion, if it is not brought into commerce and communication with the realities of man's collective life. This necessity and possibility of fusing moral and political insights does not, however, completely eliminate certain irreconcilable elements in the two types of morality, internal and external, individual and social. These elements make for constant confusion but they also add to the richness of human life. We may best bring our study of ethics and politics to a close by giving them some further consideration.

From the internal perspective the most moral act is one which is actuated by disinterested motives. The external observer may find good in selfishness. He may value it as natural to the constitution of human nature and as necessary to society. But from the viewpoint of the author of an action, unselfishness must remain the criterion of the highest morality. For only the agent of an action knows to what degree self-seeking corrupts his socially approved actions. Society, on the other hand, makes justice rather than unselfishness its highest moral ideal. Its aim must be to seek equality of opportunity for all life. If this equality and justice cannot be achieved without the assertion of interest against interest, and without restraint upon the self-assertion of those who infringe upon the rights of their neighbors, then society is compelled to sanction self-assertion and restraint. It may even, as we have seen, be forced to sanction social conflict and violence.

Historically the internal perspective has usually been cultivated by religion. For religion proceeds from profound introspection and naturally makes good motives the criteria of good conduct. It may define good motives either in terms of love or of duty, but the emphasis is upon the inner springs of action. Rationalised forms of religion usually choose duty rather than love as the expression of highest virtue (as in Kantian and Stoic morality), because it seems more virtuous to them to bring all impulse under the dominion of reason than to give any impulses, even altruistic ones, moral pre-eminence. The social viewpoint stands in sharpest contrast to religious morality when it views the behavior of collective rather than individual man, and when it deals with the necessities of political life. Political morality, in other words, is in the most uncompromising antithesis to religious morality.

Rational morality usually holds an intermediary position between the two. Sometimes it tries to do justice to the inner moral necessities of the human spirit rather than to the needs of society. If it emphasizes the former it may develop an ethic of duty rather than the religious ethic of disinterestedness. But usually rationalism in morals tends to some kind of utilitarianism. It views human conduct from the social perspective and finds its ultimate standards in some general good and total social harmony. From that viewpoint it gives moral sanction to egoistic as well as to altruistic impulses, justifying them because they are natural to human nature and necessary to society. It asks only that egoism be reasonably expressed. Upon that subject Aristotle said the final as well as the first authoritative word. Reason, according to his theory, establishes control over all the impulses, egoistic and altruistic, and justifies them both if excesses are avoided and the golden mean is observed.

The social justification for self-assertion is given a typical expression by the Earl of Shaftesbury, who believed that the highest morality represented a harmony between "self-affections" and "natural affections." "If," said Shaftesbury, "a creature be self-neglectful and insensible to danger, or if he want such a degree of passion of any kind, as is useful to preserve, sustain and defend himself, this must certainly be esteemed vicious in regard of the end and design of nature."[1]

It is interesting that a rational morality which gives egoism equality of moral standing with altruism, provided both are reasonably expressed and observe the "law of measure," should again and again find difficulty in coming to terms with the natural moral preference which all unreflective moral thought gives to altruism. Thus Bishop Butler begins his moral theorising by making conscience the balancing force between "self-love" and "benevolence." But gradually conscience gives such a preference to benevolence that it becomes practically identified with it. Butler is therefore forced to draw in reason (originally identified with conscience) as a force higher than conscience to establish harmony between self-love and conscience.[2]

The utilitarian attempt to harmonise the inner and outer perspectives of morality is inevitable and, within limits, possible. It avoids the excesses, absurdities and perils into which both religious and political morality may fall. By placing a larger measure of moral approval upon egoistic impulses than does religious morality and by disapproving coercion, conflict and violence more unqualifiedly than politically oriented morality, it manages to resolve the conflict between them. But it is not as realistic as either. It easily assumes a premature identity between self-interest and social interest and establishes a spurious harmony between egoism and altruism. With Bishop Butler most utilitarian rationalists in morals believe "that though benevolence and self-love are different . . . yet they are so perfectly coincident that the greatest satisfaction to ourselves depends upon having benevolence in due degree, and that self-love is one chief security of our right behavior to society."[3] Rationalism in morals therefore insists on less inner restraint upon self-assertion than does

---

[1] Third Earl of Shaftesbury, *An Inquiry Concerning Virtue or Merit*, Bk. 2, Part 1, sec. 3.

[2] *Cf.* Joseph Butler, *Fifteen Sermons on Human Nature.*

[3] Butler, *op. cit.*, Sermon 1.

religion, and believes less social restraint to be necessary than political realism demands.

The dangers of religion's inner restraint upon self-assertion, and of its effort to achieve complete disinterestedness, are that such a policy easily becomes morbid, and that it may make for injustice by encouraging and permitting undue self-assertion in others. Its value lies in its check upon egoistic impulses, always more powerful than altruistic ones. If the moral enterprise is begun with the complacent assumption that selfish and social impulses are nicely balanced and equally justified, even a minimum equilibrium between them becomes impossible.

The more the moral problem is shifted from the relations of individuals to the relations of groups and collectives, the more the preponderance of the egoistic impulses over the social ones is established. It is therefore revealed that no inner checks are powerful enough to bring them under complete control. Social control must consequently be attempted; and it cannot be established without social conflict. The moral perils attending such a political strategy have been previously considered. They are diametrically opposite to the perils of religious morality. The latter tend to perpetuate injustice by discouraging self-assertion against the inordinate claims of others. The former justify not only self-assertion but the use of non-rational power in reinforcing claims. They may therefore substitute new forms of injustice for old ones and enthrone a new tyranny on the throne of the old. A rational compromise between these two types of restraint easily leads to a premature complacency toward self-assertion. It is therefore better for society to suffer the uneasy harmony between the two types of restraint than to run the danger of inadequate checks upon egoistic impulses. Tolstoi and Lenin both present perils to the life of society; but they are probably no more dangerous than the compromises with human selfishness effected by modern disciples of Aristotle.

If we contemplate the conflict between religious and political morality it may be well to recall that the religious ideal in its purest form has nothing to do with the problem of social justice. It makes disinterestedness an absolute ideal without reference to social consequences. It justifies the ideal in terms of the integrity and beauty of the human spirit. While religion may involve itself in absurdities in the effort to achieve the ideal by purely internal discipline, and while it may run the peril of deleterious social consequences, it does do justice to inner needs of the human spirit. The veneration in which a Tolstoi, a St. Francis, a crucified Christ, and the saints of all the ages have been held, proves that, in the inner sanctuary of their souls, selfish men know that they ought not be selfish, and venerate what they feel they ought to be and cannot be.

Pure religious idealism does not concern itself with the social problem. It does not give itself to the illusion that material and mundane advantages can be gained by the refusal to assert one's claims to them. It may believe, as Jesus did, that self-realisation is the inevitable consequence of self-abnegation. But this self-realisation is not attained on the level of physical life or mundane advantages. It is achieved in spiritual terms, such as the martyr's immortality and the Saviour's exaltation in the hearts of his disciples. Jesus did not counsel his disciples to forgive seventy times seven in order that they might convert their enemies or make them more favorably disposed. He counselled it as an effort to approximate complete moral perfection, the perfection of God. He did not ask his followers to go the second mile in the hope that those who had impressed them into service would relent and give them freedom. He did not say that the enemy ought to be loved so that he would cease to be an enemy. He did not dwell upon the social consequences of these moral actions, because he viewed them from an inner and a transcendent perspective.

Nothing is clearer than that a pure religious idealism must issue in a policy of non-resistance which makes no claims to be socially efficacious. It submits to any demands, however unjust, and yields to any claims, however inordinate, rather than assert self-interest against another. "You will meekly bear," declared Epictetus, "for you will say on every occasion 'It seemed so to him.'" This type of moral idealism leads either to asceticism, as in the case of Francis and other Catholic saints, or at least to the complete disavowal of any political responsibility, as in the case of Protestant sects practicing consistent non-resistance, as, for instance, the Anabaptists, Mennonites, Dunkers and Doukhobors. The Quakers assumed political responsibilities, but they were never consistent non-resisters. They disavowed violence but not resistance.

While social consequences are not considered in such a moral strategy, it would be shortsighted to deny that it may result in redemptive social consequences, at least within the area of individual and personal relationships. Forgiveness may not always prompt the wrongdoer to repentance; but yet it may. Loving the enemy may not soften the enemy's heart; but there are possibilities that it will. Refusal to assert your own interests against another may not shame him into unselfishness; but on occasion it has done so. Love and benevolence may not lead to complete mutuality; but it does have that tendency, particularly within the area of intimate relationships. Human life would, in fact, be intolerable if justice could be established in all relationships only by self-assertion and counter-assertion, or only by a shrewd calculation of claims and counterclaims. The fact is that love, disinterestedness and benevolence do have a strong social and utilitarian value, and the place they hold in the hierarchy of virtues is really established by that value, though religion may view them finally from an inner or transcendent perspective. "The social virtues," declares David Hume, "are never regarded without their beneficial tendencies nor viewed as barren and unfruitful. The happiness of mankind, the order of society, the harmony of families, the mutual support of friends, are always considered as a result of their gentle dominion over the breasts of men."[4] The utilitarian and social emphasis is a little too absolute in the words of Hume, but it is true within limits. Even

---

[4] David Hume, *An Enquiry Concerning the Principles of Morals*, Part 2, sec. 2.

the teachings of Jesus reveal a prudential strain in which the wholesome social consequences of generous attitudes are emphasised. "With what measure you mete, it shall be measured to you again." The paradox of the moral life consists in this: that the highest mutuality is achieved where mutual advantages are not consciously sought as the fruit of love. For love is purest where it desires no returns for itself; and it is most potent where it is purest. Complete mutuality, with its advantages to each party to the relationship, is therefore most perfectly realised where it is not intended, but love is poured out without seeking returns. That is how the madness of religious morality, with its trans-social ideal, becomes the wisdom which achieves wholesome social consequences. For the same reason a purely prudential morality must be satisfied with something less than the best.

Where human relations are intimate (and love is fully effective only in intimate and personal relations), the way of love may be the only way to justice. Where rights and interests are closely interwoven, it is impossible to engage in a shrewd and prudent calculation of comparative rights. Where lives are closely intertwined, happiness is destroyed if it is not shared. Justice by assertion and counter-assertion therefore becomes impossible. The friction involved in the process destroys mutual happiness. Justice by a careful calculation of competing rights is equally difficult, if not impossible. Interests and rights are too mutual to allow for their precise definition in individual terms. The very effort to do so is a proof of the destruction of the spirit of mutuality by which alone intimate relations may be adjusted. The spirit of mutuality can be maintained only by a passion which does not estimate the personal advantages which are derived from mutuality too carefully. Love must strive for something purer than justice if it would attain justice. Egoistic impulses are so much more powerful than altruistic ones that if the latter are not given stronger than ordinary support, the justice which even good men design is partial to those who design it.

This social validity of a moral ideal which transcends social considerations in its purest heights, is progressively weakened as it is applied to more and more intricate, indirect and collective human relations. It is not only unthinkable that a group should be able to attain a sufficiently consistent unselfish attitude toward other groups to give it a very potent redemptive power, but it is improbable that any competing group would have the imagination to appreciate the moral calibre of the achievement. Furthermore a high type of unselfishness, even if it brings ultimate rewards, demands immediate sacrifices. An individual may sacrifice his own interests, either without hope of reward or in the hope of an ultimate compensation. But how is an individual, who is responsible for the interests of his group, to justify the sacrifice of interests other than his own? "It follows," declares Hugh Cecil, "that all that department of morality which requires an individual to sacrifice his interests to others, everything which falls under the heading of unselfishness, is inappropriate to the action of a state. No one has a right to be unselfish with other people's interests."[5]

This judgment is not sufficiently qualified. A wise statesman is hardly justified in insisting on the interests of his group when they are obviously in unjust relation to the total interests of the community of mankind. Nor is he wrong in sacrificing immediate advantages for the sake of higher mutual advantages. His unwillingness to do this is precisely what makes nations so imprudent in holding to immediate advantages and losing ultimate values of mutuality. Nevertheless it is obvious that fewer risks can be taken with community interests than with individual interests. The inability to take risks naturally results in a benevolence in which selfish advantages must be quite apparent, and in which therefore the moral and redemptive quality is lost.

Every effort to transfer a pure morality of disinterestedness to group relations has resulted in failure. The Negroes of America have practiced it quite consistently since the Civil War. They did not rise against their masters during the war and remained

---

[5] Hugh Cecil, *Conservatism,* p. 182.

remarkably loyal to them. Their social attitudes since that time, until a very recent date, have been compounded of genuine religious virtues of forgiveness and forbearance, and a certain social inertia which was derived not from religious virtue but from racial weakness. Yet they did not soften the hearts of their oppressors by their social policy.

During the early triumphs of fascism in Italy the socialist leaders suddenly adopted pacifist principles. One of the socialist papers counselled the workers to meet the terror of fascism with the following strategy: "(1) Create a void around fascism. (2) Do not provoke; suffer any provocation with serenity. (3) To win, be better than your adversary. (4) Do not use the weapons of your enemy. Do not follow in his footsteps. (5) Remember that the blood of guerilla warfare falls upon those who shed it. (6) Remember that in a struggle between brothers those are victors who conquer themselves. (7) Be convinced that it is better to suffer wrong than to commit it. (8) Don't be impatient. Impatience is extremely egoistical; it is instinct; it is yielding to one's ego urge. (9) Do not forget that socialism wins the more when it suffers, because it was born in pain and lives on its hopes. (10) Listen to the mind and to the heart which advises you that the working people should be nearer to sacrifice than to vengeance."[6] A nobler decalogue of virtues could hardly have been prescribed. But the Italian socialists were annihilated by the fascists, their organisations destroyed, and the rights of the workers subordinated to a state which is governed by their enemies. The workers may live "on their hopes," but there is no prospect of realising their hopes under the present regime by practicing the pure moral principles which the socialistic journal advocated. Some of them are not incompatible with the use of coercion against their foes. But inasfar as they exclude coercive means they are ineffectual before the brutal will-to-power of fascism.

The effort to apply the doctrines of Tolstoi to the political

---

[6] Quoted by Max Nomad, *Rebels and Renegades*, p. 294.

situation of Russia had a very similar effect. Tolstoi and his disciples felt that the Russian peasants would have the best opportunity for victory over their oppressors if they did not become stained with the guilt of the same violence which the czarist regime used against them. The peasants were to return good for evil, and win their battles by non-resistance. Unlike the policies of Gandhi, the political programme of Tolstoi remained altogether unrealistic. No effort was made to relate the religious ideal of love to the political necessity of coercion. Its total effect was therefore socially and politically deleterious. It helped to destroy a rising protest against political and economic oppression and to confirm the Russian in his pessimistic passivity. The excesses of the terrorists seemed to give point to the Tolstoian opposition to violence and resistance. But the terrorists and the pacifists finally ended in the same futility. And their common futility seemed to justify the pessimism which saw no escape from the traditional injustices of the Russian political and economic system. The real fact was that both sprang from a romantic middle-class or aristocratic idealism, too individualistic in each instance to achieve political effectiveness. The terrorists were diseased idealists, so morbidly oppressed by the guilt of violence resting upon their class, that they imagined it possible to atone for that guilt by deliberately incurring guilt in championing the oppressed. Their ideas were ethical and, to a degree, religious, though they regarded themselves as irreligious. The political effectiveness of their violence was a secondary consideration. The Tolstoian pacifists attempted the solution of the social problem by diametrically opposite policies. But, in common with the terrorists, their attitudes sprang from the conscience of disquieted individuals. Neither of them understood the realities of political life because neither had an appreciation for the significant characteristics of collective behavior. The romantic terrorists failed to relate their isolated acts of terror to any consistent political plan. The pacifists, on the other hand, erroneously attributed political potency to pure non-resistance.

Whenever religious idealism brings forth its purest fruits and places the strongest check upon selfish desire it results in policies which, from the political perspective, are quite impossible. There is, in other words, no possibility of harmonising the two strategists designed to bring the strongest inner and the most effective social restraint upon egoistic impulse. It would therefore seem better to accept a frank dualism in morals than to attempt a harmony between the two methods which threatens the effectiveness of both. Such a dualism would have two aspects. It would make a distinction between the moral judgments applied to the self and to others; and it would distinguish between what we expect of individuals and of groups. The first distinction is obvious and is explicitly or implicitly accepted whenever the moral problem is taken seriously. To disapprove your own selfishness more severely than the egoism of others is a necessary discipline if the natural complacency toward the self and severity in the judgment of others is to be corrected. Such a course is, furthermore, demanded by the logic of the whole moral situation. One can view the actions of others only from an external perspective; and from that perspective the social justification of self-assertion becomes inevitable. Only the actions of the self can be viewed from the internal perspective; and from that viewpoint all egoism must be morally disapproved. If such disapproval should occasionally destroy self-assertion to such a degree as to invite the aggression of others, the instances will be insignificant in comparison with the number of cases in which the moral disapproval of egoism merely tends to reduce the inordinate self-assertion of the average man. Even in those few cases in which egoism is reduced by religious discipline to such proportions that it invites injustice in an immediate situation, it will have social usefulness in glorifying the moral principle and setting an example for future generations.

The distinction between individual and group morality is a sharper and more perplexing one. The moral obtuseness of human collectives makes a morality of pure disinterestedness impossible. There is not enough imagination in any social group to render it amenable to the influence of pure love. Nor is there a possibility of persuading any social group to make a venture in pure love, except, as in the case of the Russian peasants, the recently liberated Negroes and other similar groups, a morally dubious social inertia should be compounded with the ideal. The selfishness of human communities must be regarded as an inevitability. Where it is inordinate it can be checked only by competing assertions of interest; and these can be effective only if coercive methods are added to moral and rational persuasion. Moral factors may qualify, but they will not eliminate, the resulting social contest and conflict. Moral goodwill may seek to relate the peculiar interests of the group to the ideal of a total and final harmony of all life. It may thereby qualify the self-assertion of the privileged, and support the interests of the disinherited, but it will never be so impartial as to persuade any group to subject its interests completely to an inclusive social ideal. The spirit of love may preserve a certain degree of appreciation for the common weaknesses and common aspirations which bind men together above the areas of social conflict. But again it cannot prevent the conflict. It may avail itself of instruments of restraint and coercion, through which a measure of trust in the moral capacities of an opponent may be expressed and the expansion rather than contraction of those capacities is encouraged. But it cannot hide the moral distrust expressed by the very use of the instruments of coercion. To some degree the conflict between the purest individual morality and an adequate political policy must therefore remain.

The needs of an adequate political strategy do not obviate the necessity of cultivating the strictest individual moral discipline and the most uncompromising idealism. Individuals, even when involved in their communities, will always have the opportunity of loyalty to the highest canons of personal morality. Sometimes, when their group is obviously bent upon evil, they may have to express their individual ideals by disassociating themselves from their group. Such a policy may easily lead to political irresponsibility, as in the case of the more extreme sects of non-resisters. But it may also be socially useful. Religiously inspired pacifists who protest against the violence of their state in the name of a sensitive individual conscience may never lame the will-to-power of a state as much as a class-conscious labor group. But if their numbers grew to large proportions, they might affect the policy of the government. It is possible, too, that their example may encourage similar non-conformity among individuals in the enemy nation and thus mitigate the impact of the conflict without weakening the comparative strength of their own community.

The ideals of a high individual morality are just as necessary when loyalty to the group is maintained and its general course in relation to other groups is approved. There are possibilities for individual unselfishness, even when the group is asserting its interests and rights against other communities. The interests of the individual are related to those of the group, and he may therefore seek advantages for himself when he seeks them for his group. But this indirect egoism is comparatively insignificant beside the possibilities of expressing or disciplining his egoism in relation to his group. If he is a leader in the group, it is necessary to restrain his ambitions. A leadership, free of self-seeking, improves the morale of the whole group. The leaders of disinherited groups, even when they are avowed economic determinists and scorn the language of personal idealism, are frequently actuated by high moral ideals. If they sought their own personal advantage they could gain it more easily by using their abilities to rise from their group to a more privileged one. The temptation to do this among the abler members of disinherited groups is precisely what has retarded the progress of their class or race.

The progress of the Negro race, for instance, is retarded by the inclination of many able and educated Negroes to strive for identification and assimilation with the more privileged white race and to minimize their relation to a subject race as much as possible. The American Labor Movement has failed to develop its full power for the same reason. Under the influence of American individualism, able labor men have been more ambitious to rise into the class of owners and their agents than to solidify the laboring class in its struggle for freedom. There is, furthermore, always the possibility that an intelligent member of a social group will begin his career in unselfish devotion to the interests of his community, only to be tempted by the personal prizes to be gained, either within the group or by shifting his loyalty to a more privileged group. The interests of individuals are, in other words, never exactly identical with those of their communities. The possibility and necessity of individual moral discipline is therefore never absent, no matter what importance the social struggle between various human communities achieves. Nor can any community achieve unity and harmony within its life, if the sentiments of goodwill and attitudes of mutuality are not cultivated. No political realism which emphasizes the inevitability and necessity of a social struggle, can absolve individuals of the obligation to check their own egoism, to comprehend the interests of others and thus to enlarge the areas of co-operation.

Whether the co-operative and moral aspects of human life, or the necessities of the social struggle, gain the largest significance, depends upon time and circumstance. There are periods of social stability, when the general equilibrium of social forces is taken for granted, and men give themselves to the task of making life more beautiful and tender within the limits of the established social system. The Middle Ages were such a period. While they took injustices for granted, such as would affront the conscience of our day, it cannot be denied that they elaborated amenities, urbanities and delicate refinements of life and art which must make our age seem, in comparison, like the recrudescence of barbarism.

Our age is, for good or ill, immersed in the social problem. A technological civilisation makes stability impossible. It changes the circumstances of life too rapidly to incline any one to a reverent acceptance of an ancestral order. Its rapid developments and its almost daily changes in the physical circumstances of life destroy the physical symbols of stability and therefore make for restlessness, even if these movements were not in a direction which imperil the whole human enterprise. But the tendencies of an industrial era are in a definite direction. They tend to aggravate the injustices from which men have perennially suffered; and they tend to unite the whole of humanity in a system of economic interdependence. They make us more conscious of the relations of human communities to each other, than of the relations of individuals within their communities. They obsess us therefore with the brutal aspects of man's collective behavior. They, furthermore, cumulate the evil consequences of these brutalities so rapidly that we feel under a tremendous urgency to solve our social problem before it is too late. As a generation we are therefore bound to feel harassed as well as disillusioned.

In such a situation all the highest ideals and tenderest emotions which men have felt all through the ages, when they became fully conscious of their heritage and possible destiny as human beings, will seem from our perspective to be something of a luxury. They will be under a moral disadvantage, because they appear as a luxury which only those are able to indulge who are comfortable enough to be comparatively oblivious to the desperate character of our contemporary social situation. We live in an age in which personal moral idealism is easily accused of hypocrisy and frequently deserves it. It is an age in which honesty is possible only when it skirts the edges of cynicism. All this is rather tragic. For what the individual conscience feels when it lifts itself above the world of nature and the system of collective relationships in which the human spirit remains under the power of nature, is not a luxury but a necessity of the soul. Yet there is beauty in our tragedy. We are, at least, rid of some of our illusions. We can no longer buy the highest satisfactions of the individual life at the expense of social injustice. We cannot build our individual ladders to heaven and leave the total human enterprise unredeemed of its excesses and corruptions.

In the task of that redemption the most effective agents will be men who have substituted some new illusions for the abandoned ones. The most important of these illusions is that the collective life of mankind can achieve perfect justice. It is a very valuable illusion for the moment; for justice cannot be approximated if the hope of its perfect realization does not generate a sublime madness in the soul. Nothing but such madness will do battle with malignant power and "spiritual wickedness in high places." The illusion is dangerous because it encourages terrible fanaticisms. It must therefore be brought under the control of reason. One can only hope that reason will not destroy it before its work is done.

PROJECTS

1. Debate: The concept of a "just war" has a validity for contemporary society.

2. Write an essay relating Ellul's five laws of violence to the theological (seven conditions) basis for a "just war." Is there any rationale for the violence of a "just war" in view of Ellul's laws of violence?

3. How would Aquinas and Ellul evaluate the participation of the United States in the Vietnam conflict?

4. Arrange a panel discussion where the members evaluate Ellul's five laws of violence.

   (a) Is there a continuity to violence?
   (b) Is there a reciprocity involved with violence?
   (c) Is there a sameness about violence?
   (d) Does violence beget violence?
   (e) Does the man who uses violence attempt to justify both it and himself?

5. Ellul states that the laws of violence are laws of necessity, rules for the existence of societies. Man, when he uses violence in any form or for any reason, is participating at the level of necessity and is involved in the inevitabilities of violence. The only way to avoid the laws of violence is to refuse as an individual to participate knowingly at this level and to challenge its very necessity.

(a) What is your reaction to Ellul's position? Is it possible to challenge necessity?

(b) In your evaluation consider Niebuhr's position that to some degree there must always remain a conflict between the purest individual morality (ethic of unselfishness and love) and an adequate political morality (ethic of social duty and justice).

(c) Do you think Niebuhr is more "realistic" than Ellul concerning the matter of violence?

6. Georges Sorel writes in his book, *Reflections on Violence:* "During the Terror, the men who spilt most blood were precisely those who had the greatest desire to let their equals enjoy the golden age they had dreamt of, and who had the most sympathy with human wretchedness: optimists, idealists, and sensitive men, the greater desire they had for universal happiness the more inexorable they showed themselves."[1]

How would Niebuhr analyze such a statement in view of his distinction between individual and group morality? Would you agree or disagree with Niebuhr's analysis?

7. Debate Niebuhr's position: "Every effort to transfer a pure morality of disinterestedness to group relations has resulted in failure. The Negroes of America have practiced it quite consistently since the Civil War. They did not rise against their masters during the war and remained remarkably loyal to them. Their social attitudes since that time, until a very recent date, have been compounded of genuine religious virtues of forgiveness and forbearance, and a certain social inertia which was derived not from religious virtue but from racial weakness. Yet they did not soften the hearts of their oppressors by their social policy."[2]

8. Jean-Paul Sartre believes that evil is a product of man's ability to make abstract that which is concrete. Write an essay indicating (a) the reaction of Ellul and Niebuhr to this concept of evil, and (b) using an illustration—a dehumanized war, the violence of a hate-campaign, the violence of a race-riot—indicate your own reaction to Sartre's statement.

---

[1] Sorel, Georges, *Reflections on Violence*, Paris, 1905. New York: The Macmillan Company, 1961, p. 38.

[2] Niebuhr, Reinhold, *Moral Man and Immoral Society*, New York: Charles Scribner's Sons, 1932, p. 268.

9. For a contrast to the western religious view of violence, arrange to see the Japanese film *Woman in the Dunes.* (123 minutes, black-and-white, distributed by Contemporary Films, 267 West 25th Street, New York, N.Y.)

(a) Notice the types of violence in this film.

(b) What is the resolution for this violence?

(c) What responses would Ellul, Niebuhr and you make to this type of resolution of violence?

Bibliography

BERGER, PETER, AND NEWHAUS, RICHARD. *Movement and Revolution.* New York: Doubleday and Co., 1970. (Dialogue regarding the possibility of violence both in the movement and in revolution.)

BERRIGAN, DANIEL. *The Trial of the Catonsville Nine.* Boston: Beacon Press, 1970. (Reflections on the destruction of the Selective Service records by the priest who participated in the act.)

BERRIGAN, DANIEL, AND LEWIS, THOMAS. *Trial Poems.* Boston: Beacon Press, 1970. (Two members of the Catonsville Nine expressing in poetry and art their convictions regarding the act.)

BERRIGAN, PHILIP. *Punishment for Peace.* London: Macmillan Co., 1969. (Brother of Daniel Berrigan; reactions to a type of violence for peace.)

BONHOEFFER, DIETRICH. *Letters and Papers from Prison.* New York: The Macmillan Company, 1962. (Writings of the German Protestant minister who was executed for participating in the plot to kill Hitler.)

BUBER, MARTIN. *Pointing the Way.* New York: Harper and Row, 1963. (Part III of this book has relevant essays by Buber, Jewish writer and religious philosopher, on politics, community and peace.)

ELLUL, JACQUES. *Violence.* New York: The Seabury Press, 1969.

NIEBUHR, REINHOLD. *Moral Man and Immoral Society.* New York: Charles Scribner's Sons, 1932, rev. pref., 1960.

———. *Love and Justice.* Philadelphia: Westminster Press, 1957.

NOSS, JOHN. *Man's Religions.* New York: The Macmillan Company,

1949, rev. ed., 1967. (Excellent resource for primary and secondary sources regarding history and literature of religion.)

NOVAK, MICHAEL. *The Experience of Nothingness.* New York: Harper and Row, 1970. (Reflections on nihilism in the face of violence.)

———. *A Theology for Radical Politics.* New York: Herder and Herder, 1969.

RUETHER, ROSEMARY. *The Radical Kingdom.* New York: Harper and Row, 1970.

SOREL, GEORGES. *Reflections on Violence.* Paris, 1905. New York: The Macmillan Company, 1961.

The Political Polemic

Introduction

When social and political scientists discuss violence, their primary task is to define the term itself. The opening chapters in H. L. Nieburg's book, *Political Violence,* confront this task, indicating critical distinctions among the meanings of the words "power," "force," and "violence." "Power," Nieburg writes, "is the application of energy to do work and as raw physical power it becomes functional and legitimate in the hands of some kind of centralized authority as a means of providing internal and external security."[1] "Force" is the reserve capacity and means of exercising physical power; it is a threat of violence or counterviolence. "Violence," in contrast to these terms, is the most direct and severe form of physical power. The distinction, however, between "force" as the capability and threat of action and "violence" as the application of that action is often difficult to make in life's exacerbating situations. This is especially true when we consider "political violence," for, as Nieburg indicates, "force" and "violence" merge imperceptibly when men are involved in passionate confrontations which affect their political rights. When does force become violence in provocative demonstrations, counterdemonstrations, acts of deterrence or disruption? Reinhold Niebuhr analyzes Gandhi's famous Salt March with precisely these concerns—when did the nonresistance of his followers turn from force into violence as the result of the counterdemonstration?[2]

Man is a political animal, Aristotle reminds us, and in this sense perhaps all violent acts are violent political acts. The Na-

---

[1] H. L. Nieburg, *Political Violence* (New York: St. Martin's Press, 1969), p. 11.

[2] Reinhold Niebuhr, *Moral Man and Immoral Society* (New York: Charles Scribner's Sons, 1932), Ch. 9: "The Preservation of Moral Values in Politics."

tional Commission on the Causes and Prevention of Violence confirms this notion by describing violence as an ambiguous term whose meaning is established through political processes. "The concept of violence always refers to a disruption of some condition of order; but order, like violence, is politically defined."[3] Nieburg's definition of political violence is analogous to this opinion. Political violence involves:

> acts of disruption, destruction, injury whose purpose, choice of targets or victims, surrounding circumstance, implementation, and/or effects have political significance, that is, tend to modify the behavior of others in a bargaining situation that has consequences for the social system.[4]

The obvious question for our study is: are the consequences of political violence ethical? It is the familiar problem of means and ends—can violence (in this case, political violence) as a means produce ethical consequences (ends)? Again, Nieburg points out the difficulty involved in answering this question by reminding us (as Gandhi did) that social action of the human species always moves along a continuum between violence and nonviolence simply because social life is dynamic.[5] If we could stop the continuum—STOP THE WORLD! I WANT TO GET OFF!—then we could offer final judgments regarding the ethical dimensions of all political violence. But the world does not stop for the living, and as actors in the drama we are identified with the consequences of our actions. Being conscious of and sensitive to this fact, we become the judges of our acts and of the actions of others.

Hannah Arendt writes about the now undeniable glorification of violence in her book, *On Violence.* To glorify violence before understanding it (being conscious of and sensitive to its consequences) is to be irrational. Such irrationality, she believes,

---

[3] Jerome Skolnick, *The Politics of Protest* (Commission's Report), (New York: Ballantine Books, 1969), pp. 4–5.

[4] Nieburg, *Political Violence,* p. 13.

[5] Nieburg, p. 16.

has its roots in the confusion between the terms "power" and "violence" in our mind. Power is the ability to act as a group and in this sense, it is the essence of all government. Violence is only instrumental, a means to an end, and is the absence of power. It is impotent compared to power.

> Power and violence are opposites; where the one rules absolutely, the other is absent. Violence appears where power is in jeopardy, but left to its own course it ends in power's disappearance. This implies that it is not correct to think of the opposite of violence as nonviolence; to speak of nonviolent power is actually redundant. Violence can destroy power; it is utterly incapable of creating it.[6]

Arendt's thesis presents violence as an ineffectual instrument for attaining long-term goals. Intelligent social change is related to power, not violence. Thus violence as a means for attaining social change is limited, impotent, and noncreative ("Violence can destroy power; it is utterly incapable of creating it."), and if this is not realized by the advocates of political violence, the result will be more violent social orders.

The writings of Nieburg and Arendt are examples of critical thinking that is concerned with man's use of political violence as a means for attaining social justice. This criticism demands that we carefully define the terms we use in the defense or prosecution of political violence and that we make an analysis of the legitimacy of its activity. The three essays in this section on *The Political Polemic* give you such an opportunity.

The first selection, "No Rights, No Duties," by Truman Nelson, a historian and novelist, comes from his book, *The Right of Revolution*. Nelson has written six books on revolutionary themes, among them *The Surveyor: John Brown in Kansas* and *The Sin of the Prophet: Theodore Parker and the Boston Slave Riot.*

The second reading, "Solidarity," comes from Herbert Mar-

---

[6] Hannah Arendt, *On Violence* (New York: Harcourt, Brace and World, Inc., 1969), p. 56.

cuse's *An Essay on Liberation*. Born in Berlin, Marcuse came to the United States in 1934, became a citizen in 1940, and has taught at Columbia, Harvard and Brandeis Universities and the University of California at San Diego. In addition to *Eros and Civilization,* Marcuse is author of *One-Dimensional Man, Reason and Revolution,* and *Negations,* and with co-authors Barrington Moore and Robert Wolff, *A Critique of Pure Tolerance.*

The final selection, "Existential Politics," taken from *The Crisis of Confidence: Ideas, Power and Violence in America* is by Arthur Schlesinger, Jr. Professor of History at Harvard University from 1946–1954 (Recipient, Pulitzer Prize for History in 1945), Schlesinger became a political adviser to Adlai Stevenson and to President Kennedy, 1961–1964. Now the Schweitzer Professor of Humanities at the City University in New York, he has written such familiar books as *A Thousand Days; John Kennedy in the White House; The Politics of Hope; The Bitter Heritage; Vietnam and American Democracy.*

No Rights, No Duties

TRUMAN NELSON

Thomas Jefferson, when queried about the authority, legal and otherwise, for his revolutionary assertion that people have a right to overthrow their government under certain conditions, said:

> All its authority rests then on the harmonizing sentiments of the day, whether expressed in conversation, in letters, printed essays, or the elementary books of public right, as Aristotle, Cicero, Locke, Sidney, etc. . . . it was intended to be an expression of the American Mind.

It was just as plainly understood by the founding fathers that all government is a contract, and if it gives no rights, or even diminished rights, you owe it no duties. What allegiance, really, can this government demand of a group commonly known as *second-class citizens?* The same is true of *paupers* and *minors.* They are never given the equal protection of the laws. The poor are confined by economic attrition in slums where violations of housing and health codes are carried on with impunity every day. They could not exist as slums, otherwise. The minors, healthy young boys under voting age, are forced into an involuntary servitude in the military establishment, which demands of them that they kill or be killed in countries far away for purposes which they consider irrelevant to the point of madness. As minors, they have no rights that a legislator needs to respect.

The American people as a whole, even the affluent, seem to have lost control over their own politics. They know that faceless men at the levers of power in the Pentagon can throw a switch to oblivion for the world without even considering asking for the consent of the governed. Many of us are finally getting this straight in our heads, but they have got to us lower down and made us political eunuchs. We are so squeezed by our "responsibility to the free world" that we cannot have a free thought but what we are warned that the whole "free world" will go down if we act on it.

Political emasculation is not our only organic change. The simple facts of the Newark rebellion reveal that the total organism of American life is rotting faster and faster into putrefaction. The stinking decay grows in our guts, and when we try to cure it, they break in our hands. One of our most sacred rights, that of the individual, *individualism,* forsooth, is now debased and swept away with the full connivance of the elected powers.

The crimes, if any, in Newark, were carried out by individuals. A few armed men, estimated by the police as not over ten men, with names, personalities, and motives of their own (men feeling perhaps, that they owed no more duty to this government than the Irish did to the British Government in the beginning of their revolution) fired at our police and our soldiers. A whole people was punished for this. Mortal punishment in a rain of fire went sweeping into the apartment houses and killing the innocent.

It is nowhere known for certain if any snipers were killed by the police, and it never will be known because the police have moved into simple warfare where the trajectory of function is to find the locus of the enemy and flush him out with firepower. And to act, with the greatest immediacy, not against a suspected individual, but against a flawed totality. Thus our nationalism has reached its apogee. No longer can a man stand and bargain with his government over the extent of his rights and duties, his innocence or guilt, as our forefathers did, even with their God.

This new point of view, the consciousness now formed which demands that we punish collectively for individual guilt, we are acting out all over the world. The most important task assigned to us as a nation, the leading and generating fact of our lives, is the war we are carrying on in Vietnam, a war against a total people, wherein it is a routine function to bomb and burn a whole village because it is suspected that one or two of the active enemy are located there, or have always lived there.

How can we think that in performing this, which even our apologists characterize as a cruel and *dirty* war, that our actions will not stain through our whole consciousness and benumb and degenerate us in our wholeness and make us act toward ourselves as we do toward others?

The fact is, what the rich man does to the poor man, what the landlord does to the tenant, what the merchant does to the consumer, what the boss does to the worker, what the policeman does to the suspect, what the jailor does to the helpless criminal in his power is only a local reflection of what we are doing as a nation abroad with our armies. And as the merchants, police, judges, landlords, bosses, jailors increase at home, while our soldiers escalate their presence abroad, so does the scope and intensity of their action against their victims.

And all the time we are told that to suffer this is part of the *duty* we must pay for our *rights*. That these acts which they say they perform only as a cruel necessity are saving us from being the victims of evil men, somewhere else, or evil systems, over there . . . who will only use us for their gratification. That if they let up for a moment their heavyhanded control of our lives, it will provide the vicious and unprincipled a chance to oppress the innocent. So, although some individuals may question some of the acts performed by those in power . . . they must continue to rule us for the greater good.

This means that they, our overlords, are all virtuous, all compassionate, all understanding public servants who took up the cross to suffer and sacrifice in carrying out their tasks and duties to us . . . that it is their duty to curtail our rights because they are carrying out a responsibility to law and order and the greatest good.

We, on the other hand, have to accept their acts of usurpation and control as our *duty* and promise on our oaths that we will unquestioningly obey their commands as spoken and enforced by their myriads of overseers, spies, interrogators, and whippers-in, from the President to the local draft board and social worker. And cheerfully recognize their rights to the lion's share of our daily labor so they can carry out their duty to control us with a maximum efficiency and have a gracious surrounding in which they can unwind, after a wearisome day of holding us in an appropriate system of checks and balances.

And we must carry out, proudly and cheerfully, our right to mark, every four years, a cross beside some names printed on a ballot . . . names of men either completely unknown to us, or only too well known as scoundrels, windbags, and embezzlers who have lived all their lives on the public payrolls and prospered well beyond the million mark. And although we know, from the experiences of ourselves, our fathers, and grandfathers, that regardless of the inane speeches they utter, promising change, they will do the same as the men in office before them and before them and before them, and they will plead the same crises of the Republic, plead the same urgencies and imperatives about the obscene Vietnam War of 1967 as they did about the obscene Mexican War of 1847, and in about the same words.

We must also perform the right and duty of serving voluntarily in the courts, and sitting in judgment on other frail humans; knowing that by the time the government prosecutor and the government judge get through with the case we will still not know much about the guilt or innocence of the accused or be able to do anything about it if we did. All we have to do is be the face of the rubber stamp which the clerk pounds on the face of the man on trial which says, The people find you guilty and sentence you to prison and torture for your life's duration.

And finally, we must always consider it part of our rights and duties that, no matter how decent, how politically and economically advanced, how humane, gentle, and loving we know people in other nations to be, and no matter if the cause they are fighting and dying for is to overthrow the yoke of centuries of exploitation and despotism, we must be prepared at a moment's notice to look on them as deadly enemies threatening the very foundations of our homes and be prepared to burn them, starve them, torture them, kill them, and do the same to all others who do not regard them as deadly enemies because of government fiat, even though these others may be our own sons, brothers, fathers, lovers, and friends. Laws, lawmakers, or law-enforcers who do this are not to be considered laws, nor lawmakers, nor law-enforcers, and should be resisted as any usurpation or usurper should be, at all times.

The self-evident American right of revolution lies in this: that an unconstitutional law is not a law. An unconstitutional law can be defined, in revolutionary terms, as one against the people en masse, and for special privilege. It should be just as opposable when it is against *a people,* living within the confines of the United States. It is thus clearly not agreed on by all the people.

An officer of the government is as any officer "of the law" only when he is proceeding according to law. When he is killing a woman in an apartment house that may or may not be the location of a sniper, he is not acting in a lawful way. The moment he ventures beyond the law he becomes like any other man. He forfeits the law's mantle of immunity and protection. He may then be resisted like any other trespasser. A law that is palpably against the peace and security of all the people, such as all the racist laws on the books of the Southern States, laws limiting the rights and privileges of privacy and movement of the blacks in the Northern States, the laws against the Indians in the Western States, and those against the poor in all the states, is really not a law at all, constitutionally, and is thus void and confers no authority on anyone, and whoever attempts to execute it, does so at his own peril.

Common sense, the conscience of the mass, will tell you if this doctrine is not valid; then anyone with police power can usurp authority, and sustained by these unconstitutional laws, can treat people as he pleases. Many have already done this, are doing this, and still we wonder why we can't get these usurpers off our backs. A self-proclaimed "law-making body" or "law-enforcing agency" can beat, rape, torture or kill at will—as such bodies do now, in Mississippi, and have for over a century—and the people have no right to resist them. It simply does not make sense. The best of our founding fathers wanted the law to make sense . . . wanted a "government and policy on such plain and obvious general principles, as would be intelligible to the plainest rustic. . . ."

The true revolutionary, then and now, holds that the Declaration and the Constitution contemplate no submission by the people to gross usurpation of civil rights by the government, or to the lawless violence of its officers. On the contrary, the Constitution provides that the right of the people to keep and bear arms shall not be infringed. This constitutional right to bear arms implies the right to use them, as much as the constitutional right to buy and keep food implies the right to eat it.

The Constitution also takes it for granted that, as the people have the right, they will also have the sense to use arms, whenever the necessity of the case justifies it; this is the only remedy suggested by the Constitution, and is necessarily the only remedy that can exist when the government has become so corrupt that it can offer no peaceful solution to an intolerable way of life.

It is no answer to this argument on the right of revolution to say that if an unconstitutional act be passed, the mischief can be remedied by a repeal of it, and that this remedy can be brought about by a full discussion and the exercise of one's voting rights. The black men in the South discovered, generations ago, that if an unconstitutional and oppressive act is binding until invalidated by repeal, the government in the meantime will disarm them, plunge them into ignorance, suppress their freedom of assembly, stop them from casting a ballot and easily put it beyond their power to reform their government through the exercise of the rights of repeal.

A government can assume as much authority to disarm the people, to prevent them from voting, and to perpetuate rule by a clique as they have for any other unconstitutional act. So that if the first, and comparatively mild, unconstitutional and oppressive act cannot be resisted by force, then the last act necessary for the imposition of a total tyranny may not be.

The right of the government "to suppress insurrection" does not conflict with this right of the people to resist the execution of laws directed against their basic rights. An insurrection is a rising against the law, and not against usurpation. The actions, for example, of native fascist groups can be demonstrated by their own public acts and statements to be designed for privilege for themselves and to be defamatory and oppressive to other groups among the people. The black people don't want the police to shoot into white working-class apartments either.

The right of resistance to usurping laws is in its simplest form a natural defense of the natural rights of people to protect themselves against thieves, tyrants, monomaniacs, and trespassers who attempt to set up their own personal, or group, authority against the people they are supposed to serve. It is the threat of the power of the people to remove them by force that keeps officeholders from perpetuating themselves. Not that they are any worse than other men, but the rewards are great and most of them act as though they were trying to discover the utmost limit of popular acquiescence to their self-exploitation and small tyrannies. In sum, if there is no right of revolution there is no other right our officials have to respect.

By no means am I saying that this is the prevailing concept of our organic law among the leaders and pundits of the country. Although they might, if pressed hard enough, give lip service to it. Arthur Schlesinger said in the *Atlantic Monthly* that the American concept of the right of revolution was the greatest idea we have given to the world:

> First and foremost stands the concept of the inherent and universal right of revolution . . . proclaimed in the Declaration of Independence: the doctrine that "all men are created equal . . . possessing inalienable rights to life, liberty and the pursuit of happiness" with the corollary that governments derive their just powers from the consent of the governed and that therefore the people have a right to supplant any government "destructive of these ends" with one they believe most likely to effect their safety and happiness. True, the history of England provided precedents

to the men of 1776, and the Age of Enlightenment supplied intellectual support; but the flaming pronouncement, followed by its vindication on the battlefield, made the doctrine ever afterwards an irrepressible agency "in the course of human events." Europe was the first to respond . . . A series of revolts overturned, or strove to overturn, illiberal governments through most of the Continent, and hastened popular reforms in other lands to forestall popular upheavals. These convulsions all had their internal causes but in every instance the leaders derived inspiration from America's achievement of popular rule, as well as from its freely expressed interest in their similar aspirations.

"The Declaration of Independence is our Creed," Supreme Court Justice Douglas said, in an article on "The U.S. and the Revolutionary Spirit." He said we should not be afraid to talk revolution and to voice our approval of it. He tells us to become the active protagonist of the independence of all people. Go up against the darkness and pain of continuing feudalism. "There is a political feudalism where a dynasty has the trappings of a parliamentary system but manipulates it for the benefit of a ruling class . . . Revolution in the twentieth century means rebellion against another kind of feudalism . . . economic feudalism . . . the United States should promote democratic revolutions against these conditions of economic feudalism."

Going back, we find John Locke's dictum, in his essay on government, that when the natural rights of man are violated, the people have the right and the duty of suppressing or changing the government. "The last recourse against wrongful and unauthorized force is opposition to it."

It is the massiveness of the display of force against them that has brought the black people to their revolutionary flash point more than anything else. They know, as soon as they hear the sounds of masses of police sirens that their little insurrection, or their little rebellion, or their small act of resistance will turn into a massacre, not of the enemy, but of themselves. But yet they go on resisting until the local police sirens are replaced by the clank of tanks, or personnel carriers; the clubs, the police revolvers are superseded by bayonets and death-spitting machine guns. And still their exultation grows, an exultation that is absolutely inexplicable to the whites, seeing them surrounded by the massacre of their own people. Sartre speaks of this; of how the Frenchmen of the Resistance never felt freer than when they were under the attacks of the Nazi S. S. How the more they were condemned to silence, the more they felt that they were approaching liberation.

These rebellions by the blacks are a minority action: they cannot succeed militarily, and nobody thinks they will. The whole process is a *telling* revolution, a way of stating something buried under centuries of apathy and indifference far worse than omnipresent opposition. A *Life* magazine interview with a black sniper reveals this. He is not trying to kill cops and Guardsmen. When they are struck down it is by accident. He is trying, he says, to tell "our people we are here." And in the process, "the firing of five or six shots in the air is enough to draw cops thick as fleas on a dog and still give time to get away." Then the people take what they want.

But it is much more than that: the black insurrection-white massacre method of telling revolution is in some ways comparable to the Buddhists burning themselves to tell of their to-the-death commitment to their country's revolution.

I always felt that an enormous amount of time, money, and effort was wasted in the last years of the civil-rights crisis, while the leaders, black and white, were trying to convince the American black man that he was really a downtrodden Hindu, a palpitating mass of ingrained and inborn submission, a victim of a caste society which stretches back, almost to prehistory. The Hindu, or to be more specific, the followers of Gandhi, were victims in a land so impoverished and barren that a lifetime of starvation was, and still is, their common lot . . . a land where living is so hard that men want a God so they can hate him as the father and ordainer of their degradation.

The American black man is a citizen in a rich land, with a citizen's rights and duty to resist, resist all attempts to deprive him of its manifold blessings. Even if he doesn't *want* to resist, he must; it is his duty, as it is the duty of all honest whites to urge him and support him in the process. Why should he have been urged to go through all this Hinduizing to regain the rights he already had in 1776? He was here then and fought alongside of the whites out of the same revolutionary morality, for the same revolutionary rights he is dying for right now . . . the idea that men before the law are exactly equal and that no man can take away these equalities except as forfeiture for a crime adjudged and confirmed by ancient and democratic due process.

Legally he has always had these rights. They were taken away from him by force and fraud. When the racist laws were written and enforced and then upheld finally by the Supreme Court of the United States, it was the lawbreaker and should have been resisted. The black man did resist these racist laws, but in vain. Police, militia, Federal troops beat him until he went down, over and over again, a victim of blood and violence, his land looted, his home burned, his daughter raped, his son lynched, his babies starved, his progeny for generations suffering automatically the same fate.

When he was finally handed the weapon of "soul force" he tried it; no one can deny that he honestly gave it a try. But we are living in a lunatic society, a racist society that will never stop hiring cops and soldiers to beat him until he stops them . . . or we stop the hiring. If we say the black man is a citizen, then he has a clear duty to resist tyranny and dictatorship, legally and peacefully if he can, forcibly if he must. He is the birthright possessor of the same rights we have. He cannot give them up if he wants to. He was not born to be a victim to test the longevity of our desire to oppress him.

Take a good look at the *Life* magazine for July 28, 1967. Look at it before it lies dog-eared in the dentist's office, or slides to oblivion in the trash trucks. Before the eyes of one of its reporters and cameramen, a police cruiser drew up on a littered street, surrounded by stores so gutted and debased that they are simply valueless: they are not stores anymore, they are piles of trash. A twenty-four-year-old black man took a six-pack of beer from one of them. He saw the cops. He had been arrested before, so he ran.

A yellow-helmeted cop with a shotgun leaped out of the cruiser. He aimed the gun with *his kind* of all deliberate speed and shot the black man dead . . . for a six-pack of beer! And the spreading pellets from the murderous blast tore their way into the soft flesh of Joe Bass, Jr., a black shoe-shine boy, twelve years old, with nothing in his hands. He was struck in the neck and the thigh and fell bleeding to the pavement, his eyes open and staring straight ahead, his body almost finding a restful embrace in the dirty asphalt.

The Newark policeman, his shotgun still at the ready, turns away from the murdered Billy Furr, the looter of a six-pack of beer. There is no anguish in his face, his mouth is relaxed, almost soft as he reaches into the side pocket of his blue shirt for a cigar. The story is told accurately and compassionately, even to the point of telling how when little Joey was struck down fifty sobbing black men and women tried to get to him, to help him, and were clubbed back by a small squad of police with rifle butts. But the name of the murderer in the blue uniform shirt is not reported. And it is possible he will never be known, and his face will be forgotten, for the police in this country, when they are acting against the black people, are usually faceless and nameless and omnipotent, infallible and unpunishable, like Yahweh.

There was the Boston Massacre and there was the Newark Massacre. The last took place yesterday, in our time, in our country; the men who carried it out bore our faces, the bullets that found their way anonymously into black bodies were paid for, in part by us. It is our consciousness, our heritage, vibrating in the air we breathe.

Let us examine again the rules we live by . . . the life, liberty and pursuit of happiness guarantees. These rules say, if these guarantees are not forthcoming . . . "that whenever any form of government shall become destructive of these ends, it is the right of the people to alter or abolish it, and to institute a new government."

Certainly, no one in his right mind will deny that this form of government has been highly destructive to the life, liberty, *et cetera* of the black people. This, above all things, is self-evident. The black people are still in a social, economic, and political bondage. After a great war was fought to free them, they are not free. There is no excuse for the brute fact that our parliamentary system has not been able to bring them into the mainstream of American life. Not only that, their story can only be told in times of upheaval and self-slaughter. And even after these take place, the only comment made on it, or the only ones asked about it, are old crocks like Senator Dirksen, someone who is supremely irrelevant to what is going on, anywhere, and who yet is considered one of the two or three leading spokesmen of our government. All he can say is that we, the whites, are "getting impatient with this disregard of law and order." This fact alone, that Dirksen is speaking for it, shows the complete idiocy and futility of the Congress.

We say over and over again that the solving of the race question will take time, but there is no excuse for this. We establish new forms of government because it took too much time before, in the old form, to resolve an accursed question of human suffering. New governments are not to create a continuation of the same wrongs and social stultifications that made the new form a bloody imperative. We have had long enough . . . enough, enough to see ourselves as white-skinned racists creating and maintaining a society where some get all the good of it while others deeply suffer . . . where the good of one comes out of the evil put upon another . . . where we exist in a prison of our white skin as inescapable as that of our black neighbors. What we do to the black people, daily, makes me want to secede from the white race! It makes me, down deep, hate myself, and my color. All decent whites especially the young whites, abhor having to bear the burden of racist guilt their fathers have placed upon them.

And they hate white racist America and their own fathers for sustaining it, for stealing from them what should have been a birthright of human brotherhood, alienating them from young blacks by white cruelty to them, in their white image. For setting up impassable barriers between young whites and young blacks, areas of suspicion coming from a constant betrayal. They want to clasp hands with the blacks, if only in admiration of the dignity, patience, and restraint they have shown up to this breaking point. If we let them alone they will offer them love and support for their bloody struggle to rise to a level of liberation and privilege which whites accept as due to them by their birth alone.

And we adults: we hate white racist America because it has blocked out of the culture of our time the unfettered expression of the wisdom of a people to whom the meaning of life has had to be privation, suffering and alienation, but who have lived, somehow, with moments of ecstasy, with spurts of infectuous and inexplicable joy. White racist America makes me ashamed of my own country, which not only presents to a vibrant, revolutionary world the complacent facade of a sluttish society whose mass ideal is the unlimited consumption of all possible goods and services . . . but has lost all of its revolutionary virtues in an hour when the darker people are finally climbing into the light, and are forced to seek elsewhere the encouragement which some of our revolutionary fathers meant for us to bestow upon mankind. And in the losing of this revolutionary virtue, we have turned despicably into our opposites and are murdering revolutionaries all over the world.

And all the time we are doing this we are telling the little white children, and some of the little black children, that Abe Lincoln said in 1848: "Any people anywhere being inclined and having the power, have the right to rise up and shake off the existing government, and form a new one that suits them better. This is a most valuable and sacred right, a right we hope and believe is to liberate the world."

And we are teaching high school students, black and white, that Abe Lincoln, the great emancipator, said, in his First

Inaugural Address: "This country, with its institutions, belongs to the people who inhabit it. Whenever they shall grow weary, of the existing government, they can exercise their constitutional right of amending it, or their revolutionary right to dismember, or overthrow it."

They tell us that we have this great and basic right, but if we so much as suggest the use of it, we are punished . . . we are imprisoned. So that it serves as an entrapment, a vicious provocation to smoke out radicals and revolutionaries. Why do they say this . . . why do they so piously quote the forefathers and then blame and hurt people under an unforgivable longevity of oppression . . . obviously getting worse instead of better . . . for trying to act under it?

The United States House of Representatives has just demonstrated its imbecility and outright betrayal of the Bill of Rights, which it has sworn to uphold, by passing a bill which makes traveling from one state to another and saying anything that might be, after the fact, twisted into a connection with a riot, a criminal offense. It carries a fine of ten thousand dollars or imprisonment for five years, or both.

It was written by a white racist from Florida and forced onto the floor by the white racist from Mississippi, who said, the insurrections in the black ghettos were "organized conspiracies backed by the Communists . . . if you vote against this bill, what are you going to say when you go home and meet the policeman and fireman who risked their lives, and in many instances, lost them. . . ." As if it was not already clear that the lawless, conspiratorial, rioting element in the community is the police themselves.

This does not mean that the Southern racist congressmen were responsible for the bill. Charles W. Sandman, Jr., a Republican from New Jersey, was one of its most ardent supporters and said the police in Newark had told him that rioters had crossed the Hudson River in buses, were picked up in cars and taken to the center of Newark, where the trouble occurred. There is no proof in existence that this did occur, while on the other hand it is well known that the police will say anything that will develop their own positions. So the bill was passed by a vote of 347 to 70 . . . and they were not all Southern congressmen who voted for it.

This is how we put off, again and again, truth and resolution for some dishonest and shoddy solution. And then we snivel and hurt the helpless when the chickens come home to roost. It was not outside agitators behind the guns of Newark . . . it could be the inflammatory boasts and texts of our daily education. Now they will have to prevent Thomas Jefferson, in the form of his writings, from crossing state lines, for he said: "What country can preserve its liberties if their rulers are not warned from time to time that this people preserve the spirit of resistance. Let them take arms. . . ."

Or if the agitator from New Jersey crosses the line into Pennsylvania, he will find the Pennsylvania Declaration of Rights already there, saying: "The Community hath an indubitable, inalienable, and indefeasible right to reform, alter or abolish government in such manner as shall be by that community judged most conducive to the public weal."

Henry Clay of Kentucky, the Great Commoner, said: "An oppressed people are authorized, whenever they can, to rise and break their fetters."

John Adams, the second President of the United States, said: "It is an observation of one of the profoundest inquiries into human affairs that a revolution of government is the strongest proof that can be given by a people, of their virtue and good sense."

His son, also a President of the United States, said: "In the abstract theory of our government, the obedience of the citizen is not due to an unconstitutional law: he may lawfully resist its execution."

And Henry D. Thoreau, a good revolutionary, an artist of the revolutionaries, said: "All men recognize the right of revolution, that is the right to refuse allegiance to and to resist, the government where its tyranny or its inefficiency are great and unendurable."

In Maryland its Declaration of Rights reads: "Whenever the ends of government are perverted, and public liberty manifestly endangered, and all other means of redress are ineffectual, the people may, and of right ought to, reform the old or establish a new government; the doctrine of nonresistance against arbitrary power and oppression is absurd, slavish and destructive of the good and happiness of mankind."

General and President U. S. Grant said: "The right of Revolution is an inherent one. When people are oppressed by their government, it is a natural right they enjoy to relieve themselves of the oppression if they are strong enough, either by withdrawing from it, or by overthrowing it and substituting a government more acceptable."

And Emerson, talking of affairs in Kansas, when white settlers in 1856 had to knuckle down to racist tyrants and live like people in the black ghettos today, said:

> I think there never was a people so choked and stultified by forms. We adore the forms of law, instead of making them vehicles of wisdom and justice. Language has lost its meaning in the universal cant. . . . *Representative Government* is really misrepresentative. *Democracy, Freedom*, fine names for an ugly thing. They call it attar of roses and lavender,—I call it bilge water. They call it Chivalry and Freedom; I call it the stealing of all the earnings of a poor man and the earnings of his little girl and boy, and the earnings of all that shall come from him his children's children forever. But this is union and this is Democracy, and our poor people, led by the nose by these fine words, dance and sing, ring bells and fire cannon, with every new link of the chain which is forged for their limbs by the plotters in the Capital. . . . What are the results of law and Union? There is no Union. The judges give cowardly interpretation to the law, in direct opposition to the known foundation of all law, *that every immoral statute is void!* If that be law, let the ploughshare be run under the foundations of the Capitol—

> and if that be Government, extirpation is the only cure. I am glad that the terror at disunion and anarchy is disappearing. . . .

Now I submit that somewhere, every day in this country, some schoolboy is reading about these men; that their words, revolution and all, are passing into their consciousness. This being undeniably true . . . how can we stop these dangerous thoughts from crossing state lines, color lines, or lines of any kind? We could not stop them from entering the icy legal mind of Mr. Justice Jackson, late of the Supreme Court, who gave, in 1950, the most concrete modern juridical opinion of the right of revolution based on the Declaration of Independence.

> . . . we cannot ignore the fact that our own government originated in revolution, and is legitimate only if overthrow by force can sometimes be justified. That circumstances sometimes justify it is not Communist doctrine, but an old American belief. The men who led the struggle forcibly to overthrow lawfully constituted British authority found moral support by asserting a natural law under which their revolution was justified, and they bravely proclaimed their belief in the document basic to our freedom. Such sentiments have also been given ardent and rather extravagant expression by Americans of undoubted patriotism.

So there it is, deep in the hide of the Republic, and you can talk about it all you want, having a revolution, that is, just as long as it is in a classroom, and you are white. But don't say it, as William Epton did, on the streets of Harlem before a group of silent men, whose eyes have a tiny glow like the stirring of a long-banked fire.

Solidarity

HERBERT MARCUSE

The preceding attempt to analyze the present opposition to the society organized by corporate capitalism was focused on the striking contrast between the radical and total character of the rebellion on the one hand, and the absence of a class basis for this radicalism on the other. This situation gives all efforts to evaluate and even discuss the prospects for radical change in the domain of corporate capitalism their abstract, academic, unreal character. The search for specific historical agents of revolutionary change in the advanced capitalist countries is indeed meaningless. Revolutionary forces emerge in the process of change itself; the translation of the potential into the actual is the work of political practice. And just as little as critical theory can political practice orient itself on a concept of revolution which belongs to the nineteenth and early twentieth century, and which is still valid in large areas of the Third World. This concept envisages the "seizure of power" in the course of a mass upheaval, led by a revolutionary party acting as the avant-garde of a revolutionary class and setting up a new central power which would initiate the basic social changes. Even in industrial countries where a strong Marxist party has organized the exploited masses, strategy is no longer guided by this notion—witness the long-range Communist policy of "popular fronts." And the concept is altogether inapplicable to those countries in which the integration of the working class is the result of structural economic-political processes (sustained high productivity; large markets; neo-colonialism; administered democracy) and where the masses themselves are forces of conservatism and stabilization. It is the very power of this society which contains new modes and dimensions of radical change.

The dynamic of this society has long since passed the stage where it could grow on its own resources, its own market, and on normal trade with other areas. It has grown into an imperialist power which, through economic and technical penetration and outright military intervention, has transformed large parts of the Third World into dependencies. Its policy is distinguished from classical imperialism of the preceding period by effective use of economic and technical conquests on the one hand, and by the political-strategic character of intervention on the other:

the requirements of the global fight against communism supersede those of profitable investments. In any case, by virtue of the evolution of imperialism, the developments in the Third World pertain to the dynamic of the First World, and the forces of change in the former are not extraneous to the latter; the "external proletariat" is a basic factor of potential change within the dominion of corporate capitalism. Here is the coincidence of the historical factors of revolution: this predominantly agrarian proletariat endures the dual oppression exercised by the indigenous ruling classes and those of the foreign metropoles. A liberal bourgeoisie which would ally itself with the poor and lead their struggle does not exist. Kept in abject material and mental privation, they depend on a militant leadership. Since the vast majority outside the cities is unable to mount any concerted economic and political action which would threaten the existing society, the struggle for liberation will be a predominantly military one, carried out with the support of the local population, and exploiting the advantages of a terrain which impedes traditional methods of suppression. These circumstances, of necessity, make for guerrilla warfare. It is the great chance, and at the same time the terrible danger, for the forces of liberation. The powers that be will not tolerate a repetition of the Cuban example; they will employ ever more effective means and weapons of suppression, and the indigenous dictatorships will be strengthened with the ever more active aid from the imperialist metropoles. It would be romanticism to underrate the strength of this deadly alliance and its resolution to contain subversion. It seems that not the features of the terrain, nor the unimaginable resistance of the men and women of Vietnam, nor considerations of "world opinion," but fear of the other nuclear powers has so far prevented the use of nuclear or seminuclear weapons against a whole people and a whole country.

Under these circumstances, the preconditions for the liberation and development of the Third World must emerge in the advanced capitalist countries. Only the internal weakening of the superpower can finally stop the financing and equipping of suppression in the backward countries. The National Liberation Fronts threaten the life line of imperialism; they are not only a material but also an ideological catalyst of change. The Cuban revolution and the Viet Cong have demonstrated: it can be done; there is a morality, a humanity, a will, and a faith which can resist and deter the gigantic technical and economic force of capitalist expansion. More than the "socialist humanism" of the early Marx, this violent solidarity in defense, this elemental socialism in action, has given form and substance to the radicalism of the New Left; in this ideological respect too, the external revolution has become an essential part of the opposition within the capitalist metropoles. However, the exemplary force, the ideological power of the external revolution, can come to fruition only if the internal structure and cohesion of the capitalist system begin to disintegrate. The chain of exploitation must break at its strongest link.

Corporate capitalism is not immune against economic crisis. The huge "defense" sector of the economy not only places an increasingly heavy burden on the taxpayer, it also is largely responsible for the narrowing margin of profit. The growing opposition against the war in Vietnam points up the necessity of a thorough conversion of the economy, risking the danger of rising unemployment, which is a by-product of technical progress in automation. The "peaceful" creation of additional outlets for the productivity of the metropoles would meet with the intensified resistance in the Third World, and with the contesting and competitive strength of the Soviet orbit. The absorption of unemployment and the maintenance of an adequate rate of profit would thus require the stimulation of demand on an ever larger scale, thereby stimulating the rat race of the competitive struggle for existence through the multiplication of waste, planned obsolescence, parasitic and stupid jobs and services. The higher standard of living, propelled by the growing parasitic sector of the economy, would drive wage demands toward capital's point of no return. But the structural tendencies which determine the development of corporate capitalism do not justify the assumption that aggravated class struggles would terminate in a socialist revolution through organized political action. To be sure, even the most advanced capitalist welfare state remains a class society and therefore a state of conflicting class interests. However, prior to the disintegration of the state power, the apparatus and the suppressive force of the system would keep the class struggle within the capitalist framework. The translation of the economic into the radical political struggle would be the consequence rather than the cause of change. The change itself could then occur in a general, unstructured, unorganized, and diffused process of disintegration. This process may be sparked by a crisis of the system which would activate the resistance not only against the political but also against the mental repression imposed by the society. Its insane features, expression of the ever more blatant contradiction between the available resources for liberation and their use for the perpetuation of servitude, would undermine the daily routine, the repressive conformity, and rationality required for the continued functioning of the society.

The dissolution of social morality may manifest itself in a collapse of work discipline, slowdown, spread of disobedience to rules and regulations, wildcat strikes, boycotts, sabotage, gratuitous acts of noncompliance. The violence built into the system of repression may get out of control, or necessitate ever more totalitarian controls.

Even the most totalitarian technocratic-political administration depends, for its functioning, on what is usually called the "moral fiber": a (relatively) "positive" attitude among the underlying population toward the usefulness of their work and toward the necessity of the repressions exacted by the social organization of work. A society depends on the relatively stable and calculable sanity of the people, sanity defined as the regular, socially coordinated functioning of mind and body—especially at work, in the shops and offices, but also at leisure and fun. Moreover, a society also demands to a considerable extent, belief in one's beliefs (which is part of the required sanity); belief in the operative value of society's values. Operationalism is indeed an indispensable supplement to want and fear as forces of cohesion.

Now it is the strength of this moral fiber, of the operational values (quite apart from their ideational validity), which is likely to wear off under the impact of the growing contradictions within the society. The result would be a spread, not only of discontent and mental sickness, but also of inefficiency, resistance to work, refusal to perform, negligence, indifference—factors of dysfunction which would hit a highly centralized and coordinated apparatus, where breakdown at one point may easily affect large sections of the whole. To be sure, these are subjective factors, but they may assume material force in conjunction with the objective economic and political strains to which the system will be exposed on a global scale. Then, and only then, that political climate would prevail which could provide a mass basis for the new forms of organization required for directing the struggle.

We have indicated the tendencies which threaten the stability of the imperialist society and emphasized the extent to which the liberation movements in the Third World affect the prospective development of this society. It is to an even greater extent affected by the dynamic of "peaceful coexistence" with the old socialist societies, the Soviet orbit. In important aspects, this coexistence has contributed to the stabilization of capitalism: "world communism" has been the Enemy who would have to be invented if he did not exist—the Enemy whose strength justified the "defense economy" and the mobilization of the people in the national interest. Moreover, as the common Enemy of *all* capitalism, communism promoted the organization of a common interest superseding the intercapitalist differences and conflicts. Last but not least, the opposition within the advanced capitalist countries has been seriously weakened by the repressive Stalinist development of socialism, which made socialism not exactly an attractive alternative to capitalism.

More recently, the break in the unity of the communist orbit, the triumph of the Cuban revolution, Vietnam, and the "cultural revolution" in China have changed this picture. The possibility of constructing socialism on a truly popular base, without the Stalinist bureaucratization and the danger of a nuclear war as the imperialist answer to the emergence of this kind of socialist power, has led to some sort of common interest between the Soviet Union on the one side and the United States on the other.

In a sense, this is indeed the community of interests of the "haves" against the "have nots," of the Old against the New. The "collaborationist" policy of the Soviet Union necessitates the pursuance of power politics which increasingly reduces the prospect that Soviet society, by virtue of its basic institutions alone (abolition of private ownership and control of the means of production: planned economy) is still capable of making the transition to a free society. And yet, the very dynamic of imperialist expansion places the Soviet Union in the other camp: would the effective resistance in Vietnam, and the protection of Cuba be possible without Soviet aid?

However, while we reject the unqualified convergence thesis, according to which—at least at present—the assimilation of interests prevails upon the conflict between capitalism and Soviet socialism, we cannot minimize the essential difference between the latter and the new historical efforts to construct socialism by developing and creating a genuine solidarity between the leadership and the liberated victims of exploitation. The actual may considerably deviate from the ideal, the fact remains that, for a whole generation, "freedom," "socialism," and "liberation" are inseparable from Fidel and Ché and the guerrillas—not because their revolutionary struggle could furnish the model for the struggle in the metropoles, but because they have recaptured the truth of these ideas, in the day-to-day fight of men and women for a life as human beings: for a new life.

What kind of life? We are still confronted with the demand to state the "concrete alternative." The demand is meaningless if it asks for a blueprint of the specific institutions and relationships which would be those of the new society: they cannot be determined a priori; they will develop, in trial and error, as the new society develops. If we could form a concrete concept of the alternative today, it would not be that of an alternative; the possibilities of the new society are sufficiently "abstract," i.e., removed from and incongruous with the established universe to defy any attempt to identify them in terms of this universe. However, the question cannot be brushed aside by saying that what matters today is the destruction of the old, of the powers that be, making way for the emergence of the new. Such an answer neglects the essential fact that the old is not simply bad, that it delivers the goods, and that people have a real stake in it. There can be societies which are much worse—there are such societies today. The system of corporate capitalism has the right to insist that those who work for its replacement justify their action.

But the demand to state the concrete alternatives is justified for yet another reason. Negative thinking draws whatever force it may have from its empirical basis: the actual human condition in the given society, and the "given" possibilities to transcend this condition, to enlarge the realm of freedom. In this sense, negative thinking is by virtue of its own internal concepts "positive": oriented toward, and comprehending a future which is "contained" in the present. And in this containment (which is an important aspect of the general containment policy pursued by the established societies), the future appears as possible liberation. It is not the only alternative: the advent of a long period of "civilized" barbarism, with or without the nuclear destruction, is equally contained in the present. Negative thinking, and the praxis guided by it, is the positive and positing effort to prevent this utter negativity.

The concept of the primary, initial institutions of liberation is familiar enough and concrete enough: collective ownership, collective control and planning of the means of production and distribution. This is the foundation, a necessary but not sufficient condition for the alternative: it would make possible the usage of all available resources for the abolition of poverty, which is the prerequisite for the turn from quantity into quality: the creation of a reality in accordance with the new sensitivity and the new consciousness. This goal implies rejection of those policies of reconstruction, no matter how revolutionary, which are bound to perpetuate (or to introduce) the pattern of the unfree societies and their needs. Such false policy is perhaps best summed up in the formula "to catch up with, and to overtake the productivity level of the advanced capitalist countries." What is wrong with this formula is not the emphasis on the rapid improvement of the material conditions but on the model guiding their improvement. The model denies the alternative, the qualitative difference. The latter is not, and cannot be, the result of the fastest possible attainment of capitalist productivity, but rather the development of new modes and ends of production —"new" not only (and perhaps not at all) with respect to technical innovations and production relations, but with respect to the different human needs and the different human relationships in working for the satisfaction of these needs. These new relationships would be the result of a "biological" *solidarity* in work and purpose, expressive of a true harmony between social and individual needs and goals, between recognized necessity and free development—the exact opposite of the administered and enforced harmony organized in the advanced capitalist (and socialist?) countries. It is the image of this solidarity as elemental, instinctual, creative force which the young radicals see in Cuba, in the guerrillas, in the Chinese cultural revolution.

Solidarity and cooperation: not all their forms are liberating. Fascism and militarism have developed a deadly efficient solidarity. Socialist solidarity is autonomy: self-determination begins at home—and that is with every I, and the We whom the I chooses. And this end must indeed appear in the means to attain it, that is to say, in the strategy of those who, within the existing society, work for the new one. If the socialist relationships of production are to be a new way of life, a new Form of life, then their existential quality must show forth, anticipated and demonstrated, in the fight for their realization. Exploitation in all its forms must have disappeared from this fight: from the work relationships among the fighters as well as from their individual relationships. Understanding, tenderness toward each other, the instinctual consciousness of that which is evil, false, the heritage of oppression, would then testify to the authenticity of the rebellion. In short, the economic, political, and cultural features of a classless society must have become the basic needs of those who fight for it. This ingression of the future into the present, this depth dimension of the rebellion accounts, in the last analysis, for the incompatibility with the traditional forms of the political struggle. The new radicalism militates against the centralized bureaucratic communist as well as against the semi-democratic liberal organization. There is a strong element of spontaneity, even anarchism, in this rebellion, expression of the new sensibility, sensitivity against domination: the feeling, the awareness, that the joy of freedom and the need to be free must precede liberation. Therefore the aversion against preestablished Leaders, apparatchiks of all sorts, politicians no matter how leftist. The initiative shifts to small groups, widely diffused, with a high degree of autonomy, mobility, flexibility.

To be sure, within the repressive society, and against its ubiquitous apparatus, spontaneity by itself cannot possibly be a radical and revolutionary force. It can become such a force only as the result of enlightenment, education, political practice—in this sense indeed, as a result of organization. The anarchic element is an essential factor in the struggle against domination: preserved but disciplined in the preparatory political action, it will be freed and *aufgehoben* in the goals of the struggle. Released for the construction of the initial revolutionary institutions, the antirepressive sensibility, allergic to domination, would militate against the prolongation of the "First Phase," that is, the authoritarian bureaucratic development of the productive forces. The new society could then reach relatively fast the level at which poverty could be abolished (this level could be considerably lower than that of advanced capitalist productivity, which is geared to obscene affluence and waste). Then the development could tend toward a sensuous culture, tangibly contrasting with the gray-on-gray culture of the socialist societies of Eastern Europe. Production would be redirected in defiance of all the rationality of the Performance Principle; socially necessary labor would be diverted to the construction of an aesthetic rather than repressive environment, to parks and gardens rather than highways and parking lots, to the creation of areas of withdrawal rather than massive fun and relaxation. Such redistribution of socially necessary labor (time), incompatible with any society governed by the Profit and Performance Principle, would gradually alter society in all its dimensions—it would mean the ascent of the Aesthetic Principle as Form of the Reality Principle: a culture of receptivity based on the achievements of industrial civilization and initiating the end of its self-propelling productivity.

Not regression to a previous stage of civilization, but return to an imaginary *temps perdu* in the real life of mankind: progress to a stage of civilization where man has learned to ask for the sake of whom or of what he organizes his society; the stage where he checks and perhaps even halts his incessant struggle for existence on an enlarged scale, surveys what has been achieved through centuries of misery and hecatombs of victims, and decides that it is enough, and that it is time to enjoy what he has and what can be reproduced and refined with a minimum of alienated labor: not the arrest or reduction of technical progress, but the elimination of those of its features which perpetuate man's subjection to the apparatus and the intensification of the struggle for existence—to work harder in order to get more of the merchandise that has to be sold. In other words, electrification indeed, and all technical devices which alleviate and protect life, all the mechanization which frees human energy and time, all the standardization which does away with spurious and parasitarian "personalized" services rather than multiplying them and the gadgets and tokens of exploitative affluence. In terms of the latter (and only in terms of the latter), this would certainly be a regression—but freedom from the rule of merchandise over man is a precondition of freedom.

The construction of a free society would create new incentives for work. In the exploitative societies, the so-called work instinct is mainly the (more or less effectively) introjected necessity to perform productively in order to earn a living. But the life instincts themselves strive for the unification and enhancement of life; in nonrepressive sublimation they would provide the libidinal energy for work on the development of a reality which no longer demands the exploitative repression of the Pleasure Principle. The "incentives" would then be built into the instinctual structure of men. Their sensibility would register, as biological reactions, the difference between the ugly and the beautiful, between calm and noise, tenderness and brutality, intelligence and stupidity, joy and fun, and it would correlate this distinction with that between freedom and servitude. Freud's last theoretical conception recognizes the erotic instincts as work instincts—work for the creation of a sensuous environment. The social expression of the liberated work instinct is *cooperation,* which, grounded in solidarity, directs the organization of the realm of necessity and the development of the realm of freedom. And there is an answer to the question which troubles the minds of so many men of good will: what are the people in a free society going to do? The answer which, I believe, strikes at the heart of the matter was given by a young black girl. She said: for the first time in our life, we shall be free to think about what we are going to do.

Existential Politics

ARTHUR M. SCHLESINGER, JR.

This new creed has two parts. The negative part is an attempt to clear away what its theorists regard as the noxious rubbish of the Bill of Rights. The new creed thus perceives the First Amendment as the keystone not of liberty but of a cunning apparatus of tolerance employed by an oppressive social order to thwart basic change. I do not wish to do this new doctrine an injustice, so I will state in the words of its leading advocate—that is, Herbert Marcuse—the belief that it is *necessary* and *right,* as a matter of principle, to howl down views with which one disagrees and to suppress those who utter such views.

Mr. Marcuse begins with the proposition that contemporary society, in his idiom, is defined by "the passing of the historical forces which, at the preceding stage of society, seemed to represent the possibility of new forms of existence." In other words, contemporary society has absorbed and abolished the historic means of social revolution. It has learned the secret of "containing social change—qualitative change, which would establish essentially different institutions, a new direction of the productive process, new modes of human existence." It has done this, Mr. Marcuse argues, through an ingenious and despicable combination of welfarism, tolerance and manipulation. Capitalism, in short, subverts potential opponents by offering them a measure of apparent economic security and personal freedom. Mr. Marcuse regards this as a terrible state of affairs. As he sees it, any improvement in the condition of the powerless and the oppressed only plays into the hands of the rulers—and is therefore to be regretted. "The totalitarian tendencies of the one-dimensional society render the traditional ways and means of protest ineffective—perhaps even dangerous because they preserve the illusion of popular sovereignty."

Tolerance is evil because it dissipates the force of protest. It is also evil because it permits the promulgation of evil ideas. Therefore, Mr. Marcuse suggests, the way to revive the dream of social change is to strike at the root of the evil. He is candid about his repudiation of the Bill of Rights.

> The traditional criterion of clear and present danger seems no longer adequate to a stage where the whole society is in the situation of the theater audience when somebody cries: "Fire." . . . The whole post-fascist period is one of clear and present danger. Consequently, true pacification requires the withdrawal

> of tolerance before the deed, at the stage of communication in word, print, and picture. . . . Certain things cannot be said, certain ideas cannot be expressed, certain policies cannot be proposed, certain behavior cannot be permitted without making tolerance an instrument for the continuation of servitude.

And he is specific about what he would forbid. His program, as he states it:

> would include the withdrawal of toleration of speech and assembly from groups and movements which promote aggressive policies, armament, chauvinism, discrimination on the grounds of race and religion, or which oppose the extension of public services, medical care, etc. Moreover, the restoration of freedom of thought may necessitate new and rigid restrictions on teachings and practices in the educational institutions.[1]

Mr. Marcuse's call for the forcible suppression of false ideas is, I have suggested, the first part of the new creed. No one can

---

[1] Mr. Marcuse, enjoying the protection of the Bill of Rights, regards tolerance with contempt and intellectual freedom as a sham and sees American society as far down the road to totalitarianism. How grotesque his arguments must seem to people living in truly totalitarian societies! The Russian physicist Andrei D. Sakharov, writing at great personal risk his underground pamphlet "Thoughts on Progress, Peaceful Coexistence and Intellectual Freedom," is a good deal less disdainful about the disadvantages of liberty. "Intellectual freedom," he says, "is essential to human society—freedom to obtain and distribute information, freedom for open-minded and unfearing debate and freedom from pressure by officialdom and prejudices. . . . The key to a progressive restructuring of the system of government in the interests of mankind lies in an intellectual freedom."

In the summer of 1968, some California reactionaries, perhaps following the Marcuse argument too closely, threatened to murder this champion of intolerance. Subsequently (in the *New York Review of Books*, August 22, 1968) Mr. Marcuse signed a letter about the impending Democratic convention, concluding, "We demand an open Convention," thereby claiming in a somewhat lordly manner for himself what, as a matter of principle, he has argued should be denied to those whose views he dislikes. Ordinarily this would have to be accounted an extraordinary act of impertinence. But perhaps his recent California experience has persuaded my old friend that there may be some point in the Bill of Rights.

doubt the relish with which activists have seized the mantle of intellectual respectability thus offered them. So Paul Krassner, editor of a popular underground paper, the *Realist,* in a yippie manifesto: "No more marches. No more speeches. The dialogue is over, baby. Tolerance of rational dissent has become an insidious form of oppression. The goal now is to disrupt an insane society." Of course, this sort of assault on the Bill of Rights is not new, even for radicals. The Stalinists of the thirties, for example, had no compunction in arguing in much the same way that civil freedom should be denied those who rejected the Stalinist truth. What particularly distinguishes the New Left of the sixties from previous American radicalisms is the second part of its creed—and here not the summons to revolution, which again is familiar, but the refusal to state revolutionary goals except in the most abstract and empty language. To put it more precisely, what distinguishes the New Left is not only its unwillingness to define what its aims for after the revolution but its belief that such mystification is a virtue.

On its positive side the new creed becomes, so to speak, a kind of existentialism in politics—a rudimentary kind, no doubt, but still rooted in some manner in the existential perception that man dwells in an absurd universe and defines himself through his choices. In extreme cases, this perception may lead to *voyages au bout de la nuit:* as Nietzsche said, "Nihilism represents the ultimate logical conclusion of our great values and ideals—because we must experience nihilism before we can find out what value these 'values' really had." In its serious form, existentialism can lead to an immense and intense sense of individual responsibility as every man realizes that only he can provide his own escape from the enveloping nothingness around him. In its vulgar form, however, with which we are dealing here, existential politics becomes the notion that we must feel and act before we think; it is the illusion that the experience of feeling and action will mysteriously produce the insight and the policy.

Our contemporary existential politics springs much more from Sorel than from Kierkegaard. Sorel drew a distinction between myths, which, he said, were "not descriptions of things, but expressions of a determination to act," and utopias, which were intellectual products, the work of theorists who "seek to establish a model to which they can compare existing society." Sorel regarded utopias—that is, rational programs—as contemptible. The myth must be the basis of action; the myth would produce the revolution, which would thereafter produce its own program; and "the myth," Sorel emphasized, "must be judged as a means of acting on the present; any attempt to discuss how far it can be taken literally as future history is devoid of sense."[2] So, in the footsteps of Sorel, the New Leftists believe in the omnipotence of the deed and the irrelevance of the goal. The political process is no longer seen as the deliberate choice of means to move toward a desired end. Society is to evolve through the process of struggle itself. Where libertarian democracy ideally demands means consistent with the end, and where the Stalinist Left of the thirties had contended that the end justified the means, the New Left propounds a different doctrine: that the means *create* the end.

Let us not ignore the attractions of the existential approach. After all, there are many absurdities in our world. Our country has never undertaken anything more absurd in its history than the Vietnam war. After all, man does make himself by his decisions. After all, our conventional liberalism is to a discouraging degree a liberalism of promises and excuses. After all, social renewal can only come from personal commitment.

All these things help explain, I think, the appeal of the terrible idealism of the new creed. Yet this creed contains so much in the way of fakery and fallacy—to put it bluntly, it is so preposterous and so depraved—that I do not see how it can long be entertained by any serious democrat.

Let us look first at the negative part: the demand for the forcible suppression of false ideas. This immediately raises a self-evident question: How is one to tell which ideas are O.K.

---

[2] *Reflections on Violence*, Introduction, Ch. 4.

and which are to be suppressed? "In the interplay of theory and practice," Mr. Marcuse replies, "true and false solutions become distinguishable. . . . Freedom is liberation, a specific historical process in theory and practice, and as such it has its right and wrong, its truth and falsehood." But who is to make this determination? What agency is the repository of final judgment on truth and falsehood? Here, alas, Mr. Marcuse lets us down, except to introduce hopelessly vague standards, as, for example, that "what is *not* conducive to a free and rational society, what impedes and distorts the possibilities of its creation" should be forbidden. He does not exclude repression: "there is a social and political repression which can foster human progress, which can lead toward a true democracy and a true freedom." In the end, he places his confidence in what he mystically calls "the democratic educational dictatorship of free men."

This is not very satisfactory; so let us pursue the question a step further. I suppose that the new creed does not expect to make such judgments through a man. But, if not through a man, these judgments must be made through a mechanism, which means through men. Such a mechanism would plainly have to have an extraordinary degree of power. What assurance can there ever be that this power would be used disinterestedly—that is, for the good and the true, should there ever be a means of defining the good and the true—rather than in the interests of the men operating the mechanism? What will this mechanism become—what have such mechanisms ever become—but a means to suppress criticism of the manipulators of the mechanism? So the mechanism, in the end, rests on an assumption of human infallibility.

But the assumption of human infallibility has never been justified in the long and varied history of mankind. It implies the rule of those whom Mr. Dooley long ago defined as men who do what they think "th' Lord wud do if He only knew the facts in th' case"—and Mr. Dooley was defining a fanatic. Jefferson in his First Inaugural made a relevant comment: "Sometimes it is said that man cannot be trusted with the government of himself. Can he, then, be trusted with the government of others? Or have we found angels in the form of kings to govern him? Let history answer this question." History has answered the question: man has never found angels in the form of kings, or even of philosopher-kings, to govern him. And, if he should, "the unfortunate thing," Pascal said, "is that he who would act the angel acts the brute."

Not only do men who claim infallibility in politics do far more evil than good, but the systematic suppression of supposedly false ideas would deeply impoverish human knowledge and understanding. "There is no error so crooked," Tupper said, "but it hath in it some lines of truth." Or, as Norman Mailer recently put it, "Sometimes a profound idea is buried in a particularly ugly notion." Human creativity takes a marvelous and sinister diversity of forms. How dare anyone assume the right to deny the unlimited freedom of human expression? "I tolerate with the utmost latitude the right of others to differ from me in opinion without imputing to them criminality," wrote Jefferson. "I know too well the weakness and uncertainty of human reason to wonder at its different result."

The demand for the forcible suppression of "false" ideas would be an enormously effective way of calling a halt to human progress. And the other half of the new creed makes no more sense: that is, the conviction that one should feel and act first and think later, that the struggle generates the program and the means create the end. The kind of action supremely required to strike through the mask of official society, we are told, is violence. Without violence, official society, in its present sophistication, will calmly co-opt and emasculate the opposition. Only violence will force official society to drop the smiling mask of tolerance and reveal its inner viciousness. More than this, violence becomes a means of social and individual redemption. As Frantz Fanon has written, "Violence is a cleaning force. It frees the native from his inferiority complex and from his despair and inaction; it makes him fearless and restores his self-respect. . . .

Violence alone, violence committed by the people, violence organized and educated by its leaders, makes it possible for the masses to understand social truths."

This is hardly, of course, a novel doctrine. Others in this century have eloquently propagated the cult of the deed. It was, after all, Mussolini who used to distinguish between "a violence that liberates, and a violence that enslaves . . . a violence that is moral and a violence that is immoral." And it was Hitler who wrote, "The very first essential for success is a perpetually constant and regular employment of violence." It is perfectly obvious why Mussolini and Hitler favored violence: because violence, by abolishing the procedures and civilities of society, opens the way for those who are most adept in the mobilization of force. I do not know about the situation in developing countries; there violence in certain contexts may be an indispensable means of establishing a sense of national identity. But surely little is more pathetic than the view that in American society violence will benefit the left.

A limited amount of collective violence may stimulate the process of democratic change; but, if the left, through the cult of the deed, helps create an atmosphere which destroys the process of democracy itself, the only winners will be those who use violence best, and they will be on the right. "If they want blood to flow from our heads," Tom Hayden cried bravely in Chicago, "the blood will flow from a lot of other heads around this city and around this country. We must take to the streets, for the streets belong to the people. . . . It may well be that the era of organized, peaceful and orderly demonstrations is coming to an end, and that other methods will be needed." If the New Left should finally succeed in making American politics a competition in hysteria and force, does any New Leftist really suppose that Tom Hayden and Eldridge Cleaver will bring more armed men into the streets than George Wallace?

The new creed, with its dismissal of free discussion and its conviction that violence will mystically generate policy and program, represents an assault on rationality in politics—an assault based on the ultimate proposition that rights and wrongs in public affairs are so absolute and so easily ascertainable that opposition can be legitimately forbidden. This assault on the Bill of Rights and on libertarian democracy is in my judgment wrong, because no one is infallible. It is stupid, because the beneficiaries will not be the idealists of the left but the brutalists of the right. It is dangerous because it represents a reversion to and rationalization of the strain of hatred and violence in our own national tradition: the politics of lynch law against the politics of Lincoln. The New Left, in this respect, casts its vote for the worst against the best in our political ethos.

Above all, the new creed overlooks the fact of human frailty. "Men are not flattered," wrote Lincoln, "by being shown that there has been a difference of purpose between the Almighty and them." Yet men are not gods. That is why absolutism always fails in human society. Democracy requires consent—it insists, that is, that a majority of the electorate eventually be persuaded that one course is preferable to another. If men or mechanisms were infallible, there would be no need for such persuasion. But, because they are not, the discipline of consent is indispensable to civilized society. The discipline of consent means that policies must triumph not through the divine right of kings or of a "democratic educational dictatorship" but through making sense to a majority of the people; and the condition of bringing a majority along is the best guarantee that policies relate, not to private fantasy or personal power, but to the greatest good of the greatest number.

Nietzsche once wrote, "Gaze not too deeply into the abyss, lest the abyss gaze into you." Those who claim to *know*—to be the bearers of absolute truth—are men who have gazed too deeply into the abyss. They have committed what Hawthorne called the Unpardonable Sin—the sin of self-pride, which enslaves people, breeds fanaticism and concludes in madness and catastrophe. It is sad when the derelicts of our society surrender to the Unpardonable Sin; it is contemptible when our intellectuals exemplify it. Worse, these intellectuals who have gazed into the abyss see nothing except the virtue of destruction-for-destruction's-sake; and they then present the absence of intelligible objectives as evidence of the purity of their cause. They should remember Tocqueville: "In a rebellion, as in a novel, the most difficult part to invent is the end."

Let us strike out against the concrete evils of our time. But let us not yield to that awful despair which dissolves all distinctions in thought and action and hurtles us on to the politics of apocalypse. In the long run, any sane society must rest on freedom and reason. If we abandon this, we abandon everything.

PROJECTS

1. Using the discipline of the political scientist, write an evaluation of Truman Nelson's "No Rights, No Duties" indicating (a) his use of the terms "power" and "revolution" (implicit or explicit definitions of these terms), (b) why, in your opinion, he does not use the word "violence" in his essay.

2. Debate: The constitutional right of revolution in the United States involves the right to use political violence for the cause of social justice (illustration: denial of civil rights to a minority group).

3. What, according to Nelson, is revolutionary virtue? How is it attained and sustained by an individual, by a society? Would you agree with Nelson that the American society has lost its revolutionary virtue?

4. "So there it is, deep in the hide of the Republic, and you can talk about it all you want, having a revolution, that is, just as long as it is in a classroom, and you are white. But don't say it, as William Epton did, on the streets of Harlem before a group of silent men, whose eyes have a tiny glow like a stirring of a long-banked fire." If this is the case, how *realistic* is it for Nelson to write about (a) the natural law of the people to make a revolution against an immoral government and (b) asking "the people" to unite against that immoral contract it has with such a government?

5. Herbert Marcuse writes: "Violence, I confess, is very dangerous for those who are the weakest. But first we should examine our

terminology. People are always talking about violence, but they forget that there are different kinds of violence, with different functions. There is a violence of aggression and a violence of defense. There is a violence of police forces or armed forces or of the Ku Klux Klan, and there is a violence in the opposition to these aggressive manifestations of violence. The students have said that they are opposing the violence of society, legal violence, institutionalized violence. Their violence is that of defense. They have said this, and I believe it is true. Thanks to a kind of political linguistics, we never use the word violence to describe the actions of the police, we never use the word violence to describe the actions of the Special Forces in Vietnam. But the word is readily applied to the actions of students who defend themselves from the police, burn cars or chop down trees. This is a typical example of political linguistic, utilized as a weapon by this established society."[1]

Write a critical essay evaluating this statement in terms of: (a) its implication for the use of political violence and (b) your reaction to his analysis. What is implied in Marcuse's reference to violence being very dangerous for those who are the weakest?

6. Discuss: There are many signs in the American society which indicate the disintegration of its moral fiber. These are hopeful signs in the sense that they will provide the opportunity for a new political climate and a new "solidarity" (Marcuse's type of socialistic solidarity).

(a) What specific signs do you think indicate a disintegration of the American moral fiber?

(b) Do you agree with Marcuse that these signs may be hopeful within the same context (a new socialistic solidarity) or within a different context?

(c) Do you think that a sign of disintegration is reflected by Marcuse's thinking itself in "Solidarity"?

7. Do you think that Marcuse's reliance on the Pleasure Principle rather than the Reality Principle as the foundation of the liberated

---

[1] Jean-Louis Ferrier, Jacques Boetsch, Francoise Giroud, "Marcuse Defines His New Left Line," *New York Times Magazine*, October 27, 1968, p. 90.

society of solidarity is the prelude to a rationale for violence? In your evaluation refer to Schlesinger's statement in "Existential Politics" that half of Marcuse's creed rests on "the conviction that one should feel and act first and think later, that the struggle generates the program and the means create the end."

8. At the conclusion of his essay, Marcuse refers to that liberated society based on the Pleasure Principle which allows us to be free to think about what we are going to do. Schlesinger criticizes Marcuse's position as being naive in this regard: "To put it more precisely, what distinguishes the New Left is not only its unwillingness to define what it aims for after the revolution but its belief that such mystification is a virtue."

(a) What reaction do you have in regard to these two positions?

(b) What position(s) would Nieburg or Arendt take regarding the creative potential of violence?

(c) Do you think political violence has a creative potential?

9. "Let us strike out against the concrete evils of our time. But let us not yield to that awful despair which dissolves all distinctions in thought and action and hurtles us on to the politics of apocalypse. In the long run, any sane society must rest on freedom and reason. If we abandon this, we abandon everything."

(a) How is Schlesinger defining the terms "freedom" and "reason" in the context of this paragraph?

(b) How would Marcuse define these terms?

(c) How would you define freedom and reason with reference to the "politics of apocalypse"?

10. Several provocative films in this area are:

a. Lebert Bethune's *Malcolm X: Struggle for Freedom* (22 minutes—rental $22.50)

b. Agnes Varda's *Report on Black Panthers* (26 minutes—rental $60.00)

c. Roberta Hodes' *The Game* (17 minutes—$15.00 rental)

d. Robert Machover's *Good Times, Wonderful Times* (73 minutes—$135.00 rental)

e. Harold Becker's *Interview with Bruce Gordon* (discussion by a young SNCC organizer on experiences which motivated him to become active in the civil rights movement in Alabama) (17 minutes —$12.50 rental) Write to Contemporary Films, Princeton Road, Hightstown, New Jersey, 08520.

For other films listed above write to Grove Press Film Division: 85 Bleecker Street, New York, New York, 10012.

Bibliography

ARENDT, HANNAH. *On Violence.* New York: Harcourt, Brace and World, Inc., 1969.

BROWN, RICHARD MAXWELL, ed. *American Violence.* Englewood Cliffs, N.J.: Prentice Hall, 1970.

DOUGLAS, WILLIAM O. *Points of Rebellion.* New York: Random House, 1970.

FANON, FRANTZ. *The Wretched of the Earth.* New York: Grove Press, 1963.

FERRIER, JEAN-LOUIS, BOETSCH, JACQUES, AND GIROUD, FRANCOISE. "Marcuse Defines His New Left Line," *New York Times Magazine,* October 27, 1968.

FORTAS, ABE. *Concerning Dissent and Civil Disobedience.* New York: Signet Books, 1968.

FOX, GEORGE. "Counter-Revolution," *Playboy,* March 1970.

FRANKEL, MAX. "Introduction," *Rights in Conflict.* New York: Bantam Books, 1968. (Violence in Chicago: The Walker Report).

GRAHAM, HUGH DAVIS, AND GURR, TED ROBERT. *The History of Violence in America.* New York: Bantam Books, 1970.

HOFSTADER, RICHARD, AND WALLACE, MICHAEL. *American Violence: A Documentary History.* New York: Alfred A. Knopf, Inc., 1970.

LANE, ROBERT, AND LERNER, MICHAEL. "Politics and Polarities: Why Hard-Hats Hate Hairs," *Psychology Today,* November 1970.

MARCUSE, HERBERT. *An Essay on Liberation.* Boston: Beacon Press, 1969.

NELSON, TRUMAN. *The Right of Revolution.* Boston: Beacon Press, 1968.

NIEBURG, H. R. *Political Violence.* New York: St. Martin's Press, 1969.

Rubenstein, Richard. *Rebels in Eden: Mass Political Violence in America*. Boston: Little, Brown & Co., 1970.

Schlesinger, Arthur M., Jr. *The Crisis of Confidence; Ideas, Power and Violence in America*. Boston: Houghton Mifflin Co., 1969.

Sennett, Richard. "Urban Peace Through Disorder or The Uses of Anarchy," *Psychology Today,* November 1970.

Skolnick, Jerome. *The Politics of Protest* (*National Commission on the Cause and Prevention of Violence*). New York: Ballantine Books, 1969.

Slark, Rodney, and McEvoy, James. "Middle-Class Violence," *Psychology Today,* November 1970.

Taylor, Telford. *Nuremberg and Vietnam, An American Tragedy*. New York: Quadrangle Books, 1970.

Zinn, Howard. *Disobedience and Democracy: Nine Fallacies on Law and Order*. New York: Vintage Books, 1968.

The Social Polemic

Introduction

The complexity of violence as a social phenomenon involves the biological, psychological, religious, and political aspects that we have included in Part II, *The Polemics of Violence*. In fact, to limit the study of violence to only one area of concern is to reduce violence to a theory but not to its existential reality. Frederic Wertham's essay, "The Goddess of Violence," warns against this type of limitation. It is only within the total context of our existence as social beings that we can begin to hope to understand the complexity of violence. From his experiences as chief resident psychiatrist at Johns Hopkins, senior psychiatrist at Bellevue Hospital in New York, and director of psychiatric services at Queens General, Dr. Wertham finds abundant evidence to support this concern for the complexity of violence. Perhaps his own role as the sole psychiatric consultant to the Kefauver Senate Subcommittee for the Study of Organized Crime reinforced his conviction. In addition to his book, *A Sign for Cain* (from which "The Goddess of Violence" is taken), he is author of *Dark Legend: A Study in Murder, The Show of Violence, Seduction of the Innocent,* and *The Circle of Guilt.*

The essays which follow Wertham's "The Goddess of Violence" support his thesis that this "Goddess" appears in many forms including the pressure of a "baiting" social order, random violence on the street, "revolution" on the campus, and the impersonal brutality of the media.

French-born Romain Gary, author of "The Baiting Society," received his law degree from the University of Paris and a diploma in Slavic languages from the University of Warsaw. In addition to writing such novels as *Company of Men, Colors of the Day, The Roots of Heaven* and *The Ski Bum,* Gary has served as the first secretary spokesman for the French Delegation to the United Nations (1952–1955), as Secretary of the French

Embassy in London (1955), and as consulate general of France in Los Angeles (1956). In "The Baiting Society," Gary presents social violence as a natural part of a society which "baits" its members with particular, and often unattainable, desires. The unavoidable and cruel logic, which follows from the facts described by both Wertham and Gary, is depicted with candor and horror in "Random Violence: Is That Man Coming Down the Street to Kill You?" Its author, Herbert Gold, involves himself personally and the irrationality of random violence. Gold is an essayist and novelist, whose books include *The Optimist, Therefore Be Bold, Salt,* and *Father.*

"Salvation Through Revolution" applies the social polemic of violence to the campus scene. Donald Rogan, Associate Professor of Religion and Chaplain at Kenyon College in Ohio, examines violence as a revolutionary model for social salvation in his book, *Campus Apocalypse, The Student Search Today*—chapter seven being "Salvation Through Revolution."

The final selection, "Reflections on Violence as a Literary Tool," is by Morris Renek. Author of the novel, *The Big Hello,* Renek also writes short stories, reviews, and articles including this one, which invites us to examine violence in its literary form as "the ultimate metaphor of a frightened and bewildered age of humanity."

Perhaps the social phenomenon of violence in the media is one of the most seductive metaphors of the "Goddess of Violence." It appears as spontaneous, joyous revolution in the Living Theater (but not violent revolution, Julian Beck claims), which begins in the theater and ends in the streets.[1] Guerrilla (theater of the streets) Theater presents its own disarming metaphor by acting out the violence of our society in local parks and on the sidewalks. Films such as *The Strawberry Statement* and *Getting Straight* are sexy metaphors for revolution which bring violent

[1] Elinore Lester, "The Living Theater Presents: Revolution! Joy! Protest! Shock! Etc.!" *New York Times Magazine,* October 13, 1968.

solutions to complex problems as quickly as "Mr. Clean."[2] And television, that ever-present metaphor of our frustration and bewilderment, offers exciting and incessant recipes for violent solutions to problems rather than reasonable alternatives to violence.[3] In addition, the artists of protest compel us to make a commitment against social injustice with the brutal conclusions of their songs, words, and designs. With their artistry, evil and violence are sometimes reduced to simple and childlike forms, and we react to these forms by longing for an immediate and, if necessary, violent solution to such evil. In this sense, the social polemic of violence as found in the media is deeply emotive and intimately related to everyday experiences—and therefore is a very seductive and paradoxical metaphor of the goddess of violence.

---

[2] David Denby, "Commercials for Revolution," *The Atlantic*, October 1970.

[3] Arnold Arnold, *Violence and Your Child*, Chicago: Henry Regnery Company, Chicago, 1969 (see Chapter Two).

The Goddess of Violence

FREDERIC WERTHAM

Birth is the beginning of life, death is its end. But violent death is an end before the end. Often it is an end with great physical pain and suffering. It is this latter aspect that has motivated me, as a physician, to make a comprehensive study of the subject of violence. It was in the course of these studies that I learned that violence is not only physical suffering and annihilation, as it is in such catastrophes of nature as an earthquake or the eruption of a volcano. Violence has far greater effects on the lives of the survivors and on society. Whether the victims are forgotten or not (and they are often not even properly counted), violent deaths have deeper and more enduring consequences than we like to concede. Violence corrupts. We need to realize how insidious it is. We also have to make clear to ourselves the connections between the manifold phenomena related to it.

If I had to compare violence with a medical disease, I would compare it with cancer. Cancer can start insidiously in any part of the body. It becomes known to us through a local manifestation, but it can spread all over the body. It is deadly if not arrested in time. And it requires all the ingenuity of science to diagnose early, to treat, and to prevent.

There is an old saying that "nothing matters until a fool starts violence." That has a certain validity, except that before anybody starts violence, many others must have prepared the ground. The aggressor is not the only, and sometimes not even the chief, transgressor. He comes onstage and fires the shot, but the script has been written long before. One single actor does not make a play.

According to the legend, which, whatever else it may constitute, embodies some element of anthropological truth, the earliest family—Adam, Eve, and their children—was beset by three major troubles: first, what has been described as a "turmoil of thought," especially about good and evil (the tree of the knowledge of good and evil); secondly, sex (the serpent of lust); thirdly, violence (Cain's murder of Abel).

It is an interesting fact that the philosophers, the scientists, and the theologians have focused their attention on the first two. There are innumerable treatises on moral philosophy and, of course, on sex. But violence as a general subject has been neglected. This despite the fact that we are today nearer to mass violence than ever in the history of the world. Even the sign of Cain, or mark of Cain, is sometimes misunderstood. I have heard district attorneys asking for the death penalty while pointing to the "sign of Cain" on the accused's forehead. They did not realize that this sign does not stamp a man as one fit for the death penalty, but on the contrary is a device *against* continued violence: "a sign for Cain, lest any finding him should smite him."

The chain of the continuity of violence reaches from the most ancient times to today's headlines. Can we break this chain?

Recently two middle-aged women in Brooklyn on a summer evening were walking on a side street toward one of the larger avenues, after visiting a friend nearby. They intended to take a taxi home. About 250 feet from the avenue, a group of boys came up, crowding the sidewalk. The women drew back to let them pass. The last boy grabbed the right arm of one woman, to take her purse, then knocked her down on the sidewalk and jumped on her again and again. When she was taken to the hospital, it was found that she had a broken shoulder, broken elbow, broken arm, and a compound fragmented fracture of her right thighbone, for which an elaborate operation was necessary. She needed three nurses around the clock. And when she recovers, she will have to wear a brace from her hip to her heel and will be permanently crippled, with one leg shorter than the other. In my professional contact with this case, I learned what terrible pain and shock were caused—and that the expenses involved wiped out a family's savings. There was no sexual connotation to this attack. Since the boy had the pocketbook, there was no reason for pure gain to explain his stomping the woman so mercilessly.

Twenty-five years ago this would have been an exceptional case and would have caused a sensation. Now it did not raise a ripple and was not even reported as news. It happens too often. The boys were never caught; if they had been caught, the authorities would not have known what to do with them. This is today's violence in pure culture. I have known a number of similar cases. They are as a rule not fully reported, far less solved or resolved. Those who use the fashionable explanations for violence, that it is due to domineering mothers or inadequate ones, to pent-up aggressive instincts or a revolt against early toilet training, do not know the current facts of life in big American cities. They try to reduce ugly social facts to the level of intriguing individual psychological events. In this way they become part of the very decadence in which present-day violence flourishes.

Psychology has an important role to play, in its place, but no violent act can be fully explained by psychology alone. We must take into account the society, the various influences which surround the individual and family. Violence is always a historical fact; that is to say, it is always relative to the prevailing social-historical conditions. It is futile to try to translate it into some superhistorical principle in individual human nature. If on the streets of Brooklyn a young boy wantonly stomps a woman, much more is at work than a little imp in his brain.

Violence is destructive physical action against another person. But there is another kind of violence in the broadest sense which may be called figurative violence. It may be somewhat intangible, but it is neither invisible nor inaudible. We say smilingly, "I'll break your neck," or "I'll punch you in the nose," or speak of giving somebody a "tongue-lashing." It is merely verbal, but it has psychological implications. A prominent writer just now advocates in a column printed in many papers that youths who commit violent crimes be "fried" (meaning electrocuted). We use as a matter of course such crude and almost obscene expressions as "population explosion."

Language itself helps us to trace the ramifications of figurative or symbolic violence. We speak of "doing violence" to a text, an idea, or a principle. That means to misrepresent it or distort it unscrupulously. Disagreements are necessary, but they are often expressed in violent invective. The noise of loudspeakers, overshrill music, leaving the radio turned on very loudly, overloud commercials on television—they all belong to this violence in the broader sense. What corresponds to it is a kind of ruthlessness in thought and feeling.

This radiates into many spheres: politics, economic life, art and literature, and the ordinary relations between human beings. Henry James spoke of the American business scene as characterized by a "boundless ferocity of battle." We are becoming so enveloped by this whole atmosphere that we hardly realize it any more.

The influence of figurative violence on actual physically violent occurrences is hard to trace in detail, but as a matter of social psychology this influence undoubtedly exists. When the environment tolerates, approves, propagates, or rewards violent expressions, violent behavior is more apt to happen.

Figurative violence also implies a larger issue, the dominance in our society of the principle of success-at-any-price. This ruthless striving for success is permeated with violencelike elements. As James Baldwin has expressed it, "The American equation of success with the big time reveals an awful disrespect for human life." To put something over on the other person, to overpower him, is rewarded socially and economically. There is a whole philosophy of self-expression and "self-actualization" popular in some academic and intellectual circles which in part teaches the young to live out their aggressive drives regardless of what that may do to other people. In a book that is part of a series edited by a professor of psychology at Harvard University, we find this revealing statement: "Necessary to the concept of self-actualization is a certain selfishness and self-protectiveness, a certain promise of necessary violence, even of ferocity." It is significant for the spirit of our time that the same term, "ferocity," which was used by Henry James in condemnation is used here by a modern psychologist with scientific approval.

The success-at-any-price principle debases man. Rabindranath Tagore, whose thinking was much occupied with questions of violence and nonviolence, wrote in one of his last poems of

> This play of losing and winning
> This false magic of life

The magic of losing and winning, of success-at-any-price, is closely related to violence. For anybody who wishes to help stem the tide of physical violence in the world, great effort is required to escape the standardized ways of success-thinking in our social life.

It is a paradox that while physical violence is such a definite, decisive, and irrevocable act, writing about it is often evasive and unrealistic. Violence, individual or multiple, is not an idea, not a psychological-philosophical abstraction. It is not an eternal, universal constituent of all human existence, as some philosophers seem to assume. It is part of the harsh reality of our historically developed social life.

There is not one scientific or scientifically oriented book in any language on the general subject of physical violence as such and its prevention. This is a significant gap. And if you look over recent books in fields like sociology, social science, psychology, and psychopathology, the word "violence" is usually not in the index. In school and college courses and textbooks, violence is presented only in patriotic garb, with heavy emphasis on dates, geographical places, names of rulers and commanders. We learn a lot in school about the violence of conquest, but little about the conquest of violence.

The fact that no scientific book on violence has been written is a problem that itself becomes a part of the study of violence. There are a number of significant reasons for this neglect. Violence is an emotionally loaded subject. It has more extensive implications than are apparent on the surface. The details that lead up to it are even more disconcerting because they concern us all. Its distant roots and runners reach into the life space of almost everybody, in the form of ultimate gain from it or responsibility for it. This is dimly felt by many people, though not often fully realized or easily admitted. Sweeping and comforting generalizations replace concrete research. Do we perhaps, as the columnist Henry Butler expressed it, "privately cling to the promise of some kind of magic fulfillment through savagery?"

We need to keep in mind the critical role of violence in human affairs. An important aspect of human development, past and present, could be outlined by the history of the occurrence of violence, the reasons for it, and the evolution of ideas about it. When we look beneath the surface for the causes of violence, including seemingly remote ones, we are apt to find raw truths not easily acceptable. We may learn that less lofty forces are at work than we thought. In chemistry, if you put sulfuric acid on a lump of sugar, it becomes black and you reveal the carbon coal underneath. No feelings are hurt, no interests impinged upon. But if you investigate violence, you are likely to trespass on touchy ground.

The study of violence may, in a restricted way, begin in the laboratory. You can put mice in a cage with an electrically wired floor. When you send a painful electric current through the wires, the mice begin to fight and bite one another. That, by analogy, may be some clue to why men fight. But the study has to reach much further, away from the laboratory and into the home, the street, the forum.

One reason for the neglect of violence is that it is regarded as too isolated and restricted a subject. We have learned about the many disguises, pre-stages, and finer ramifications of sex. We have not yet learned that the murder drive also has many masks, that temptation, seduction, and many other influences play a role, that its causes and its effects are as widespread as those of sex.

Another obstacle to seeing violence concretely and frankly is the aspect of its so-to-say official standing. When the government wants to prevent violence, it speaks of law and order. But law and order are themselves maintained by the potential threat of violence. As Barbara Wootton expressed it, our society, and every civilized society, is in the last resort founded on violence. According to the sociologist Max Weber, the state is the monopoly for all legitimate physical violence, and all political structures are structures of violence. Surely that is insufficient for explaining either the state or violence, but it is a view, widely held, which has done its part to prevent our seeing violence as a whole. After all, there is a prospect—not an illusion, but a scientific prognosis—that with the progress of science and morality, nonviolent structures of society will be built.

Perhaps the strongest reason for the neglect of the subject of violence is a growing disregard for the victim. Surely when a murder is committed we owe it to the victim to settle it properly, either showing our condemnation by punishment or our understanding by psychiatric or social treatment—all in an effort to prevent future violence. When a war is ended we owe it to the victims to build quickly a proper peace and at least try to prevent thereby a repetition. This is all far from the reality around us. Rarely is a murder case fully studied in its complete context. As for wars, the creation of the Polish Corridor after the First World War is a good example of a settlement which any schoolboy who could look at a map would know was dangerously unstable. Two decades after the Second World War, there was no peace settlement. Again, any schoolboy could see by a glance at a map that the island of Taiwan can no more represent the whole of China than the tail can wag the dog and that the current fashion of dividing countries in half is in the long run unworkable. Such arrangements are permanent invitations to violence.

Monuments to the Unknown Soldier may assuage our conscience, but they do not fulfill our duty to the victims. The Soldier has no name, and his death becomes something impersonal, distant, and general. Actually his death was anything but impersonal. He did have a name, and an address, and people who loved him. Were he to come back to life, would we be able to answer his legitimate questions about violence? Moreover, considering London, Hiroshima, Dresden, and many other cities and villages, there should also be monuments to the Unknown Civilian, especially to the Unknown Children, the greatest and most innocent sufferers. Is it not significant, considering the thousands of child victims, that nobody seems ever to have thought of erecting a monument to the Unknown Child?

In the light of the number of victims and the reality of their suffering, writers' discussions of subtle differences about what anxiety really is or what existence really means become less important. These abstruse disquisitions have lost a good deal of their meaning for us. It is as if nothing had happened and all these dead had not really died. The disregard for victims is related to a general lack of feeling for the average man. We have become interested in the elites, the exceptional, the specially gifted, the consumer, the glamorously neurotic, *et al.,* but not in the average man, his wife, and his child.

The lack of serious concern for the victim is illustrated by a recent case. A young man of prominent family in New York was accused of drunken driving, reckless driving, and leaving the scene of an accident in which five people, including a six-year-old child, were killed. Some witnesses said he was driving ninety miles an hour and later was unsteady on his feet. He had previously been guilty of thirteen traffic violations and had been deprived of his driver's license once. Yet it took a panel of three criminal-court judges only five minutes of deliberation to acquit him. *One minute per victim* is not enough. Young people who read about this in the newspapers or hear about it on the radio or on television can learn from this neither respect for law nor sympathy for victims.

Another point has contributed to the neglect of violence as a subject of scientific and serious literature. With regard to violence we are apt to deceive ourselves—and be deceived—about the degree of civilization we have reached. It seems a small error, but it may be a fatal one, to believe that we are already living in an era of nonviolence or even that a time of true nonviolence has begun. Most of the victims of the First World War had not the faintest idea, and would not have believed, that another big war could break out and last for more than four years. The countless civilians who perished prior to and during the Second World War in bombardments, concentration camps, euthanasia proceedings, extermination camps, jails, and slave-labor camps could not imagine that such a development was possible in the modern world. Far less could these victims believe that this would happen to their children. This is their tragic guilt. Their disbelief made them even more defenseless. They listened to those who in the early labor movement were called the "all-righters," those who say that everything is all right or at any rate by itself soon will be all right. The study of violence as such should help to dispel these illusions in the future.

We live at present in an era of the greatest potential violence in the history of the world. No, it has *not* always been so. There are many symptoms from diverse fields to bear that out. This is an age when a postwar period has drifted imperceptibly into a prewar period. The name we give it is peace. Wedged between the barbarism of yesterday and that of the morrow, we can kill more and faster than any previous generation.

The study of violence cannot rely merely on the historical data known prior to two decades ago. There are entirely new facts from which we can learn. Violence is not history, it is the present. First, of course, are the technological advances, atomic bombs, and missiles, which have made violence a mass threat of hitherto unimagined proportions. But we have learned (or maybe it is better to say we have had a chance to learn) about other circumstances which a generation ago would have seemed inconceivable; for example, even before the advent of atomic arms, unprecedented large-scale killings, especially of civilians, took place with what are called conventional weapons, like fire bombs. Related to this there have been changes in psychological and sociological attitudes which are not yet recognized officially and academically. These changes have played a part in bringing about the events, and the events in turn have reinforced the changes. These new attitudes can be easily summed up: the readiness for violence and brutality has increased in recent years. Not to recognize this is a form of social blindness. That is true technologically, socially, psychologically, and politically.

It is often said that the real danger lies in the unalterable nature of man. Recent history disproves that. Since it can be documented that the readiness to violence has increased, man can evidently be conditioned either upward or downward. When a serious modern playwright like Arthur Miller writes of "human nature as the only source of violence" and François Mauriac (referring to Nazi massacres) speaks of "the inherent ferocity of human nature," they unwittingly make themselves part of the atmosphere of violence of our time. For if it is all in human nature, and if we are all guilty, then nobody is guilty. And if we are all responsible, no man is responsible. We make it too easy for ourselves. We want to confess and participate at the same time. Such authors are in effect reverting to Spengler, a prophet of violence, who told the German people two years before Hitler came to power: "The tactics of man's life is that of a splendid, brave, cunning, cruel beast of prey. He lives attacking, killing, destroying. He has wanted to be master as long as he has existed."

Others like to isolate in their minds those who act brutally or violently and put them into ready-made categories—psychological, sociological, political, geographical, national, ethnic, racial. The facts of our time do not bear out such facile generalizations. The labels prevent us from seeing the often less palatable truths.

Romantic poets and dogmatic psychoanalysts believe that everybody who kills has severe guilt feelings afterward, consciously or unconsciously. That may have been true for some times and some places. It certainly is not always true today. Justification feelings bolstered by false social-philosophical ideas frequently replace guilt feelings. Freud described unconscious guilt feelings in a very restricted sense. He did not generalize them for almost all crime and violence as is often done now.

It has been widely stated by psychiatrists and lay writers that in our culture every killer must be psychopathic. That implies a rosy view of our society. It leaves out the terrible aspects of normality (however defined) in a violent age. We flatter ourselves if we believe that our social conditions are so far above reproach that only mentally ill adults and children can commit violence.

In trial after trial of men who committed mass murder during the Nazi regime, it has now been ascertained, some fifteen or twenty years after the crime, that the perpetrators were educated, respected citizens who lived typical, ordinary, successful lives with their wives and happy children. They were well-adjusted family men. To label them psychopathic personalities merely serves to obscure the issue. We come much closer to the truth if we realize with historian James Parks that the facts of these mass murders show "what man could organize and do, could watch and plan, and could find allies for in the whole operation among all the civilized countries of Europe." A British Member of Parliament, Maurice Edelman, expresses it this way: "The plague of our generation is this passion to give pain: to torture as in Algeria; to mass extermination as in Hitler's Germany; to mass obliteration, as in the preparations for atomic war."

Nor can one still say that mass murders and atrocities were committed only by violence-indoctrinated party fanatics. We learn differently from eyewitnesses. For example—and this is by no means an isolated or exceptional instance—when the German Army had to evacuate a Russian village, they herded all the inhabitants who had been left behind, old men and women, children, the disabled, into houses and set the houses afire. One little boy jumped from a window through the flames to the ground. He wept, terrified. He was picked up by the legs and tossed back into the flames. All this was not carried out by the specially trained SS troops, as is so often assumed, but was done by ordinary soldiers. In civilian life they were workers, peasants, artisans, clerks, businessmen.

To subsume this under the convenient term "individual sadism" would mean to misunderstand its essential nature. To label it "mob action" would also be misleading. It was routine. As a matter of fact, one of the German soldiers later stated quite truthfully that they had acted on orders. If you have to destroy a village with all its inhabitants, you cannot let one little boy escape. It would be like appearing at parade with unpolished shoes. What propaganda had been put into these men's heads, from cradle to Krupp, that they were able and willing to do this? A concrete study of that is necessary to understand them. However, what obedience to orders means in an ordinary soldier's head was clearly expressed about another mass killing in Poland. A corporal stated: "I did not think about my orders. I thought that they must be right and everything in order because they came from the highest quarters." The vast majority of those who committed such acts have never been called to account. They still think they acted right.

We bar the way to understanding if we assume that this can be explained by national characteristics. We may not be willing to concede this—until it is too late—but a very similar type of violence-thinking pervades our own "highest quarters," and a similar type of propaganda influences those who will think it right to obey orders. What is being thought of and prepared today is not only the destruction of villages, but that of large cities and whole provinces. No child will be able to crawl through those flames. The prediction of Michael Innes is about to become true: "We scrap a generation by violent and costly means, and very soon it is the cost and not the scrapping that troubles us."

Force and violence are deeply embedded in our whole economic process. A very substantial part of production, employment, economic planning, and research is devoted to the means of violence. We live in a violence economy. If this were to cease suddenly, the greatest economic dislocation would follow. The fear of violence is counterbalanced unconsciously by a fear that the production of the means for it would also cease. We are drawn into this stream and will continue to be until we have learned to dam it and put its water to better use.

Our cultural and psychological atmosphere is charged with the electricity of violence. The old know about death because they have seen their friends and acquaintances die. But many of them have not been exposed to violence. The young know all about violence but nothing about death. The big manifestations of violence, such as the mass killings of the recent past or those prepared for the future, are too big for us to visualize. Who can see in his mind's eye the reality of a million killed? Yet the statistical knowledge of this reality makes the little manifestations of violence seem too banal and insignificant. In large cities young salesgirls living in reputable neighborhoods have learned to keep revolvers in their apartments for protection. They feel they have to guard themselves not only from robbery or sexual attacks but also from the fierce cruelty so frequently shown on the streets and in the buildings. Perpetrators of these acts are usually very young. These youngsters in turn have been exposed through mass media to violent images continuously and relentlessly, in every context and every costume. No previous civilization can equal the amount or the degree of brutality.

We are victims of the hydrogen bomb before it is ever used, for the psychological fallout comes far in advance of the physical one. We are entering an era in which overnight the innocent become guilty, the murderer and the victim become one. Poets have called this the age of anxiety. More accurately but less poetically, one can say it is an age of complacence. It has also been called the age of space flight, but that has as a prerequisite that we stay alive to go there. According to my diagnosis, this is the age of violence.

The goddess of violence is a strong and alluring woman. She stands on a pedestal of granite, the granite of human indifference. Her emblem is not the sword, for she will use any weapon. Her eyes are not bandaged, for she chooses her victims. In one hand she holds a smoking, smoldering torch of hate. In the other she has a graven tablet with an inscription that reveals the secret of her power: "Let mankind continue in the false belief that violence will cease by itself."

From my psychiatric and sociological studies I have arrived at a double thesis. On the one hand, violence is becoming much more entrenched in our social life than people are willing to believe. On the other hand, it is in our power eventually to conquer and abolish it.

The following propositions may be formulated:

Violence is not so complicated and difficult a subject as those who do not want to do anything about it would have us believe. We must learn to understand it, not in its complexity but in its simplicity. Violence has to be seen as a whole. That is to say, all its manifestations have to be taken seriously, from little toy guns, military toys, and violent mass media to political murders, riots, and wars. These are very different matters, but they are not entirely unrelated. All forms of human violence are in some way connected with one another. The task is to trace the connections and to uncover the violence potential in whatever disguise it appears.

Violence and violence-mindedness are deeply embedded in our whole social life. Explosions of violence occur because we live in a peaceful dream about ourselves and permit the explosive material to accumulate. None of our traditional safeguards against violence have kept pace with the reality of violence.

Violent acts cannot be explained by human nature alone. Their roots reach further than the individual. All psychological forces operate in a social environment, and it is necessary in scientific studies to achieve a balance between the psychological and the social.

Violence is not over when it is over. It is always part of a process. If the process is not halted and the violence resolved, it will break out again, maybe in a different place or at a different time.

We underestimate the extent of violence in our time, do not give sufficient recognition to its inconspicuous prestages, and neglect decisive and rational measures afterward.

In different periods of history, the pattern of violence changes and the factors leading up to it change too.

The whole fabric of our civilization rests in the last analysis on the avoidance of violence.

The Baiting Society

ROMAIN GARY

As I sat in front of my television set watching the second invasion of Czechoslovakia, this time by the Communist storm troopers, resentment and despair, shame, indignation and the frustrated awareness of my total impotence were racing wildly through the corridors of my mind, like the "hounds of heaven" in the famous Housman poem. I was trying to control my breathing and to clear my throat; my whole body was tense, and in my hands there was a kind of physical longing for the controls of the bomber I had flown against the other Nazis during the War. Then, out of some even darker corner of my psyche, there suddenly arose a monstrous thought: This, if ever, was a case for the use of the atom bomb. Under the impact of intolerable provocation, faced with this cynical baiting of my helplessness and weakness through a combination of total frustration and powerless sense of injustice, I was crossing the border of sanity and falling prey to the obscure forces within a Lee Harvey Oswald, a Hitler or a Sirhan Sirhan.

My own reaction is the answer to all those who wonder how violence has become our daily companion, why students are running amuck in every city of the world. Our consciousness and conscience, our inbred belief in the existence of some kind of honor among men are mercilessly teased, baited, provoked day by day, hour by hour, through the instant audio-visual contact with the world we live in. This world may be no more ugly than it was 50 years ago, but its beastliness was then ignored or unknown to a colossal degree, and this ignorance protected our psyche. But two generations of mass media and communications have exposed both the world to us and us to the world in such a brutal way that our conscience has become an exposed nerve. An adjustment to such a situation becomes not only impossible but immoral; that is why Freud and psychoanalysis are more and more rejected by the young, as Miss Anna Freud herself so courageously pointed out some time ago. In the world of Prague, Biafra, Vietnam and Harlem, can anyone tell me what could possibly be meant by an adjusted man? Brainwashed at best; more likely, a passive accomplice. For the youth of today, to be ill adjusted is a term of praise, a first necessity in terms of dignity, of moral and psychological survival, as well as the first prerequisite to a radical change of the total environment.

Not long ago, I heard an 18-year-old boy say ironically, looking at his father with an unbelievable expression of scorn: "Yeah, he's always been well adjusted."

One of the most absurd arguments advanced against the 16,000 rioting students in Paris last May ran as follows: "We are feeding them, clothing them, we are giving them all the opportunities to learn and to occupy a place in society, then they go and throw stones at us." It is true that 90 percent of the rioters were *fils à papa.* It is, however, the most stupidly selfish argument ever employed by the French *bourgeoisie* in blind self-defense. For the so-called French revolution of 1968 had its roots precisely in the fact that the young intellectuals of Nanterre and Paris could no longer stand to be well fed, well clothed, well educated and settled in jobs in a world where 700,000,000 people are suffering from malnutrition. It was said that the rioting students had no purpose in sight. True enough, they were merely vomiting the world.

Being a violent person myself, I am no less aware than other observers of the pathological character of all violence and I would be the last to defend it or to sing its praise. But, on the other hand, we cannot drive people mad and then condemn them for being insane. I am also aware that violence derives either from our own self-righteous conviction that we are absolutely right or from our reaction to others who feel and behave as if they are absolutely right. Such an attitude excludes all margin of tolerance. The belief in one's cause becomes so strong that all other moral considerations are swept aside, usually together with some butchered or burned bodies of men, women and children. My moral convictions become so overwhelming that I no longer let ordinary morality stand in my way. For the holder of absolute truth, everything else ceases to matter. During the last War, I spent five years more or less continuously at the controls of a bomber in England, Abyssinia, Libya, Syria, France and Germany. In 1943, I dive-bombed and missed an enemy submarine. I have often heard of bomber pilots who, years later, experience a recurrent nightmare: They see the victims of their bombing. I suffer from an even more terrible recurrent nightmare: Twenty-six years later, I still dream that I miss that submarine. I wake up screaming in a cold sweat because I have *not* killed. My anti-Nazi convictions and my belief in what I was fighting for were so absolute that I had become a highly decorated killing machine. Even today, my painfully abstract remorse stems from the fact that I feel no remorse.

Albert Camus has written what to me is one of the two key sentences of our or, for that matter, any other time: "I am against all those who think they are absolutely right." And I may as well quote the other key sentence in the same context: "You condemn to the death penalty a guilty man, but you always carry out the sentence on an innocent one." I know of no greater truth; and yet, as I was watching the rape of Czechoslovakia, I felt so absolutely right in my indignation that I caught myself longing for the absolute weapon.

I do not believe that this is a time when one can have a conscience and be entirely sane. Brutality is merely the opposite pole of this escape from reality, the oversensitive individual always dreams of toughness, of virility, and can become a pathological killer merely to escape from his own feeling of impotence.

My contention is that we are in the midst of the greatest psychological, moral and spiritual crisis that our civilization has ever known. Ideology has become associated with mass murder. Materialistic society finds nowhere to go, except to more of the same, and there is neither God nor man in sight any longer. Humanism is dead and Man, with a capital M, died with it. I myself believe in an extraordinary spiritual revolution and renaissance in the next century, and it probably will be of a scientific origin or, if you prefer, a revelation. Man cannot live by man alone. The new civilization will have to find outside help. I do, however, feel that our traditional religions are all deeply associated with our fiasco and that our spiritual rebirth will have very little to do with them.

One of the most obvious reasons for our angst is, of course, the fact that we are truly opening our eyes for the first time. For thousands of years, civilizations prospered on a happy mixture of limited knowledge and unlimited ignorance. The most frightening, shocking single event in Voltaire's life and time was the Calcutta earthquake. Today, an earthquake is a reassuring thing: At least there is one horror for which we are not responsible. We are living in a state of instant and constant awareness. Let me give you an example of the power of the mass media. Last May, in Paris, a few hundred students occupied the Sorbonne. It so happened that while Dean Roche, Chief of Police Grimaud and Sauvageot—the handsome Ché Guevara of the students' revolt—were negotiating inside the building, unknown to them, Radio Luxembourg had its mikes there and every word of the angry discussion was on the air. Within a matter of hours, the 400 students were 16,000 and the May revolution began.

It would, of course, be absurd and totally unacceptable that the realities of the world we live in should be deliberately hidden from us. But it is no less true that we are overexposed. By its very nature, television dwells on dramatic events. There is no show element in peace. Nondrama, the nonhappening, is not something upon which movies, radio and television can feed and prosper. Our conscience and consciousness are therefore constantly bombarded with the worst: The very nature of showmanship, of the spectacular, of the arresting, of the dramatic, is shock. Overemphasis sets in with the necessity to conquer new audiences and to fight the competition of other media. All those who listened to the hysterical radio report on the assassination of Senator Robert Kennedy soon found themselves reacting hysterically to the tragedy. Superevents provoke overreactions.

Even the voices of the majority of news commentators in the United States are almost constantly keyed up; they tend to overplay the drama already emphatic enough in itself. The accent is always on tragedy, and the more peaceful and happy aspects of life are largely ignored. There is an old saying in France: "Happy people have no history." There is no story in the absence of drama. We are, therefore, being served day-by-day overdoses of tragedy and we like, through mass media, a permanent show, with the consequence that a lack of entertainment, which was our normal way of life for thousands of years, leaves us in a vacuum. It is not so much the violence on the television screen or in the movies, as is too often said, that leads to crime and violence; it is a craving for a constant happening, the conditioning by the constant dramatic vibration on the screen, which, in the end, equates nondrama with a feeling of nonexistence. As often as not, violence in the streets is a form of self-provided entertainment.

I understand that after the assassination of Robert Kennedy, many Hollywood personalities took an oath to renounce violence in the movies in which they star. It may be a valid personal reaction against our gun society, but it has no relevance to the murder of Robert Kennedy. The young Senator was assassinated —probably as was his brother—because his glamorous personality, wealth, power, good looks and unlimited prospects had been overdramatized by mass media to the point that they were begining to act as provocation on a paranoid personality with an inherent feeling of inferiority and frustration, always on the lookout for dramatic self-assertion. In such a situation, the assassin feels that he has avenged himself and has achieved greatness by his act, and that he has risen above the status of his victim.

As for violence in films, its influence is probably highly overestimated. And can anyone tell me what effect *Bonnie and Clyde* had on the sadistic behavior of the Chicago police during the convention?

During last spring's riots in Washington, I was fortunate

enough to be able to witness an example of a truly curious rapport between the television addicts and the magical box. Several houses were burning around 14th Street. A few blocks from the nearest and clearly visible fire, I saw a crowd in front of a store. The crowd was watching a television set in the window, and do you know what they were looking at? They were looking at a house burning in the neighborhood. They had only to turn their heads to see the fire live, but they obviously preferred to watch it on TV. Maybe they were confident that the network had picked the *best* fire for them. Or maybe they wanted to see the commercial that would follow. I do not pretend to be able to explain this phenomenon. At one moment, I even began to suspect that the crowd was not watching the fire on the screen but the TV set itself. Or perhaps they were just waiting for someone to break the window, so that they could take the set and the fire home with them.

The power of the transistor radio in the underdeveloped countries is fantastic. It can be argued that Egypt and the whole Arab Middle East are held together only by transistor radio. A few words can throw millions of people into the streets, as happened in Cairo during Nasser's "abdication" speech, and in Paris, in the Champs Elysées, during De Gaulle's challenging speech against the Communist Party.

The power of the mass media is snowballing through the democratic explosion and coincides with the appearance on the social scene of a completely new and extremely receptive class —youth, with its own economic power and leadership, its own mechanized transport, vocabulary, heroes and tribal organizations, with its more sensitive and militant elements refusing any form of integration. Youth power is in the process of radically changing the patterns of behavior in our society; and the adults are simply unable to meet the challenge of the young and to compete with them, if only because they are almost physiologically incapable of the same reflexes, vitality, eagerness and freshness of outlook. All they seem able to do is to call the police. In such a situation, mass reactions are bound to become endemic and explosive, unpredictable and beyond the grasp of traditional reason. In France, the average age at a mass meeting 35 years ago was 42. Today, it is 24. A huge turnout 40 years ago meant 100,000 people; today, it means nearly 1,000,000. A large minority of this new class, youth, seeks a deliberate alienation from the rest of society, develops new codes of behavior and reinvents something akin to tribalism. The recourse to tribalism—hippies, black angels, psychedelic clans, gangs, sects, each with its own way of living, of dressing, each with its own customs, language, signs and symbols—is a reaction of the individual against the sucking-in pressures of a homogenized society endowed with unlimited power and authority over him. The individual regroups himself within the tribe and tries to create a world of his own. This form of retreat will be prevalent as long as a prosperous society permits such marginal living, which is feeding essentially on surplus and offal: The same forces will become revolutionary when marginal forms of escape living become economically impossible. Add to this the demographic congestion in urban areas and the evidence that our unreconstructed society is largely incapable of coping with the growth of its own birth rate, and it becomes apparent that we will either have to reconstruct the society entirely or establish a police state. Our civilization remains static and clings to sameness, while all its components, from technology to communications media, are in constant change, which can only mean an explosion, a breakdown or rapid, deliberate progress. The whole refuses to follow the changes of its components.

Within the U. S. A., the combined psychological pressures of advertising and of the constant show of wealth surrounding the poor are so strong that they amount to an invitation to looting or to robbery. The baiting never stops. Buy! Consume! You cannot do without this; this is the newest and the best and you must have it! Come on, it's waiting for you! How can we act indignant after that when the ghetto kid, submitted to such a teasing, at the first opportunity goes on a looting spree? America has laid out the rule for the successful consumers' society: Get rich. Yet it refuses both within its national boundaries and throughout the world to play its own game. Willing or not, it finds itself, therefore, constantly baiting, taunting and provoking millions of its own economically abandoned nonconsumers, as well as all the underdeveloped countries. The attitude of the destitute masses of South America, Asia and Africa toward the U. S. A. is that of the average looter toward a Fifth Avenue store.

The alternative to crime would be revolutionary, it would consist of an attempt to overthrow a society that at the same time baits you with its riches and denies you economic access to them. Crime is a form of adjustment to society. It's a pathological way of accepting this society and of answering to its pressures. Crime is not, as is often said, the left hand of idealism: It is the right hand of ignorance.

Each of us can compose his own list of overwhelming forces active as a tease within our baiting society. Authority, for instance, has become a dirty word because of the sheer exhibitionistic, overactive and ever-present aspects of it. For young people everywhere, revolutionary and nonrevolutionary alike, from Moscow to Belgrade, from Prague to Paris, from Chicago to Montreal, authority is the number-one enemy. No wonder: Living has become an exercise in bureaucracy. Individual freedom has all the scope of a pedestrian crossing: Walk, Don't Walk. During the students' May revolt, when spring in Paris was blossoming with slogans on all walls in the flickering light of burning cars, one of the graffiti I read was: "Down with the bureaucracy of living!" It was impossible to find out what the students were fighting for, in terms of actual politically constructive changes. They were merely reacting to the daily baiting of our civilization, reaching for an overexposed and unacceptable reality; and they reminded me once more of Kafka's most moving prophecy, those few words that have been my greatest inspiration as a writer and whose echo can be heard in all my books: "The power of the human scream is so great that it will smash all the iron laws decreed against man."

"La puissance, voilà l'ennemi!" ("Power, that's the enemy!") ran another bit of writing on the wall. The individual is surrounded by the evidence of too much implacable power around him—nuclear, economic, military, industrial, mechanized, organized, anonymous, impudent power. The individual either capitulates to the power machine and becomes a kind of "insert one" coin in its entrails or tries to destroy the machine itself, with nothing in mind to replace it. Violence, then, becomes a kind of groping for self-respect, a self-assertion, a proclamation of independence. Victory becomes irrelevant; what counts is the old-fashioned, seldom-heard today word "honor." The rebellious Jews of the Warsaw ghetto could not hope for any victory over the German war machine. But they attained dignity and honor.

Each of us is exposed day by day to increasing doses of historical fallout. After all, there is no reason a French student should feel guilty and responsible for what happens, let us say, in Biafra. But when a mass-circulation magazine prints on its cover the picture of a tiny skeleton still stirring and staring at you under the caption, "Within two hours this child will be dead," unless you have become completely amorphous, with your sensitivity killed by overexposure and you no longer care or react (which is the first step toward a police state), any human being, and particularly the young, feels like smashing something, a typical reaction of frustration and impotence.

I vividly remember other slogans scribbled on the dirty old walls of Paris: "The word is a born liar," which is an approximate translation of *"Le mot ment comme il respire."* "The word comes with police protection and tear gas." "Truth cannot be expressed in words without lying." "Unlearn the words: Go back to before ABC." "Stop the word before it makes another million dead." As I write this, I wonder how the politicians and the warmakers everywhere would feel about this. The disillusionment of the young is entirely justified, and the indisputable fact is that the Communists and the capitalists, all the democrats and nondemocrats, all the revolutionaries and conservatives alike have betrayed their beautiful words and promises. Remember "Freedom from fear, freedom from want"? I wonder what happened to *them*.

To many people, this verbal aggression against words may appear as mere literature; but then, what they are really shrugging off is literature itself, which they cannot do without admitting that they have capitulated in their relationship with spiritual values and that those values are in the process of rotting in the vast Marxist and non-Marxist cemetery of "culture." It is characteristic that the leaders of the Paris revolt and most of the rank and file were students of literature and philosophy. Unquestionably, the revolution had its roots in the very dynamics of all artistic creation: the need for self-expression under the onslaught, baiting and pressures by our unacceptable reality. All art and literature is an answer to the taunting or challenge by reality. All craving for justice is an artistic pursuit, a craving for beauty and harmony. Frustration and inability to change the real world can lead both to violence and to artistic creation. This age will probably see more music, art and literature—and more young people, talented or not, devoted to those pursuits—than any other age, simply because there is no other way out. From the furious action painting of Jackson Pollock to Picasso's pictorial aggression against reality, from the theatrical Happening to the students' riots in the streets, the means of self-defense and self-expression may differ vastly, but the motivation is the same: a refusal to accept the taunting of our consciousness and of our conscience by a monstrous environment. Psychodrama, Happening, Living Theater—the riots and violence in our cities were and will continue to be what art and literature have always been: an attempt at a rebirth, a spiritual self-cleansing, a deliberate alienation from the present-day social reality. Art is what is not there but should be there.

To me, the most hopeful sign is that our generation of protest and of negation has outgrown national frontiers, races, creeds and ideologies. It's nothing more than one great big, emotional *No!* And it unites Christians and atheists alike. Not long ago, I stood in the midst of a crowd of Catholic dissenters near Notre

Dame, the day after the Pope's ban on the contraceptive pill was announced. As I stood pushing the mike of my tape recorder toward the white face of a young Dominican priest, these were exactly the words I heard:

"The contraceptive pill means the rebirth of man. It means resurrection. It means the end of genocide; of genocide through hunger, through oppression, through squalor, through ignorance. It means the reassurance that the reborn Jesus will not die of hunger in some small corner of the world. The prohibition of the contraceptive pill is genocide."

My contention is that the real danger to our future is not the violent, rioting youth, still a vocal minority magnified through the mass media, always on the watch for drama. The real danger is our indifferent masses. The pattern of violence is, in my view, insufficient to force our society toward a real change; but its positive aspect is that it may awaken some stupefied, apathetic people. Every Communist and every politician have always and will always speak of the people with sobs of emotion in their voice, and the people have responded with self-righteous self-esteem almost to the point of no return. This passive, cowed, hypnotized majority may still be awakened from its slumber by the so-called violent fringe. Up to now, both in Soviet slave-land and deep between the layers of our Western fat, the people have refused to budge. We hear every day about the rioters and killers in our midst, about the troublemakers, but we never hear a word about the 95 percent of the population who are merely for law and order. The question is: *what* law and *what* order? The same as before and more of the same? Then we will soon need a police state to protect our goodies and our rights.

Random Violence: Is That Man Coming Down the Street to Kill You?

HERBERT GOLD

A few weeks ago, a nice young bureaucrat who suffered from stomach trouble took a rifle into his offices at the Labor Department in Albany, N.Y. When he was finished with his ramble, he had killed five people, four of them women, the last himself.

He has colleagues all over America. Not long ago, a group of amiable artists and rock musicians came together to plan a grand free outdoor festival of their joyful crafts in San Francisco, but a man who called himself Mother John appeared at their meetings and said he'd tear them apart, he'd burn them down: "I ain't rational, and I'll wipe you out."

"What's your last name, sir?"

"Mother John from Out-of-Town."

Then, their insurance went up, and the folks got scared. There were ten or twenty or thirty of these mothers (or maybe the same one with ten, twenty or thirty faces), but they were all talking about burning, ripping, exploding and such. The festival in the park was canceled.

Why did the mothers threaten? They wanted to hurt. *Why?* Well, maybe they were Fascist third-world Meth-freak Maoist hippie deviationist paranoids, or maybe they were just out-people wanting in, fearing that someone might find fun and profit in the festival. They really don't know or can't say. They are rebels without a pause.

The man who commits random violence always thinks his attack is justified, of course. "He gave me a lotta lip"—the true-life explanation, folks, for shooting a fellow shopper. Or: "I just don't like guys who smile to themselves." But we know that the gesture is in excess of the provocation. Maybe logically we can't explain it, but "a lotta lip" isn't reason enough to kill in a busy department store during the January White Sale.

In my novel *The Great American Jackpot,* a young man named Al Dooley robs a bank because he's lonely and seeks meaning. Well, there are other reasons, even good ones. But *he* doesn't really know them, and to the world, too, his action seems eccentric, unpredictable, irrational. He is strung out and strange to himself and a menace to others. He wants to greet reality with an answering blow. He is a frequent American.

Traditional violence usually had a clear aim. The man with the stick hit the other man to grab his goods, land or woman. Contemporary random violence, a war against phantom enemies, has murky origins—killing without hatred, rape without lust. This is the child who hits first because otherwise somebody might hit him. Causeless violence? No, but action that is far in excess of cause.

This is a violent country. Everyone who walks the streets of America knows it. If you can't walk, you read the newspapers. If you can't read, you see it on television. The subtle mining of violence under the surface control of America goes beyond anything a law-and-order manipulation of police authority can resolve.

For a time, I accepted a wry, half-paranoid suspicion that my own person (horn-rimmed novelist, nosy face) invited attack. I've gradually come to realize that I'm no worse than others, but just being alive invites attack. For example:

I was crossing Montgomery Street, San Francisco's Wall Street, on my way to dinner. I was wearing a blue suit and therefore, in a period of stock-market decline, must have looked like a stockbroker to the man following me. "When's the market going to turn around?" he asked. "I don't know," I said. "I've got a lot of losses," he said morosely, "RCA, GE, they were supposed to be blue chips." "I'm sorry," I said, "I really don't know much about it," and hurried on my way. A moment later I woke up, sprawled in the street, with cars honking at me. The disappointed investor had slugged me from behind.

I was walking in a heavy rain. The street was deserted. A man came toward me in black-militant drag, boots, leather, beret, and his lips moving, discussing with invisible enemies. But I was visible. Our eyes met. I stopped for a moment to let him by, and he glared at me. "Hi," I said weakly.

"Man, I don't see it like that," he said. "I'm gonna *kill* you."

But there was no action. There was only the wish to murder.

And there is also, oddly enough—this is often ignored—the reciprocal wish to have violence done. I know a girl, a very pretty actress, who has been raped twice. Does she invite it? Well, she undresses at night, with shades up, and when she hears a sound at the window, she goes to open the door and see what's happening. And I was standing on the street near the San Francisco art museum when I saw an old acquaintance, the girl friend of a friend, and jokingly came up to her and said: "Hey, chick, you want to do something really filthy?"

She paused and looked up into my face with a welcoming smile: "What?" Then her face darkened with disappointment. "Oh," she said, "it's Herb. I didn't recognize you at first." She later explained that she was kind of upset that day and bored and, oh, you know, looking for something to do. I realized an odd fact about rapists and molesters. They are offering a product that not many women want to buy, *but some do.*

There is no lack, of course, of the traditional kinds of violence —between races, generations and classes.

My wife and I were strolling in Berkeley after a party. A group of cops was hassling a couple in an old station wagon decorated with hippie, love and peace insignia. The five policemen were teasing the kids, looking for drugs, it seemed, or maybe just looking. A boy of high school age, long hair, blue jeans, called out: "They don't have a search warrant! You don't have to let them!"

It was careless of him to incite the police.

One huge cop went lazily moving toward the kid. The kid started to run—very fast—ahah, he'll get away. The cop thumped after him. We kept walking in response to the other cops' jerking thumbs: *Keep moving.* But in the direction of the kid. He slipped and fell, bounced to his feet and kept running, but the cop was close now. Suddenly, to our amazement, we heard a thud of feet. *All* the five cops had abandoned the car and were chasing this boy who had yelled at them. They passed us, grinning, clutching clubs, some with hands on their pistols. They rounded the corner and I heard the boy scream, "I surrender." He stood with hands up, trembling. The first cop to reach him thumped him on the head with his club and sent him staggering and bleeding. The others, grinning, gathered around as a small Saturday night crowd appeared. He gave them his papers. He was OK. He was even white. A couple of Berkeley ladies, spinsters or schoolteachers or grandmothers, were standing nearby. The cop who had hit him said, "OK, go home now."

They didn't arrest him. They had made their investigation, administered justice and dismissed the case, all in one swift comment of billy club on skull. He was bleeding from the nose. He was vomiting. He needed to see a doctor. The ladies soothed him and led him away.

The cops were pleased that they had made another request for polite attention to one's elders. But they had also created another cop-hating radical, ready to kill. And not just the boy, of course, but the ladies, and me too.

While trying to work out an explanation for the upsurge in violence in contemporary America, random violence beyond the traditional violences, I happened to be in my bank in New York City, formerly the Fun City, during the months when it is supposed to be a Summer Festival. New York offers a natural environment for thinking about random violence. I was waiting to have a check certified (speeding ticket, speedometer defective, H. Gold the Mild-Mannered Novelist feeling morose). A mousy young man came up to the desk, wrote his name and account number on a slip of paper, and said to the bank bureaucrat, "Excuse me, sir, I'd like to know how much money I have."

"How should I know?"

"I mean in my account."

"What do you mean, don't you get a statement?"

"Yes, but there seems to be a discrepancy—"

"Can't you add?"

"I think so, but it doesn't come out the same—"

"It'll cost you a dollar. There'll be a charge of a dollar."

Timidly the supplicant said: "Won't you tell me what I have in my account?"

It was like the tide rushing through a weak place in the wall. The put-upon, underpaid, not over-bright bank clerk saw weakness and found pleasure in crushing it: "We can't just stand here all day and answer stupid questions from stupid people who can't add. I said it'll cost you a dollar. You want me to call downstairs?"

The dejected supplicant took his slip of paper with his name and number on it and walked away, gray and defeated. No matter that the bank probably wouldn't and couldn't legally charge him for the service. No matter: he believed in the authority of the Man Behind the Desk, a man exasperated and rubbed raw in the great city, a loser himself. The teller turned to me and said, "Stupid idiots, asking stupid questions, they think all I got to do here is answer them?"

I said that the supplicant walked away gray and defeated, but I'm sure there was also murder in his heart. Not against the bank or the teller, not a cop, not some authority. But against someone weaker than himself—a black man, a hippie, a kid. Isolation from power makes men look for a mob in which they can be strong.

Power is the opposite of violence. The powerful man can respect the stranger, not fear him. The sense of being cut off makes men want to find reality through the ancient pride in blood-letting. Powerlessness corrupts; absolute powerlessness corrupts absolutely. Stabbing strange women or setting drunks on fire do not seem to be the moral equivalent of war that William James said America needed. But if the tax man and your parents and your employer give you trouble, and you can't strike at them openly, why not declare war on their surrogates, on the weak or the strange, on humanity itself?

Random violence is not really random or accidental, of course, and the man or mob, kid or gang, deciding to kill the first red-haired man in sight, is not unconnected with the rest of the fate of America and the world. There are 70 or 80 million more people in America than there were when I was a child. The rat-sink theory holds that animals go crazy—perverse, violent, self-destructive—when the density of population increases beyond a certain needed living space. No reason to think that the anxiety of rats is sharper than that of overcrowded human beings. Every study of ambulatory psychosis and neurosis comes up with a large store of ticking time bombs walking the streets—and driving, waiting on people, directing traffic. They are damaged, we are told, by broken families and crippled families, by historical examples of cruelty, by rage and resentment, by boredom and anxiety, by jealousy and frustration. Now we also hear of chromosome damage and genetic defects leading men toward senseless attack. Prison systems all have isolation chambers for enraged men who snarl like beasts and want only to destroy, who must be kept apart, unreachable by therapy; and some of these seem to burn out and are released, and some have not yet committed acts that get them in prison. Repressed, suppressed, tormented, unconscious, the desire to kill is a part of the risk of city life, like postnasal drip. High school basketball games turn into rampages.

A community in Washington protects itself from the world with fences, towers, electric eyes, dogs, guards, patrols—an armed concentration camp for suburban luxury living. The statistics about senseless crime, child-beating, sniping at strangers, arson and assault, and gang sadism should make Jean-Jacques Rousseau spin in his quiet French grave. If man is naturally good, he is sure going against his nature more and more of the time. It sounds like a bad joke: the paranoids are after us.

Violence pours out of city men like water out of broken fire hydrants. And it's not just the city, of course. The small-town jukebox roars out Johnny Cash songs or *Happiness Is a Warm Gun* and the bouncers hit and the cops flail and the shards of plate glass decorate the pavements.

The psychiatrist Bruno Bettelheim argues that a misunderstood Freudianism has led to a hypocritical pseudo-permissiveness on the part of frightened parents, and this in turn leads to guilt and weak control in children. The kids know their parents want them to be decent human beings, but also that the parents are afraid to assert authority. The child needs authority to provide examples for learning. The childish temper tantrum is a common means of testing. It needs to be mastered, but often isn't by the time the child has an adult's body. The character-disordered or psychopathic personality may seem to be intelligent, controlled and in touch; but in fact, all it knows is one lesson: I want, I want at once, I want only what *I* want—and I'll take it.

As Prof. Irwin Corey, the well-known comic, says, "Hatred is lovely, because without hatred, there is no joy in revenge." When a man respects no one, and not himself either, but wants wants *wants,* there is no reason to defer his hatreds and revenges; and when he doesn't really know why he hates and needs revenge, he may express his childish storm of temper with a high-powered rifle from a rooftop or a knife in a crowd. How quickly the "love generation" turns to hating Yippies under pressure about Vietnam and cynicism about American virtue. The kids can throw flowers, turn on and make lovely rock music, but if they are goalless amid affluence, they grow impatient with a doctrinaire forever springtime designed like a record jacket. The tender communal living arrangements seem to work out fine, as they did for a sweet flower child I knew a few years ago: "We love each other, we live at peace, we share everything."

"How long has this been going on?" I asked.

"Five days," she said.

But the grooviness ended with thievery, fights, jealous rage and a contagion of breakdowns. A Panglossian reaction might be: OK, let's work out the violence, it's the price we pay for super-organization. The trouble with this is that violence *expresses* other feelings, but only *communicates* itself—the desire to hurt. It does no good to the victim, unlike the victim of a poem or a song, who may benefit from the composer's expressed rage. And it does no good to the perpetrator, who comes to understand nothing but may develop a taste for blood.

A businessman I know in Detroit hopes that holdup men are rational and want his money; he can offer money—it's the ones who just want to kill him that are a bother. A childhood friend, a funny red-haired man from Cleveland, carries a tear-gas gun in his pocket. "Why?" I asked him.

"Some people don't like red hair," he said.

Mace, karate, judo, personal weapons—HELP! Stop! The police say that the worst criminals are the amateurs, out for kicks, not purses; pleasure, not gain. A presidential report on violence released on the first anniversary of the assassination of Robert Kennedy says that Americans are a "rather bloody-minded people."

In the past, it notes, violence was generally initiated by white Anglo-Saxons against Catholics, black men, labor organizers and pacifists. Now, black violence, campus violence, anti-war violence, political assassinations and spooky random violence are added to our turbulent past. Eric Hoffer, who hollered on television that we are not a violent people, wrote in his column in the San Francisco *Examiner* (June 9, 1969): "A day of wrath is waiting around the corner, when the saturated resentment of the long-suffering majority crystallizes in retaliation." He bemoaned an "incredible submissiveness" in an age of violence, and seemed to be urging the public to rush the "foul-mouthed, bushy-faced punk." People shouldn't put limitations on the police; do-gooders are the enemy.

His solution to the problem is on a similar level to the one reported in a New York *Times* story, in which Associate Justice Paul C. Reardon of the Massachusetts Judicial Supreme Court urged a campaign in the nation's schools to search "for a brief synonym for police officer and policeman to supplant that unfortunate word all Americans currently employ." The headline reads: NEW WORD FOR "COP" SOUGHT. Clearly the word "pig" won't do, but if we call the cops "angels," it won't be long until the word "angel" means what "cop" means. If there is violence and hatred in America, new words won't make them sweeter.

How can we live with random violence? Well, one way is just to go on going on, as we do with automobiles, smog, cigarettes, airplane failures, brush-fire wars—making irritated little gestures toward improving our chances but essentially enduring what malfunction or destiny brings. In the rat-sink city, we may have to think of berserk paranoids as another health hazard, like leaking stoves. Recently, I visited a prisoner in California who was convicted of kidnapping and tormenting a child. He is intelligent, gentle, thoughtful, and says he doesn't mind prison so much because it gives him a chance to catch up on his reading. (It has also dried out the drugs in his blood.) But when he is caught up on his reading and is ready for the world once again, and maybe ready to try speeding through his mind with the help of methamphetamine hydrochloride, are we to think of him as just another hazard, like the defective automobile or the mysterious disturbances in our lungs that come from breathing city air?

Suppose we're not content with this new hazard of sudden death by twitch and impulse?

The police, either kindly or repressive, can only provide fallible remedies. Either they are not there when you need them or they are too much there. Massed police tend to riot; police power means police brutality. What about personal armament, going about with little private jets of Mace that can be bought in grocery stores and at fine cosmetic counters. There are too many quick tempers abroad. When everyone is armed to protect himself, who will protect us from the protectors? This sort of panic is a reversion to the life envisaged during the great fallout-shelter craze, a retreat to something fetal and subhuman in human nature. Then what?

Other styles of child-rearing, deeper and truer education, meaningful work, creative interchanges among people—everyone talks about the ways that might make it possible for masses of men to live together on a limited planet. Improved medicine calms the distraught, tranquilizes the defective. The reform of cities and a public life that is less hypocritical about suffering, war and injustice can influence people to meet each other without rage.

Drugs, cops, institutions and karate—well, these stopgap controls may be with us forever, and we will use them when we must. Humankind requires deep solutions to the demand for animal and spiritual joy. Rage, violence, ulcers, twitches, crying jags and melancholia reflect an imbalance of personal expression and opportunity in the world. A song of a few years ago claimed morosely, "I ain't got no sat-is-fac-tion," and I've heard that song danced and sung in Los Angeles, New York, Paris and Biafra. It's a universal anthem. The dream of love and joy seems further away than ever. Doctrinaire injunctions to love one another —love! love, goddamit!—clearly don't work. Nor does anarchic self-expression when *my* freedom binds *you* to pay the price. The others out there will find their pleasure in revenge.

The billions are here, and billions more coming fast, and we must learn to live with them. There will be more of everything, including red-haired men. Is the red-haired man coming toward you your brother? No, in fact, he's not. He may be your friend or your enemy. He takes up your space, he eats your food, he jostles you. He covets what you covet.

A few days ago, waiting at the post office, a sallow, irritable, self-absorbed young man tried to slip in line between a couple of women ahead of me. I reached out to put my hand on his shoulder. I smiled sweetly. Then I said: "OK, fella, tell you what. You take that place in line and I'll take you on, OK? agreed? fine?"

He looked at me and saw a menace to society. I wanted to kill. The ladies in line shrank away from me. I was Mother Herb from Out-of-Town. I was not rational. And worst of all, I was proud of it.

Salvation Through Revolution

And so you ask, "What about the innocent bystanders?" But we are in a time of revolution. If you are a bystander, you are not innocent.

—FREE

DONALD L. ROGAN

To call what is going on among students a "revolution" is no longer hyperbole. Activism, however saving, is simply not a decisive enough word to describe the disruptions of normal campus activity that have caused the newspapers to keep front-page box scores, and the nightly newscasts to allow the campus to displace the war for prime coverage. The search for salvation to which students are committed in the various ways that have been described has become relevant in the extreme in being focused on the educational institution itself. It has increased dramatically in seriousness to the point where "revolution" has become the terrifying but unavoidable word for it. Our task is to continue to see whether the model of the search for salvation serves to give any useful explanation of what students are doing and, by it, to come to an understanding of this revolution. Perhaps we can discover a corrective for the fact that we have long made the mistake of using the word "revolution" too loosely at the same time as we have taken the fact of revolution altogether too lightly. Because of this, society at large and the educational establishment in particular are strangely hurt and surprised, and angered, by the beginnings of literal revolution, and tend further to polarize the revolutionary ideals of students.

Revolution and the University

Revolution has begun, by anyone's definition, when tactical violence begins to appear. Blacks have rightly insisted that "rebellion" rather than "riot" is the name of the urban explosions which have marked their recognition of the futility of nonviolence and their challenge to the rest of America that they are serious in their demands. Yet substantive change rather than violence is the essence of revolution, and we do not err when we conceive of peaceful revolutions. The precise character of violence in the American self-image is much discussed and still not widely recognized. The violence of the black revolution and of the student revolution provide one more opportunity for studying, and admitting, the trust in violence which they see as characteristic of American life. Thus I see it as tactical violence whose chief purpose is to draw out the violence of the establishment in its self-defense. For, in fact, the violence that succeeds, loses. And one thing that is abundantly clear to those in revolution in America is that if they press their claims with consistent violence, they will be defeated with the greater power of the state. Any serious revolution in this country can be put down easily, if force is the only issue. Violence (as well as the threat of it on the part of those in revolution) is serious and determined, but its purpose is to draw out the innate violence of the elements of control in society and in the university so that they might be seen to be the kind of authority they are, *imperium,* not *auctoritas.*

A nonviolent protest has the disadvantage of being possible to be written off as not important, empty of real commitment, the protesters not meaning what they say. A club or a gun tends to mean what it says in America, and the response of greater, more serious violence is quickly drawn. Such a response is most clearly drawn when the university turns over to the outside society its security and safety and proves that when the chips are down it desires identification with the *status quo,* rather than with progress and change. The response of violence which the university makes in order to get back to the business of "reasoned discourse" makes it the loser. Where this is a clearcut result, more students are radicalized and greater change is imminent.

The more dependent on force the university is for its survival the more clearly does it prove itself incapable of performing its real function, and in the eyes of students it is the weakness of the educational institution, rather than its strength, that is being displayed. The crisis of trust in education which this implies is likely to be decisive. The extreme will arrive when it is discovered that students as such are "them" for the university as they are for much of American society. There will be very little left of the traditions of education on which to build a new society.

The question is not that such a disaster is likely to occur as a result of revolution. The question is whether the revolutionaries are to blame for it and, being defined as a minority unapproved of by their fellow students, should be excised from the college scene before they have their way. And this question is being addressed in ways that will surely exacerbate, not solve, the problem posed by revolution. It is being assumed that student revolutionaries are responding to some agreed master plan for disrupting the universities when in fact the conclaves at which "the revolution" is discussed are disorganized and even chaotic, and in an organization like SDS the individual chapters are so autonomous as to make many observers wonder how it survives. Within individual chapters, further fragmentation of views makes the situation even less conspiratorial. The revolution, even in its literal and violent episodes, is spontaneous and dependent on factors arising from local situations and the availability of talents for leadership that vary from place to place in the country. It is here, moreover, that those concerned must continually remind themselves that student unrest is not an American, or even a Western, phenomenon, but has appeared in all the major countries of the world. Applauding the unrest of Soviet students while imagining a Communist conspiracy informing the unrest of American students is simply ridiculous. The moral authority of the university is effectively abandoned when it fails to cry out against the legislators' desire to approach the problem on a conspiratorial theory when everyone associated with the college scene knows how continuous is the spectrum from mild dissent or indifference through vocal antagonism and specific activism to the taking over of buildings and other disruptions. The fact is that the revolution is *more serious* than a conspiratorial theory allows. The extent of alienation and the potential for radicalization is all the greater for the spontaneity and selectivity of student activism, and we are in grave danger of not realizing how little of the iceberg has actually appeared. The logical extreme of the repressive approach is an educational institution without its best students present at all. A more likely result is drearier: a university system catering only to career-dominated training programs, with no vestige left of the classical goal of education in meditation on the meaning of being human.

The revolution, at all the levels at which it appears, is directed against the institution as institution, in the name of an educational ideal of an institution as community, as people, and consequently the administration of education is the primary target. Teachers are vulnerable in their having forfeited genuine responsibility for the educational community to managers, since within the educational world learning is a credential for acceptable authority. Whether the ideal can be achieved in the context of American education, where size and universality have become values, is the question posed by the revolution. The result could be a revision of our system of regarding the college degree as a proof of maturity (the end of the puberty rite). Or it could be the destruction of educational institutions which refuse to act like the living human communities they are called to be. In either case, it is a challenge to our present concepts of educational authority and relevance, and it is the institution as such, not education as such, which is attacked. To indulge in rhetoric about the dangers which revolutionaries present to the genuine educative functions of the institutions they disrupt is to assume that these functions are being performed. The students' revolutionary claim is that they are not—as long as the institution remains a complacent and contributing participant in a society that has no apparent humane goals. The revolution, therefore, may be the only relevant effort being made to *save* education and thus create a community in which the search for salvation can be fed by any real kind of hope.

We can understand and assist the necessary revolution only if we are aware of the various levels on which revolution is taking place. In its loosest sense, all that we have been discussing in earlier chapters is revolutionary, indeed any search for salvation at all is revolutionary. As noted, it is the fact that we have failed or refused to take these appearances of revolution seriously enough that more physical, that is, more violent, revolutionary moves must appear. None of the other models for understanding what students are trying to do provides the opportunity to see the revolutionary impetus as real, but the model of the search for salvation offers an insight into student life, an insight that captures the finality with which ideals are today being pressed. "Revolution" then, as we see it, is a term that applies to many levels of student awareness and behavior that substantiate the behavior generally seen as revolutionary, chiefly tactical violence; but this insight should make it possible to realize the necessity of some other response than repression.

Revolution as Alienation and Opposition

The first level of revolution is the one which takes place in thinking. It is the revolution which has created among students, on so many issues, attitudes vastly different from those of adult society; such attitudes as those toward law, toward morality, toward authority. Alienation, I hold, is not so much a psychological condition of students as it is a conscious opposition to the rest of society; alienation is itself a revolution on this first level, the level of thinking. Clues to this revolution, and confirmation that it has already taken place, appear in all studies which attempt to discover the causes of present student attitudes, such as their having been the first television generation, the first generation raised permissively, the first affluent generation, and so on. Each of these points not so much to a cause as to a quiet revolution in the factors of which the individual personality is composed that has already taken place in our society, although the revolutionary qualities thus produced are unrecognized and unappreciated by most adults.

It is not only that students and other youth are different from their predecessors but that they know they are different (as distinct from merely feeling it) and sense the power to press their difference openly. The revolution that has already taken place has produced aspirations and ideals for the social and political arena that as rhetoric are not new, but as realizable goals are more serious than they have been for some time. *Honesty* is perhaps the key concept, and the desire for openness and honesty, for bringing together whatever disparate tracks on which life is lived, for admitting fault and working for perfection, are simply traits of those already thus radicalized. Hypocrisy is the enemy, and certain kinds of muscular authority the enemy's tools.

The revolution that has already taken place provides much of the character of the search for salvation, since it is a revolution in thinking and attitudes. It is because of this revolution that the search for salvation has no meaning when it is thought of only in terms of traditional religious institutions or the irrelevantly constituted educational world. It does have meaning, if not fulfillment, when it is pressed in adventurous experiences such as with drugs, sensory awareness, or "different" religious disciplines. It is why the concern for an authentic individuality directed toward a humane sociality has gained such a strong appeal. The salvation sought must be authentically realizable and genuinely beneficial.

Revolution for the "Hell of It"

The second level of revolution is revolution for the hell of it, as Free calls it in *Revolution for the Hell of It.* ("Free" is thought to be a pseudonym for Abbie Hoffman.) This is the game model pressed to its furthest extent, including the renunciation of any seriousness whatever. It is, we might say, the indispensable element of humor which certain kinds of intellectuals thankfully bring to any movement. It reflects at once the hopelessness of serious revolution in this society and the necessity of untiring opposition to the world as it is. The revolution of complete noncooperation in a joyous and carefree spirit, it effectively exposes the arid sobriety with which the world sees itself. It is the revolution of the Youth International Party (the Yippies, who nominated a pig for President in 1968, and who treated their subsequent investigation by the House Committee on Un-American Activities as a costume ball). It is the incredibly inventive "Fuck the System" pamphlet, which swept New York City in the summer of 1968. This pamphlet, reproduced in full in *Revolution for the Hell of It,* describes how one can have life (and have it more abundantly) utterly free of charge in a big city, if one is willing to work night and day at the kind of noncooperation that refusing to earn money requires: free food, free phone calls, free college, free entertainment, free religion. In one sense, revolution for the hell of it exposes the colossal waste seemingly demanded by affluence and obsolescence. In another, it milks the system for all its spare benefits (and some not so spare). Morally, it is the fullest expression of the widespread belief in the young that to cheat an institution is not as serious as to violate the rights of another individual, and any business or government machine is fair game. This is a moral position which I have not seen effectively criticized. It cuts to the quick of our national hypocrisy that sees morality as primarily personal, rather than social, behavior. For an individual to steal from a corporation is as deadly wrong to the average moralist as for him to steal from another individual, or so he says. For a corporation to profit from its exploitations of the individual is a fact of life less accessible to moral judgment. The student who revolts just for the hell of it is testing out a precise reversal of this anomaly, for he demands morality on the social plane while denying its relevance in his personal affairs—always, "as long as nobody is hurt."

Revolution just for the hell of it is the revolution of the clown and the gadfly. Knowing that the system is so complex that nothing he can do will actually affect it, he satisfies himself by making its efficiency more difficult to maintain, and by aggravating it, making it less painful to himself. Since most of what he attacks in society is just that element of the world which takes itself with such great seriousness, and since his own mood is one of hit-and-run frivolity, he offers a salutary commentary of his own on the factors in our life which make salvation for the young so difficult. He also insists that the other levels of revolution should not take *them*selves too seriously.

Only those who think of comic relief as a luxury will miss the benefit of this kind of revolution in keeping hope alive on the other levels, and this is the function the Yippies have performed in their parodies of the New Left. That it is really revolutionary is no problem as witness the willingness of the policeman, the salesman, and the congressman alike to stamp it out whenever it appears. "To take nothing really seriously in American life!" There should never be a time when we are without such a conscience, costly as it may be to the individual who provides it. There can never be a viable revolution unless it is accompanied by another, just for the hell of it, which takes neither the *status quo* nor the pretensions of reformers as anything more than a bowl of cherries. On our model, of course, it is in itself a rejection of any possibility of salvation except in pure escape from the demands of a hostile world, not an altogether untraditional concept. If it continues to keep a sense of humor in the revolution, it will have its salvation, perhaps that of the juggler of Notre Dame.

The Yippies remind one, on reflection, of the disembodied chuckle that haunts Jean Baptiste Clamence in Camus's *The Fall.*

Their effect on the society which cannot rid itself of them is the same as the effect of the haunting laughter on that character: a pursuing challenge of guilt to complacency, a charge of the essential sinfulness of the uptight.

Revolution as Violence and Disruption

The third level of revolution to be considered is the physical acts of violence and disruption with which we began this selection. It is revolution as in Cuba, as philosophized in Marcuse. This level of revolution is desperate and serious in the extreme, with no room for the admission of error and no place for considered contemplation of consequences or alternatives. The point so far missed in commentary upon this level of revolution is what brings it on, which is the utter and complete failure of normal means of reform. In the American context, it has appeared several times since *the* Revolution, for example in abolitionism, in the development of the labor movement, and more recently in the black movement. In each case it has arisen only after a long period of relative failure in achieving demands felt to be rights of man, and in each case has been made possible by the moral indefensibility of the *status quo* against which the demands were made. As students have become revolutionary in this sense, it is partly in cooperation with the black revolution, and partly in reaction to the growing frustration with the failures of approved forms of activism to gain any attention to their rightful claim on their lives and destinies. This level of revolution requires a fine blend of anger and hope for success, both of which cut into the institutions of society at their most vulnerable point: impatience cuts into complacency, stridency into the capacity to talk a problem to death, noise into the quiet that is really escape from reality, and ingenuousness into the protections afforded by complexity. And weapons? Weapons, as already noted, prove that you expect to be heard.

The problems of physical revolution are as great as they are obvious. Most obvious of all is the fact that a revolution needs to succeed, and the revolution of blacks and students in America is, to say the least, highly unlikely to succeed. Nonviolence, undoubtedly, is the better tactic, if it can succeed in being incisive enough to draw the fire that the world levels on the true revolutionary, but this calls for ingenuity of an almost superhuman order. Precisely the reason that revolution is necessary is that our society has discovered its infinite capacity peacefully to absorb nonviolent protest. This means that the apocalyptic lure to value one's death in proportion to how great a havoc one can wreak in dying is very great. Apocalypse has already appeared on the campus; the task is to see that it ushers in a new world rather than confirming the old one in its power, as the invented apocalypse tends to do.

The other most pressing problem of revolution is its own inner failures, its own likelihood of producing tyrannies as great if not greater than those it replaces. This is perhaps peculiarly true for American revolutionaries, since the tyranny under which we live is systematic not personal, and is hence diffused throughout a variety of institutional forms. These institutions, to protect themselves, need only turn to other institutions for assistance, which they readily do, inasmuch as they recognize that it is institutionalism as such that is under attack. But the number and variety of institutions are such that no effective revolution of a physical kind can hope for success, only pointless bloodshed. In the event that revolution did prove successful in one kind of institution, the likelihood of a personal or oligarchical tyranny appearing would seem to be inevitable. Because of the diffusion of power, the temptation would be to aim revolution at the government, which is to say, to aim it away from the kind of power the revolution seeks to usurp: the power to sway the direction of institutional life away from institutionalism, away from structure, and toward a more humane and organic style.

Above all, physical revolution suffers from the diversity and spontaneity of the revolutionary impetus. The New Left and the radical students are simply not organized for revolution, only for spasmodic revolutionary activity. There is no capacity, even if radicalism were to win a revolutionary war, to fill the vacuum of power left by its initial successes. And this vacuum would undoubtedly then yield to the "revolutionaries" of the right. This is the truth implicit in the *caveat* leveled at students that the real danger they face is backlash—they so anger the general run of hard-working Americans that they will be irrationally opposed by them unless they cease antagonism. This caution too easily means that the students should accept the point of view of those who will lash back and is thus an advice impossible to accept. Somehow a revolutionary style that will stop just short of justifying such a backlash is needed, and is as yet wanting.

And yet, there is clearly a point of view from which the level of physical revolution must be seen as more than the fancies of a few of the more radical and politicized of students. Clearly, unless a bloodless revolution is midwifed into completion and breeds a genuine enthusiasm for the future in students, a bloody revolution is inevitable and will cost us our only hope of escape from mediocrity, banality, and the continuing hatred of the rest of the world. Most students tend to shy away from any serious talk of revolution as if it were the talk of a different kind of animal than they are, yet most students are also virtually bereft of hope that the society toward which they are growing is capable of real reform. They are *pre*revolutionaries, and for them, or for those armies of the young coming after them, revolution may in time become a more acceptable, because unavoidable, reality.

The Threat of More Revolution

At this point, with the threat of more physical revolution in the future, it might serve to observe the importance of anonymity in campus disruptions for most of the students. Leaders, of course, are not anonymous and take their lumps, but those who provide the numbers in a campus disruption act anonymously. Anonymity is their opportunity. But it may well also be their complaint. Especially where the type of student has known a kind of anonymity in his family life and finds it continued in college, knowing relief from anonymity only in the revolutionary community, the seeds of revolution are effectively sown. In the very small colleges, no one is anonymous, and misery, at least within the educational system, is less. In the large state universities, though the student may be anonymous on campus, it is likely that he is not from the kind of family where he has been anonymous since childhood, and again the misery is not as great. Large and complex institutions who draw their students from families where anonymity is a style of life have had the earliest and, as yet, the most serious disruptions. For in their students converges the anger to be justly directed at an inhumane society and the personal anger at not being dealt with on a personal level.

Physical revolution may be necessary simply because we are into a revolutionary time. It may require many more paroxysms in the black-white struggle before any kind of real humanity is recognized to exist in black skin, other than through outstanding ("qualified") individuals. As student alienation continues to be encouraged by the mistakes made in reaction to their attacks on the institution, and as the institution succeeds in preserving itself *qua* institution without regard for its vocation to be a community of education transcending anonymity and structure, the identification which students will feel with the "third world" and the revolutions that are economically and politically necessary elsewhere in the world (some of them made necessary by American policies) will develop in them a more clearly revolutionary stance toward their own society. Structures that will not yield to the insistent pressure of humane demand will be brought down by inhumane means. In the educational context, the response of teachers would seem to be decisive, and few have yet shown that they are willing to regard the students who refuse merely to emulate them as anything but potential enemies.

One specific response that would seem to be called for from teachers is the insistence that time be given periodically within the academic calendar for amply long and profoundly serious discussion on each campus of the proper role of the university in society. In a search for what Harvey Cox has called "the republic of virtue" as the *sine qua non* in the absence of which the "republic of intellect" is neutralized into uselessness, such discussion would serve well. This would be a mildly revolutionary tactic, if revolution involves the displacement of existing structures, since it would dislodge the tyranny of the routine calendar and the programed order of the teaching schedule. Moreover, it would require that teachers learn and students teach in many of the areas that would be discussed. Unstructured teach-ins have promoted a great deal of education over the years. The influence in society which the educational community might be able to effect might then be saving for all concerned. Until teachers use their ingenuity to show that they are allies in the revolution, the revolution will proceed in a form least consonant with real education.

More soberly, it seems to me that the rhetoric (and sometimes the acting out) of physical revolution will continue because it is necessary to keep the *possibility* of physical revolution alive until sufficient credence is given to admittedly virtuous aims of the revolutionaries. If those in control of the institutions that are the object of revolution are as fearful of substantive change as they have so far appeared to be, the possibility of physical revolution may be the only expression of real hope for change that gets heard.

It is not my aim to invest absolute hope in physical revolution, but to express as clearly as possible my feeling that it is in some circumstances inescapable. It is made necessary not by professional revolutionists, enamored of the mystique of Che Guevara, but by the unyielding response which the ideals of reform continue to encounter. Physical revolution is inevitable unless it is recognized that the search for salvation is a determined and demanding pressure on students. Salvation through revolution, unlikely though that be when the revolution is violent, is what is being sought, not revolution for its own sake or in the systematic interests of any traditional political alternatives.

Revolution as Existential Commitment to Decisive Change

A fourth level of revolution is best thought of as an existential commitment to a decisive change in the roles which an individual will allow himself to fill in his life. It is a kind of personal revolution, spiritual revolution if you like, involving deadly challenges to the *status quo* by its noncompliance in the traditional demands of its society. The revolutionary's commitment to kinds of work and styles of living which, as they emanate from him to others around him, will bring about social changes in a less direct manner than physical revolution, but with more permanent effect. This level of revolution has been experimented with in the hippie phenomenon, but that was only a trial run, a kind of rough draft. The symbol was hair, and the rhetoric was obscene, but both of these were merely external expressions of an interior change that is basic and reducible to no single manner of expression. The level of revolution as existential commitment is the internalization of the search for salvation, but it is emphatically not the escape into the self or into unconcern for the need for social change that it might appear to be. It is a kind of "going underground" politically, and it is most likely characterized by a calm, untroubled, even joyful No to the structures we have inherited and by a quiet, provisional, even wide-eyed Yes to possibilities of the future. It is not harmless, so I do not describe it to give relief to those who may fear other kinds of revolution. It is as full of potential for destruction of much we now hold dear as is suggested in Bob Dylan's old but haunting line about something happening without our knowing what it is. Its negative judgment is that the institutions we now have, in education, politics, law, religion, and the home, may be unredeemable.

The reason that other levels of revolution are important, apart from the fact of their dominance in our thought about students, is that any one of them or all of them may be routes to this fourth level of revolution. Other levels display the search for salvation being tested in ways that simply give expression to natural or traditional patterns of behavior: the revolution that has already taken place communicates itself to the young through the media of information and entertainment, revolution for the hell of it is an expression of the indispensable lightheartedness of youth, physical revolution is modeled on real revolutions of the past; each is an understandable response to known ways of pursuing one's grail, and each has the lure of the adventurously new, but each is new only in its locale or its specific content. The fourth level of revolution is new in form with each individual person, and new in effect, as each individual works out ways of gauging his effect on the world around him. Its character can be seen with the help of Ignazio Silone's *Bread and Wine.*

The Example of Pietro Spina

Bread and Wine is the story of Pietro Spina, alias Don Paolo Spada, a revolutionary in the Italy of 1938, at the time of the conquest of Ethiopia. Against the dictatorship of the Fascist regime, Pietro has thrown in his lot with the Communists as the only hope of defeating the evil of the state. His alias is in the identity of a priest, a masquerade he takes on for security, in an irony of a high order since the church's complicity in the evil of the Fascist state is great—although Christianity, in Silone's view, is still capable of producing a real saint now and then. His development as a character includes two stages of classical revolutionary activity and a final stage that approximates the existential, fourth level of revolution under consideration. In the phase of activity in which he is occupied in the first section of the novel, Pietro displays all the elements of revolutionary practice; he has gone underground to solidify the portion of the organization for which he is responsible. He is full of anti-Fascist rhetoric, unyielding and doctrinaire; he is idealistic about "the masses," in this case the peasants of the Abruzzi of his youth who suffer greatly from the bureaucratic complications of an efficient but oppressive state; he finds natural allies in the young; he participates in a loose but ubiquitous network of contacts, and maintains from his school days a hostility to the "realistic" sellout of those who, as noted in the earlier quote, live temporary lives.

This programmatic revolutionary campaign gives way under the pressure of the problems encountered in political revolution. Some of these are the necessity of constant flight from omniscient authorities, the self-interest of most of those he thought allies, the doctrinaire rigidity encountered. The disappointment he experiences in discovering the materialism of the peasants, that they will suffer under or rise up against any society only because that is what peasants are for and they will always be peasants, is a prelude for his more gloomy discovery of the chauvinism of the young who are stimulated by the war in Africa and the prospect of solving Italy's problems by increasing Ethiopia's. After a few acts of revolutionary despair and with the revolution crumbled at his feet, Pietro launches his private, existential revolution.

Pietro Spina's "fourth level" of revolution is intimated in an incident which occurs while he is masquerading as the priest, Don Paolo. He is lying sick in an inn and in his defenseless condition is importuned by an old woman who wants to make her confession. Such acts he had avoided successfully, since honor demanded limits on his imposture, but a natural compulsion to absolve and forgive grasped him. His generosity and understanding were dominical, and news of it spread widely and quickly. Soon he was so besieged with penitents that he had to flee. But the intimation is clear that his new revolution was to be an existential stance that would destroy inimical social structures (symbolized here in the church's "power" to absolve) simply as a result of his being who he was, a function of his placing himself just so in relation to others. Those who knew him would live changed lives, perhaps respond revolutionarily themselves to their situations. As he takes on his lone and private role as existential revolutionary, what he will do and where he will do do it are not clear, and a program is not necessary. It is only necessary to resolve to be what he is, a priest of sorts (but not of the sort that is an officer of the past), a prophet. Apocalypse was avoided only because the revolution failed and that of which apocalyptic is a bastardization re-emerged, the revolutionary prophet.

Pietro's role is clarified in a breathtaking way when, to launch his new role, he calls on his old priest-teacher, whose maintenance of his own prophetic revolution has isolated him from church and society and left him bereft of any responsibilities, labeled as a dangerous man. Old Don Benedetto greets him with word of a conversation he has just had with one of Pietro's schoolmates, a doctor who had come grimly to announce to the teacher his decision to give up, to take a coveted bureaucratic medical post and silence his own yearnings for a prophetic role. In the name of realism, he has capitulated. The doctor had observed, so the old priest tells Pietro, that all is not lost since Pietro, even if alone of the schoolboys, has held on to his ideals. Don Benedetto even suggests that what Pietro pursues is a divine vocation when in response to the revolutionary's confession that he had lost his faith many years ago, he says, "In cases similar to yours it is just a silly mistake. . . . This would not be the first time that the Eternal Father felt obligated to hide Himself and take a pseudonym. As you know, He has never taken the [names] men have fastened on Him very seriously." In the spirit of such a blessing, the priest tells Pietro that the doctor had taken comfort from Pietro's continued idealism. " 'It is lucky that at least Pietro has been saved,' he had said. 'Saved?' said Pietro. 'Is there a past participle of save?' "

Is there a past participle of save? This is the question to which the existential revolutionary will never accept a systematic answer, for he identifies salvation as the extension to all men of the prophetic truth which compels him, and the full relation of all men to one another and to their environment, both social and natural. It is a task that can never be done, and this the political revolutionary never quite sees. Revolution as an existential decision requires the acceptance of salvation as an endless search and at the same time as firm a commitment to the search as any more reachable form of "salvation" might offer.

The Existential Revolutionary and the Future

The existential revolutionary, like Pietro Spina, begins by the inward act of refusing to cast himself in the roles that are provided for him. He will not act in expected and predictable ways, *not even as a revolutionary*. His first act is saying NO:

> In every dictatorship, just one man, even any little man at all, who continues to think with his own head puts the whole public order in danger. Tons of printed paper propagate the regime's order of the day, thousands of loudspeakers, hundreds of thousands of posters, and handbills distributed free, and stables of orators in the squares and crossroads, thousands of priests from the pulpit, all repeat to the point of obsession, to the point of collective stupefaction, these orders of the day. But it's enough that a little man, just one little man says NO for all that formidable granite order to be in danger.[1]

American society is not a dictatorship, and no college or university is likely to be a dictatorship for long, because of the diffusion of power that characterizes our system. This means that in our society it will take more than "just one little man" to make this kind of revolution. It might take, however, "just one little minority," and this is the power that a minority can have in America. And not just for the hell of it, but because the profferings and benefits of the system are rejected out of hand as costing too much in pain and poverty for those excluded. Both in the activism of *not doing* and in that of *doing,* the prophetic revolutionary will work out his program. Few will be as Christ-like as Pietro Spina. But this kind of revolution will, nonviolently, put any self-protective establishment up against the wall. It is also a revolution not reserved to any age or race—only to those who can realize that as long as there are victims held down by our structures, it is they who must feel victimized; and in so identifying themselves—*authentically* because of their own existential decision—they participate in the salvation of others while pressing the search for their own.

---

[1] Ignazio Silone, *Bread and Wine* (New York: Atheneum, 1962), p. 216. Used with permission.

Some examples come to mind. The young college graduate who is against the draft for reasons as moral and as substantial as any conscientious objector or guileless pacifist, but who has discovered that the easiest route is to teach school and try to get a II-S classification for an essential occupation. He accepts himself as he is, and his program is only to try to be himself wherever he can, a choice still within the realm of his own deciding. His effect on the school in which he teaches, on its curriculum, on its humanity, on its direction, can be immense, precisely because he is not "qualified" by training in education to be a teacher. He is not fitting into any role provided for him by the structures of education, and the possibility is open to him precisely because those structures have stopped working in lots of school systems. He is a revolutionary.

The Peace Corps attracted many college-age people and appealed to their idealism and interest in the non-American world. Thrown into situations which had little to do with any of the structured roles for which growing up in America had prepared them, many found that their own capacity for decision and commitment gave meaning to the technical preparation given them by the Corps. They found out in the Peace Corps that they could be educated pretty effectively to do all sorts of things for which college had not educated them, that college-as-training is not worth the time it takes in our accepted structures. More significantly, many of them returned in a condition unable to accept the complacency and self-righteousness of American life ever again. These found themselves existential revolutionaries.

Not a few Vietnam veterans were converted to an existential revolution by their experience of the American program in Southeast Asia, and will not again easily accept the role they might have fallen into had they merely accepted the standard Good Samaritanism of military interpretations of American policy. Whatever they do, it will not be predictable or traditional. Their roles will be of their own creation.

There are many student revolutionaries of this kind who

simply do not plan to do the kind of work they will be expected to do, live in the kind of neighborhood they will be expected to, or perpetuate the kind of rituals of family and community existence expected of them. They are learning, on the other levels of revolution, the necessity for change; inside them, many are learning the reality of the search for salvation, that it is really pursued in a revolutionary loneliness of personal commitment to be what they are and to become what they are to become—not to fit into someone else's conception of what they are. Some may not get married; some who do may not have children; some may not ever work for anyone else; some in professions may eschew all the rewards associated with the profession in order to serve those in need. To take only one example, the future of that social institution known as the American Medical Association may be quite exciting when the prophetic revolutionaries in that field begin to discover each other at future meetings. Catch-22 is that "they will do whatever you let them do." The revolution that is serious and that can succeed is that of those who have decided to stop letting them do it. This revolution will be an even greater affront to those who earnestly desire what more and more students are rejecting than a violent revolution would be, and I suspect it is this lack of concern for what Americans have long striven for—security and status and prosperity, without soul—that makes America so angry at students. And the only point of campus disruptions is that it makes everyone face the fact that the rejection is taking place. It behooves the educational institutions to examine this rejection closely and to decide whether, in the future, they wish to have the participation of the most articulate, the most sensitive, and the most adventurous—in other words, whether education is to be saved.

Reflections on Violence as a Literary Tool

MORRIS RENEK

When Ernest Hemingway in his well-known book about bull-fighting, *Death in the Afternoon,* invented an old lady to mock and shock with the violence in his narration, he was operating under the correct assumption that there were still readers capable of being shocked. Today, however, the violent acts presented in our fiction and nonfiction, in our drama and movies, are so numerous, so bizarre, so removed from reality that one doubts the average reader is meant to take them seriously. In Joseph Heller's *Catch-22,* for example, Americans begin deliberately bombing their own planes as part of an absurd commercial enterprise. The act is not meant to be real, but must be taken as a black humorist's satiric comment on our times, a comment on our contemporary state of mind as well as on the illusions and reality of war. Violence, then, in contemporary literature becomes a metaphor, an act of no consequence in itself, but an act that expresses our modern alienation, our rootlessness, and disorientation. It is gratuitous, unrelated to our emotions or to cause and effect, unpredictable, and, in a psychological sense, more horrifying. Are we to laugh or cry, be entertained or terrified? Do the victims really suffer, do the villains really perpetrate the crime? Are there no reasons, no assurances? The answer, it seems, is no; and herein lies the difference between the classical uses of violence and violence in present-day literature.

Hemingway belonged to the classical tradition, the tradition of Homer, Shakespeare, Sophocles, Hugo, Melville, Dreiser, O'Neill, and Faulkner. The violence was an act related to passion, to fatal flaw of character, to revenge, ambition, justice, or injustice. It developed from past acts belonging to the narration, was expected by the reader as the natural consequence of what went before, and had meaning for the future. The older, classical forms of violence were concerned with putting the world back into its proper rational perspective. At the center of the great violent acts of literature there was a crying out from what the Russian novelists called the heart of hearts. Violence could be a positive attempt to recapture the good and the beautiful. It was also a kind of communication.

In Herman Melville's *Billy Budd,* for example, the act of violence clearly takes the place of speech. Billy's blow articulates his anguish against tyranny where his tongue cannot. Violence has this illiterate coherence. Everyone understands a sock in the jaw; when language fails, there is the fist.

Traditionally, too, violence could be used as a tool to achieve real or imagined ends. In Dreiser's *An American Tragedy* the hero kills his pregnant mistress because she stands between him and his dream of social status. It is the loveless act of ambition. The world, the passions, the deeds are real; and the acts of violence are to be taken as extensions of the situation or the character, not as metaphor. Yet the author does use this violence to light up the ribbing of society, forcing us to look anew at our ideals and our idols.

This classical literary use of violence was related to a coherent view of the world and led to deep insights. It required of a writer that he know his world as a reporter (Melville, Poe, Twain, Henry James, Norris, Dreiser) and that he use this knowledge with considerable imaginative power.

However, most of our better contemporary writers are part of a new tradition, using a new violence dating from Dostoevski, Gide, Kafka, and continuing through Nathaniel West, Camus, Sartre, and Beckett, until today we have Ionesco, Genet, Albee, Robbe-Grillet, Thomas Pynchon, John Hawkes, Heller, and all the other members of the absurd, existential, black humor movements. Suddenly, the violent act is no longer related to any reality, any order in society, any particular passion. Dostoevski's Raskolnikov (in *Crime and Punishment*) gratuitously picks two old ladies to murder. Gide's Lafcadio (in *Lafcadio's Adventures*) pushes a stranger off a train, purposelessly. Kafka's characters are tormented and punished for crimes they did not commit, crimes that perhaps were not committed at all.

To most American writers in this new tradition, such purposeless acts of violence are taken as a mirror of society. Violence in their hands is an esthetic shorthand wherein one reads the dementia of the times, the universal symptom that betrays loneliness, fear, and despair.

Norman Mailer is one writer who has used both the older form of violence and the new esthetic shorthand. His first published story, "The Greatest Thing in the World," touches on a bracing, universal characteristic of violence: the celebration of feeling one's juices running, and the intense personal satisfaction that comes from knowing one is self-sufficient in a dangerous world.

But *An American Dream* written more than 20 years later, is focused through a hangover lens; it is a paste-pot nightmare with none of the cleansing quality of a Céline. Comparing it with the earlier story, we see how Mailer's diffusion of energy by writing advertisements and idea articles has made him a writer who leaves his fight in the locker room. Instead of believable characters he gives us symbolic skeletons who are run across the stage from pulleys high up on the catwalks. A fog machine blows in the violence, so it is hard to tell even the sexes: "(It) was up like a bull and like a bull (it) charges. (Its) head struck me in the stomach . . . and then (it) drove one powerful knee at my groin (She fought like a prep-school bully) . . ." This is Mailer's hero Rojack fighting with his wife. Unsurprisingly, there is nothing special about his killing her; it is simply a slight intensification of their ordinary treatment of one another.

This kind of ideal violence that gives you the scrunch, sock, and zap of the real thing without the scar of pain must be abstract to keep the real world from breaking in. Edmund Wilson has written of Hemingway, ". . . in *A Farewell to Arms* as soon as we are brought into real intimacy with the lovers, as soon as the author is obliged to see them through a searching personal experience, we find merely an idealized relationship, the abstraction of a lyric emotion." The abstraction of violence in *An American Dream* is similarly isolated in a fantasy world peopled with incredible grotesques. Perhaps the grotesques are not meant to be taken as real, but as images of a surreal world—our contemporary civilization as Mailer sees it.

Truman Capote tried to have it both ways in his book *In Cold Blood*. The reader is given an eyewash of psychologizing to show the unloved background of the two killers. But if this were really to suggest a motive for the crime or re-establish the old-fashioned, one-to-one relationship of cause and effect, the mass killing would have less power to intrigue us. There would be the brutal killings, but no mystery: the psychos did it. Yet the author clearly felt that the impact of his story depended on the possibility that there was no motive, that the crime was meaningless and absurd. So he has to keep insisting on this possibility, reminding the reader of it—because so many motives keep appearing: robbery, sexual assault, "saving face."

In Cold Blood is packaged violence, hacked up chronologically for its maximum suspense and bled for its curio items. It is a high grade of Sunday-supplement ore, a reportorial thriller that would have been far better done, because far better probed, as a genuine fiction in the hands of a writer like Graham Greene. Fiction, with its imaginative power, could have developed and expanded in just those areas where the book is dry and documentary. And what is more, since the novelist knows all he needs to know, one can at least be sure that the acts of violence he chooses to represent seem meaningless by design—not by accident or through lack of knowledge.

Between the older conventions of the use of violence and the new, there was—generally speaking—a transitional stage where writers created the very crackle of the violent atmosphere as though their characters were walking in a world with highly explosive tinfoil under their feet. William Faulkner could do it. His violence is not gratuitous; it develops directly from the roots of social deterioration—the decorum of the old South has passed away, characters like the Snopes tribe rise to power, and rapes and murders proliferate. Yet in a book like *Sanctuary,* an admitted potboiler, the shock of his descriptions of brutality becomes almost an end in itself. He is working toward the metaphorical use of random violence.

Another superb creator of the violent scene in America is Erskine Caldwell. In his short story "Saturday Afternoon," a lynching is a good place to sell soda pop and enliven a few idle hours. It is as ordinary as a baseball game. The victim happens to be a Negro who, in the American spirit, is getting ahead on his own hard work and minding his business. Being a Negro, he is lynched for these qualities. Here and elsewhere Caldwell has a way of depicting an ordinary social scene and filling it with sheer violent madness that harmonizes perfectly with the background comings and goings of daily life. It is not explained by the story, but permeates it.

The poet Leonard Cohen not only captures the slipshod, cold impersonality of this kind of world, but also goes to the heart of what's wrong. In a poem appropriately titled "What I'm Doing Here," he speaks for all these writers:

"I will not be held like a drunkard
under the cold tap of facts
I refuse the universal alibi"

"Facts" are used to justify all forms of cruelty and the breakdown of meaningful communication, but Cohen acknowledges his complicity in the things that have gone wrong:

"I don't know if the world has lied
I have lied
I do not know if the world has conspired against love
I have conspired against love"

Cohen waits for other people to own up—and this is what gives the poem its poignant quality, for he knows that they will go on observing their customary rituals. In this dead end we are alone.

We cannot be heard in a world where love doesn't work any more.

There is, however, one last alternative left—*not* to turn to violence but to retreat forever into whatever evil harbor or lighthouse will have you. This choice is dramatized with skill and childlike originality by Jean Goldschmidt in "The Testament of Uncle George." An attractive girl withdraws from the conventional college world of loneliness and intellectual posturing to a world of perversions and madness which she prefers to the normal life that will also ruin her. Though the story is told in a cheerful, down-the-rabbit-hole manner, it carries a warning at the end suitable for an arsenic bottle.

But there's a cozy, surreal humor in Goldschmidt's story that characterizes most of our sanest views of the violent world. It is as though the humor itself were the only coherent factor in a chaotic blackness. In Beckett, we are treated to insanely mundane conversations that reflect life's monotony. In Pinter's *The Homecoming,* the dull conversation amuses us because of what it says of the workaday world outside. The germinal madness is often on the other side of the door. In Albee's *Who's Afraid of Virginia Woolf?*, it is a fantasy that hallucinates the two main characters. In such cases we never actually see the villain, because the villain is the System or The Establishment or whatever Life has been compromised into. Ionesco has stretched this nonvillain approach to its laughable conclusion in *The Bald Soprano,* which opens like a tidy Victorian parlor play and ends in violent absurdity. The characters change, but the world that makes them mad remains the same. This is the same surreal humor that charges up Heller's *Catch-22*: In conforming to the military logic of their lives the men were demonstrably and admittedly crazy.

The black humorists have done their best to enlighten this corporate insanity and affirm some small sign of reason in the chaos. "Anyone! Anyone!" is a savagely comic one-act play in which seemingly meaningless acts of violence sum up the despair and frustration of our times. In it, Charles L. Mee, Jr. shows us two men ultimately stripped of power and of hope. Their building is being destroyed by the contractor's wrecking ball even as they desperately try to live peacefully in their room—working out a crossword puzzle. In explaining their trouble Arthur says, ". . . you see . . . Junior, we have no connections." But if it is partly a matter of having the right connections and the right friends, their real plight is summed up in Arthur's question: "Who cares, after all? Who cares? No one listens." Their only defense is to murder, casually and efficiently, the spokesmen for the nonvillain who is tearing down buildings without any thought for the people who live in them.

Here again is a literary use of violence that is meaningless in the old traditional sense but speaks to us powerfully about our present disconnection from a logical universe in which cause and function have a rational relationship. Outrageous, frightful, and often laughable, this new literary violence cannot be taken seriously as an extension of reality. But it must be taken seriously as the ultimate metaphor of a frightened and bewildered age of humanity.

PROJECTS

1. List Wertham's reasons for the neglect of the study of violence as a complex social problem. Evaluate these reasons indicating your agreement or disagreement. Refer to any recent studies of violence which illustrate your opinion.

2. Would you agree with Wertham that the study of violence may begin in the laboratory but only in a restricted sense? Refer to Ardrey's article, "The Violent Way," to illustrate your position.

3. "Violent acts cannot be explained by human nature alone. Their roots reach further than the individual. All psychological forces operate in a social environment, and it is necessary in scientific studies to achieve a balance between the psychological and the social."

(a) What do you think Wertham means by achieving a balance between the psychological and the social factors in the study of violence?

(b) Do you find this "balance" lacking in Bruno Bettelheim's article, "Violence: A Neglected Mode of Behavior" or in R. D. Laing's "The Mystification of Experience"?

(c) What specific statements would you use from Bettelheim's and/or Laing's articles to support your opinion?

4. Can you give examples from your own experience that violence is an alluring goddess who holds in her hand the inscription of her power: "Let mankind continue in the false belief that violence will cease by itself"? Would Lucy Komisar ("Violence and the Masculine Mystique") approve of Wertham's reference to violence as an alluring goddess?

5. Discuss Gary's statement: "As often as not, violence in the streets is a form of self-provided entertainment." Refer to Gold's article and/or your own experiences for specific illustrations.

6. Would you agree with Gary's alternative to violence: "We will either have to reconstruct the society entirely or establish a police state"? Write an essay which (a) agrees with Gary and indicates directions for this reconstruction, or (b) disagrees and offers another alternative to violence, or (c) offers another solution in the style of Marcuse or Laing.

7. Analyze Gary's statement: "My contention is that the real danger to our future is not the violent, rioting youth, still a vocal minority magnified through the mass media, always on the watch for drama. The real danger is our indifferent masses. The pattern of violence is, in my view, insufficient to force our society toward a real change, but its positive aspect is that it may awaken some stupefied, apathetic people."

(a) Does this insufficiency of force in violence indicate a lack of power (refer to Nieburg or Arendt)?

(b) Does this, in turn, reveal naiveté in Gary's thinking regarding the "positive aspect of violence as a factor which awakens stupefied, apathetic people"?

(c) Isn't this type of violence an invitation to that "need for a police state to protect our goodies and our rights"?

8. Do you believe that your own university, college, school, is performing what Donald Rogan calls "the classical goal of education —namely that opportunity to meditate on the meaning of being

human"? Discuss the pros and cons of this interpretation of classical education and the specifics of your own education which support or deny this interpretation.

9. Debate: "The revolution, therefore, may be the only relevant effort being made to *save* education and thus create a community in which the search for salvation can be fed by any real kind of hope."

(a) Be sure to define "revolution" referring to Rogan's several definitions of the term.

(b) What is "tactical violence"? What legitimate role does it play in saving education? (Refer to your answer to question eight.)

10. "Nonviolence, undoubtedly, is the better tactic, if it can succeed in being incisive enough to draw the fire that the world levels on the true revolutionary, but this calls for ingenuity of an almost superhuman order. Precisely the reason that revolution is necessary is that our society has discovered its infinite capacity peacefully to absorb nonviolent protest."

(a) Is Rogan implying that American society only responds to the irrationality of violence and not to the rational appeal of nonviolence?

(b) What are the consequences of such a belief?

(c) Does this belief produce the politics of the apocalypse?

(d) Would you consider Gandhi and Martin Luther King, Jr. "sublimely mad" because they used the tactics of nonviolence?

11. Is it indeed true that American society is rejecting its youthful students because they are, in turn, rejecting its values—security, status, and prosperity without soul? Would you agree that this rejection is more serious than the concern about violence as a revolutionary tactic?

12. Use one of the illustrations from Renek's article (or similar literary sources) to indicate your support or disagreement with his statement that violence in its literary form is "the ultimate metaphor of a frightened and bewildered age of humanity." In view of your conclusion, what is your judgment regarding violence in the media? Would you censor it? If so, at what level and to what degree?

13. Arrange to see one of the "revolutionary films" (*Getting Straight* or *The Strawberry Statement* may be released in 16mm for rental), and discuss whether or not you agree that such films are

simpleminded "commercials for revolutions." (Refer to David Denby's review of these films, "Commercials for Revolution," in *The Atlantic.*)

14. "War is the supreme test of man, in which he rises to heights never approached in any other activity." (General George S. Patton) See the film *Patton* and then discuss the social polemic of violence as it is expressed in war. (Refer to "The Case for War," *Time Magazine,* March 9, 1970, pp. 46 ff.)

Bibliography

AVORN, JERRY L. *Up Against the Ivy Wall: A History of the Columbia Crisis.* New York: Atheneum, 1969.

BELL, DANIEL, AND KRISTOL, IRVING, eds. *Confrontation, The Student Rebellion and the Universities.* New York: Basic Books, Inc., 1969.

BERKOWITZ, LEONARD. *Aggression.* New York: McGraw-Hill, Inc., 1962.

BRONOWSKI, J. *The Face of Violence.* Cleveland: World Publishing Company, 1968.

CLEAVER, ELDRIDGE. *Soul on Ice.* New York: McGraw-Hill Book Co., 1968.

EISENHOWER, MILTON (chairman). *To Establish Justice, To Insure Domestic Tranquility* (Final Report on the Causes and Prevention of Violence, Introduction by James Reston). New York: Praeger, 1970.

ENDLEMAN, SHALOM, ed. *Violence in the Streets.* Chicago: Quadrangle Books, 1968.

ERIKSON, ERIK. *Childhood and Society.* New York: W. W. Norton & Co., 1950.

A. FREE (Abbie Hoffman). *Revolution for the Hell of It.* New York: Dial Press, 1968.

GARY, ROMAIN. "The Baiting Society," *Playboy,* May 1969.

GLAZER, NATHAN. *Remembering the Answers: Essays on the American Student Revolt.* New York: Basic Books, Inc., 1970.

GOLD, HERBERT. "Random Violence: Is That Man Coming Down the Street to Kill You?", *Look,* November 17, 1970.

GRIER, W. H., AND COBBS, P. M. *Black Rage.* New York: Basic Books, 1968.

HELLER, JOSEPH. *Catch-22.* New York: Simon and Schuster, 1961.

HOOK, SIDNEY. *Academic Freedom and Academic Anarchy.* New York: Cowles Book Company, Inc., 1969.

HOPE, MARJORIE. *Youth Against the World: Contemporary Portraits of the New Revolutionaries.* Boston: Little, Brown & Co., 1965.

JONES, HOWARD MUMFORD. *Violence and Reason.* New York: Atheneum, 1969.

KENISTON, KENNETH. *The Young Radicals.* New York: Harcourt, Brace and World, 1968.

KRUTCH, JOSEPH WOOD. *Human Nature and the Human Condition.* New York: Random House, 1959.

KUNEN, J. S. *The Strawberry Statement.* New York: Random House, 1969.

LANGE, DAVID L. AND OTHERS. *Mass Media and Violence* (Vol. 9, A Staff Report to the National Commission on the Causes and Prevention of Violence). Washington, D. C.: U. S. Government Printing Office, 1969.

LEITER, ELINORE. "The Living Theater Presents: Revolution! Joy! Protest! Shock! Etc.!", *New York Times Magazine,* October 13, 1968.

LEITES, NATHAN, AND WOLF, CHARLES, JR. *Rebellion and Authority: An Analytic Essay on Insurgent Conflicts.* Chicago: Markham Publishing Co., 1970.

LEONARD, JOHN. "Che: The Making of a Movie Revolutionary," *New York Times Magazine,* December 8, 1968.

MONTAGU, ASHLEY. *Man and Aggression.* London: Oxford University Press, 1968.

MUMFORD, LEWIS. *The Transformations of Man.* New York: Collier Books, 1962.

ORTEGA Y GASSET, JOSÉ. *The Revolt of the Masses.* New York: Norton, 1932.

RADER, DOTSON. *I Ain't Marchin' Anymore!* New York: David McKay Co., 1969.

RENEK, MORRIS. "Reflections on Violence as a Literary Tool," *Story,* May 1967.

ROGAN, DONALD. *Campus Apocalypse, The Student Search Today.* New York: Seabury Press, 1969.

SILONE, IGNAZIO. *Bread and Wine*. New York: Atheneum, 1962.
STORR, ANTHONY. *Human Aggression*. New York: Atheneum, 1968.
VICKERS, GEORGE, ed. *Dialogue on Violence*. New York: Bobbs-Merrill Company, Inc.
WERTHAM, FREDERIC. *A Sign for Cain: An Exploration of Human Violence*. New York: The Macmillan Company, 1966.

PART III
An End to Violence

Revolution that is separated from honor
betrays its origins that belong to
the reign of honor.

ALBERT CAMUS
The Rebel

Introduction

Exhortations to end violence range from the carefully rational approach to the forthright emotional appeal. This concluding section, *An End to Violence,* includes three literary examples which encompass both the rational and the emotional approach, in order to awaken us to the full consequences of human violence. "The Introduction" to the Scranton Report on Campus Unrest presents the rational admonition backed up by the Commission's factual study of violence on the campus. Its chairman, William Scranton, former governor of Pennsylvania, was educated in law at Yale University and has served as legal and political adviser for many causes including the position as Presidential Advisor to the Commission on Disarmament Negotiations.

Loren Eiseley, the author of the second essay, "The Last Magician," combines scientific insight into the effects of violence with a literary skill which brings the issues of violence into an emotional as well as rational light. He has combined his interest as an anthropologist with teaching and writing producing such literary gems as *Mind as Nature, The Immense Journey, The Firmament of Time,* and *The Unexpected Universe.* His sensitive insight into the nature of man and man's relationship to his world makes his article a natural bridge between the facts of the Scranton Report and Hermann Hesse's poem, "To Children."

Hermann Hesse, who writes of the individual's search for the self, was born in Germany in 1877. His own life personified this search which is found in his novels (for example, *Demian, Siddhartha, Steppenwolf, Narcissus and Goldmund, Magister Ludi*). The violence of World War I reinforced his introspective and pacifist nature and forced him, in turn, to leave Germany for Switzerland where he lived until his death in 1962. He received the Nobel Prize in 1946 for his novel *Magister Ludi* (*The Glass Bead Game*). "To Children (At the End of 1914)" comes from a book of Hesse's poems edited and translated by James Wright. Three of Hesse's poems have been set to music by Richard Strauss (*Four Last Songs*) and recorded by George Szell and the Berlin Radio Symphony Orchestra with Elisabeth Schwartzkopf as soloist.

Introduction to Campus Unrest—The Scranton Report

To the American People

The crisis on American campuses has no parallel in the history of the nation. This crisis has roots in divisions of American society as deep as any since the Civil War. The divisions are reflected in violent acts and harsh rhetoric, and in the enmity of those Americans who see themselves as occupying opposing camps. Campus unrest reflects and increases a more profound crisis in the nation as a whole.

This crisis has two components: a crisis of violence and a crisis of understanding. We fear new violence and growing enmity.

Crisis of Violence

On the nation's campuses, and in their neighboring communities, the level of violence has been steadily rising. Students have been killed and injured; civil authorities have been killed and injured; bystanders have been killed and injured. Valuable public and private property, and scholarly products have been burned.

Too many Americans have begun to justify violence as a means of effecting change or safeguarding traditions. Too many have forgotten the values and sense of shared humanity that unite us. Campus violence reflects this national condition.

Much of the nation is so polarized that on many campuses a major domestic conflict or an unpopular initiative in foreign policy could trigger further violent protest and, in its wake, counterviolence and repression.

The Constitution protects the freedom of all citizens to dissent and to engage in non-violent protest. Dissent is a healthy sign of freedom and a protection against stagnation. But the right to dissent is not the right to resort to violence.

Repression Is Unwise

Equally, to respond to peaceful protest with repression and brutal tactics is dangerously unwise. It makes extremists of moderates, deepens the divisions in the nation, and increases the chances that future protest will be violent.

We believe it urgent that Americans of all convictions draw back from the brink. We must recognize even our bitter opponents as fellow Americans with rights upon which we cannot morally or legally encroach and as fellow human beings whom we must not club, stone, shoot, or bomb.

We utterly condemn violence. Students who bomb and burn are criminals. Police and National Guardsmen who needlessly shoot or assault students are criminals. All who applaud these criminal acts share in their evil. We must declare a national cease-fire.

There can be no more "trashing," no more rock throwing, no more arson, no more bombing by protesters. No grievance, philosophy, or political idea can justify the destruction and killing we have witnessed. There can be no sanctuary or immunity from prosecution on the campus. If our society is to survive, criminal acts by students must be treated as such wherever they occur and whatever their purpose.

Crimes committed by one do not justify crimes committed by another. We condemn brutality and excessive force by officers and troops called to maintain order. The use of force by police is sometimes necessary and legal, but every unnecessary resort to violence is wrong, criminal, and feeds the hostility of the disaffected.

Our universities as centers of free inquiry are particularly vulnerable to violence. We condemn those groups which are openly seeking to destroy them.

We especially condemn bombing and political terrorism. The full resources of society must be employed to bring to justice those who commit terroristic acts. Anyone who aids or protects terrorists, on or off campus, must share the moral and legal responsibilities for the crimes they commit.

We find ominous and shocking reports that students are laying in supplies of weapons, and that others are preparing to take the law into their hands against protesters and minorities they dislike. There can be no place in our society for vigilantes, night-riders, or militants who would bring destruction and death upon their opponents. No one serves the law by breaking it.

Violence must stop because it is wrong. It destroys human life and the products of human effort. It undermines the foundations of a just social order. No progress is possible in a society where lawlessness prevails.

Violence must stop because the sounds of violence drown out all words of reason. When students and officials resort to force and violence, no one can hear and the nation is denied a vital call to conscience. It must stop because no nation will long tolerate violence without repression. History offers grim proof that repression once started is almost impossible to contain.

Crisis of Understanding

Campus protest has been focused on three major questions: war, racial injustice, and the university itself.

The first issue is the unfulfilled promise of full justice and dignity for blacks and other minorities. Blacks, like many others of different races and ethnic origins, are demanding today that the pledges of the Declaration of Independence and the Emancipation Proclamation be fulfilled now. Full social justice and dignity—an end to racism, in all its human, social and cultural forms—is a central demand of today's students, black, brown, and white.

A great majority of students and a majority of their elders oppose the Indochina war. Many believe it entirely immoral. And if the war is wrong, students insist, then so are all policies and practices that support it, from the draft to military research, from ROTC to recruiting for defense industry. This opposition has led to an ever-widening wave of student protests.

A third target of student protest is the shortcomings of the American university. The goals, values, administration, and curriculum have been sharply criticized by many students. Students complain that their studies are irrelevant to the social problems that concern them. They want to shape their own personal and common lives, but find the university restrictive. They seek a community of companions and scholars, but find an impersonal multiversity. And they denounce the university's relationship to the war and to discriminatory racial practices.

Behind the student protest on these issues and the crisis of violence to which they have contributed lies the more basic crisis of understanding.

Americans have never shared a single culture, a single philosophy, or a single religion. But in most periods in our history, we have shared many common values, common sympathies, and a common dedication to a system of government which protects our diversity.

We are now in grave danger of losing what is common among us through growing intolerance of opposing views on issues and of diversity itself.

A "new" culture is emerging primarily among students. Membership is often manifested by differences in dress and life style. Most of its members have high ideals and great fears. They stress the need for humanity, equality, and the sacredness of life. They fear that nuclear war will make them the last generation in history. They see their elders as entrapped by materialism and competition, and prisoners of outdated social forms. They believe their own country has lost its sense of human purpose. They see the Indochina war as an onslaught by a technological giant upon the peasant people of a small, harmless and backward nation. The war is seen as draining resources from the urgent needs of social and racial justice. They argue that we are the first nation with sufficient resources to create not only decent lives for some, but a decent society for all and that we are failing to do so. They feel they must remake America in its own image.

But among the members of this new student culture, there is a growing lack of tolerance, a growing insistence that their own views must govern, an impatience with the slow procedures of liberal democracy, a growing denial of the humanity and good will of those who urge patience and restraint, and particularly of those whose duty it is to enforce the law. A small number of students have turned to violence; an increasing number, not terrorists themselves, would not turn even arsonists and bombers over to law enforcement officials.

At the same time, many Americans have reacted to this emerging culture with an intolerance of their own. They reject not only that which is impatient, unrestrained, and intolerant in the new culture of the young, but even that which is good. Worse, they reject the individual members of the student culture themselves. Distinctive dress alone is enough to draw insult and abuse. Increasing numbers of citizens believe that students who dissent or protest, even those who protest peacefully, deserve to be treated harshly. Some even say that when dissenters are killed, they have brought death upon themselves. Less and less do students and the larger community seek to understand or respect the viewpoint and motivations of the other.

If this trend continues, if this crisis of understanding endures, the very survival of the nation will be threatened. A nation driven to use the weapons of war upon its youth, is a nation on the edge of chaos. A nation that has lost the allegiance of part of its youth, is a nation that has lost part of its future. A nation whose young have become intolerant of diversity, intolerant of the rest of its citizenry, and intolerant of all traditional values simply because they are traditional, has no generation worthy or capable of assuming leadership in the years to come.

We urgently call for reconciliation. Tolerance and understanding on all sides must re-emerge from the fundamental decency of Americans, from our shared aspirations as Americans, from our traditional tolerance of diversity, and from our common humanity. We must regain our compassion for one another and our mutual respect.

There is a deep continuity between all Americans, young and old, a continuity that is being obscured in our growing polarization. Most dissenting youth are striving toward the ultimate values and dreams of their elders and their forefathers. In all Americans there has always been latent respect for the idealism of the young. The whole object of a free government is to allow the nation to redefine its purposes in the light of new needs without sacrificing the accumulated wisdom of its living traditions. We cannot do this without each other.

Violence Must End

Despite the differences among us, powerful values and sympathies unite us. The very motto of our nation calls for both unity and diversity: from many, one.

Out of our divisions, we must now recreate understanding and respect for those different from ourselves.

Violence must end.

Understanding must be renewed.

All Americans must come to see each other not as symbols or stereotypes but as human beings.

Reconciliation must begin.

We share the impatience of those who call for change. We believe there is still time and opportunity to achieve change. We believe we can still fulfill our shared national commitment to peace, justice, decency, equality, and the celebration of human life.

We must start. All of us.

Our recommendations are directed toward this end.

The Last Magician

LOREN EISELEY

Every man in his youth meets for the last time a magician, the man who made him what he is finally to be. In the mass, man now confronts a similar magician in the shape of his own collective brain, that unique and spreading force that will precipitate the last miracle or wreak the last disaster. The possible nature of the last disaster the world of today has made all too evident: Man has become a blight that threatens to efface the green world that created him.

It is of the last miracle, however, that I would write. And to do so, I have to describe my closing encounter with the personal magician of my youth, the man who set his final seal upon my character. I was 50 years old when my youth ended and it was, of all unlikely places, within that great unwieldy structure built to last forever and then hastily to be torn down: the Pennsylvania Station in New York. I had come in through a side door and was slowly descending a great staircase in a slanting shaft of afternoon sunlight when I became aware of a man loitering at the bottom of the steps, as though awaiting me there. As I descended, he swung about and began climbing toward me.

At the instant I saw his upturned face, my feet faltered and I almost fell. I was walking to meet a man ten years dead and buried, the man who had been my teacher and confidant and had not only spread before me as a student the wild background of the forgotten past but had brought alive for me the spruce-forest primitives of today. With him I had absorbed their superstitions, handled their sacred objects, accepted their prophetic dreams. He had been a man of unusual mental powers and formidable personality. In all my experience, no dead man but he could have so wrenched time as to walk through its cleft of darkness unharmed into the light of day.

The massive brows and forehead looked up at me as if to demand an accounting of that elapsed decade during which I had held his post and discharged his duties. We met and, as my dry mouth strove to utter his name, I became aware that his gaze was directed beyond me and that he was hastening elsewhere. The blind eye turned sideways was not, in truth, fixed upon me; I beheld the image but not the reality of a long-dead man. Phantom or genetic twin, he passed on and the crowds of New York closed inscrutably about him. I groped for the marble railing and braced my continued descent while, around me, travelers moved like shadows. I was a similar shadow, made so by the figure I had passed. But what was my affliction? That dead man and myself had been friends, not enemies. What terror, save the terror of the living toward the dead, could so powerfully have enveloped me?

On the slow train homeward, the answer came. I had been away for ten years from the forest. I had had no messages from its depths, such as that dead savant had hoarded even in his disordered office, where box turtles wandered over the littered floor. I had been immersed in the post-War administrative life of a growing university. But all the time, some accusing spirit, the familiar of the last wood-struck magician, had lingered in my brain. Finally, he had stridden up the stairs to confront me in the autumn light. Whether he had been imposed in some fashion upon a convenient facsimile or was a genuine illusion was of little importance compared with the message he had brought. I had starved and betrayed myself. It was this that had brought the terror. For the first time in years, I left my office in midafternoon and sought the sleeping silence of a nearby cemetery. I was as pale and drained as the Indian-pipe plants without chlorophyll that rise after rains on the forest floor. It was time for a change. I wrote a letter and studied timetables. I was returning to the land that bore me.

Collectively, man is about to enter upon a similar, though more difficult, adventure. At the climactic moment of his journey into space, he has met himself at the doorway to the stars. And the looming shadow before him has pointed backward into the tangled gloom of a forest from which it has been his purpose to escape. Man has crossed, in his history, two worlds. He must now enter another and forgotten one—but with the added knowledge he has gained on the pathway to the moon. He must learn that whatever his powers as a magician, he lies under the spell of a greater, green enchantment that, try as he will, he can never avoid, however far he travels. The spell has been laid on him since the beginning of time—the spell of the natural world from which he sprang.

Long ago, Plato told the story of the cave and the chained prisoners whose knowledge consisted only of what they could learn of flickering shadows on the wall before them. Then he revealed their astonishment upon being allowed to see the full source of the light. He concluded that the mind's eye may be bewildered in two ways, either from advancing suddenly into the light of higher things or from descending once more from the light into the shadows. Perhaps more than Plato realized in the spinning of his myth, man has truly emerged from a cave of shadows, or from comparable leaf-shadowed dells. He has read his way into the future by firelight and by moonlight; in man's early history, night was the time for thinking, for the observation of the stars. The stars traveled, men noted, and therefore they were given hunters' names; it was the way of the hunters' world and of the seasons.

In spite of much learned discourse upon the ways of our animal kin and of how purely instinctive cries slowly gave way to variable and muddled meanings in the head of protoman, I like to think that the crossing into man's second realm of received wisdom was truly a magical experience. I once journeyed for several days along a solitary stretch of coast. By the end of that time, from the oddly fractured shells on the beach, little distorted faces began to peer up at me—with meaning. I had held no converse with a living thing for many hours and, as a result, I was beginning, in the silence, to *read* again—to read like an illiterate. The reading had nothing to do with words. The faces in the cracked shells were somehow assuming a human significance.

Once again, in the night, while I was traversing a vast plain on foot, the clouds that coursed above me in the moonlight began to build into archaic, voiceless pictures. That they could do so makes me sure that the reading of such pictures long preceded what men of today call language. The reading of so endless an alphabet of forms is already beyond the threshold of the animal; man could somehow see a face in a shell or a pointing finger in a cloud. There existed in the growing cortex of man a place where, paradoxically, time both flowed and lingered, where mental pictures multiplied and transposed themselves. One is tempted to believe, whether or not it is literally true, that the moment of first speech arrived in a starburst like a supernova. To be sure, the necessary auditory discrimination and memory tracts were a biological preliminary, but the "invention" of language—and I put this carefully, having respect for both the biological and the cultural elements involved—may have come, at the last, with rapidity.

Certainly, the fossil record of man is an increasingly strange one. Millions of years were apparently spent on the African and Asiatic grassland, with little or no increase in brain size, even though simple tools were in use. Then, quite suddenly, during the 1,000,000 years or so of the Ice Age, the brain cells multiplied fantastically. One prominent linguist would place the emergence of true language at no more than 40,000 years ago. I myself would accord it a much longer history, but all scholars would have to recognize biological preparation for its emergence. What the fossil record, and perhaps even the studies of living primates, will never reveal is how much can be attributed to slow incremental speech growth associated directly with the expanding brain and how much to the final cultural invention spreading rapidly to other biologically prepared groups.

Language, wherever it first appeared, is the cradle of the human universe, a universe displaced from the natural in the common environmental sense of the word. In this second world of culture, forms arise in the brain and can be transmitted in speech as words are found for them. Objects and men are no longer completely within the natural world; they are subject to the transpositions the brain can evoke or project. The past can be remembered and caused to haunt the present. Gods may murmur in the trees; ideas of cosmic proportions can twine a web of sustaining mathematics around the cosmos. But in the attempt to understand his universe, man has to give away a part of himself that can never be regained—the certainty of the animal that what it senses is actually there in the shape the eye beholds.

By contrast, man finds himself in Plato's cave of illusion. He has acquired an interest in the whole of the natural world at the expense of being ejected from it and returning, all too frequently, as an angry despoiler.

A distinction, however, should be made here. In his first symbol making, primitive man and, indeed, even the last simple hunting cultures of today, projected a friendly image upon animals: Animals talked among themselves and thought rationally like men—they had souls; men may even have been fathered by totemic animals. Primitive man existed in close interdependence with his first world, though already he had developed a philosophy, a kind of oracular reading of her nature. Nevertheless, he was still inside that world; he had not turned her into an instrument or a mere source of materials. Christian man in the West strove to escape this lingering illusion the primitives had projected upon nature. Intent upon the destiny of his own soul, and increasingly urban, man drew back from too great an intimacy with the natural, its fertility and its orgiastic attractions. If the new religion was to survive, Pan had to be driven from his hillside or rendered powerless by incorporating him into Christianity—to be baptized, in other words, and allowed to fade slowly from the memory. As always in such intellectual upheavals, something was gained and something lost.

What was gained intellectually was a monotheistic reign of law by a single deity, so that man no longer saw distinct and powerful wood spirits in every tree or running brook. His animal confreres slunk soulless from his presence. They no longer spoke; their influence upon man was broken; the way was unconsciously being prepared for the rise of modern science. That science, by reason of its detachment, would first of all view nature as might a curious stranger. Finally, science would turn upon *man* the same gaze that had driven the animal forever into the forest. Man, too, would be relegated soulless to the wood, with all his lurking irrationalities exposed. He would know, in a new and more relentless fashion, his relationship to the rest of life. Yet, as the crust of his exploitive technology thickened, the more man thought he could withdraw from or recast nature; that by drastic retreat, he could dispel his deepening sickness. Like that of one unfortunate scientist I know—a remorseless experimenter—man's whole face has grown distorted. One bulging eye—the technological, scientific eye—was willing to count man, as well as nature's creatures, in terms of megadeaths. Its objectivity had become so great as to endanger its master, who was mining his own brains as ruthlessly as a seam of coal.

Linguists have a word for the power of language: displacement. It is the means by which man came to survive in nature. It is the method by which he created and entered his second world, the realm that now encloses him. In addition, it is the primary instrument by which he developed the means to leave the planet earth. It is a very mysterious achievement whose source is the ghostly symbols that move along the pathways of the human cortex. Displacement, in simple terms, is the ability to talk about what is absent, to make use of the imaginary in order to control reality. Man alone is able to manipulate time into past and future, to transpose objects or abstract ideas and make a kind of reality that exists only as potential in the real world. From this gift come his social structure and traditions and even the tools with which he modifies his surroundings. They exist in the dark confines of the cranium, before the instructed hand creates the reality.

There is another aspect of man's mental life that demands the utmost attention, and this is the desire for transcendence. Philosophers and students of comparative religion have often remarked that we need to seek the origins of human interest in the cosmos, the "cosmic sense" unique to man. However this sense may have evolved, it has made men conscious of human inadequacy and weakness and may be responsible for the desire for rebirth expressed in many religions. Stimulated by his own uncompleted nature, man seeks a greater role, restructured beyond nature. Thus, we find the Zen Buddhist, in the words of the scholar Suzuki, intent upon creating "a realm of Emptiness or Void" where "rootless trees grow." The Buddhist, in a true paradox, would empty the mind in order that the mind may fully experience the world. No creature other than man would question his way of thought or feel the need of sweeping the mind's cloudy mirror in order to unveil its insight. Man's life, in other words, is felt to be unreal and sterile. Perhaps a creature of so much ingenuity and deep memory is almost bound to grow alienated from his world, his fellows and the objects around him. He suffers from a nostalgia for which there is no remedy except as it is to be found in the enlightenment of the spirit—an ability to have a perceptive rather than an exploitive relationship with his fellow creatures.

After man had exercised his talents in the building of the first neolithic cities and empires, an intellectual transformation descended upon the known world, a time of questioning. It is a period fundamental to the understanding of man and has engaged the attention of such scholars as Lewis Mumford and Karl Jaspers. This period culminates in the first millennium before Christ. Here in the great centers of civilization, whether Chinese, Indian, Judaic or Greek, man had begun to abandon inherited gods and purely tribal loyalties in favor of an inner world in which the pursuit of earthly power was ignored. The destiny of the human soul became of more significance than the looting of a province. Though these dreams are expressed in different ways by such diverse men as Christ, Buddha and Confucius, they share many aspirations and beliefs, not the least of which is respect for the dignity of the common man. The period of the creators of transcendent values, the axial thinkers, as they are called, founded the world of universal thought that is our most precious human heritage. One can see it emerging in the mind of Christ as chronicled by Saint John. Here the personalized tribal deity of earlier Judaic thought becomes transformed into a world deity. Christ, the Good Shepherd, says, "Other sheep I have, which are not of this fold: Them also I must bring, and they shall hear my voice; and there shall be one fold, and one shepherd. . . . My sheep hear my voice . . . and they follow me."

These words, spoken by the carpenter from Nazareth, are

those of a world changer. They passed boundaries, whispered in the ears of galley slaves: "One fold, one shepherd. Follow me." These are no longer the wrathful words of a jealous city ravager, a local potentate god. They mark, instead, a rejection of purely material goals, a turning toward some inner light. As these ideas diffused, they were, of course, subject to the wear of time and superstition; but the human ethic of the individual prophets and thinkers has outlasted empires. These men speak to us across the ages. In their various approaches to life, they encouraged the common man toward charity and humility. They did not come with weapons; instead, they bespoke man's purpose to subdue his animal nature and, in so doing, to create a radiantly new and noble being. These were the dreams of the first millennium B.C., and tormented man still pursues these dreams today.

Earlier, I mentioned Plato's path into the light that blinds the man who has lived in darkness. Out of just such darkness arose the first humanizing influence. It was genuinely the time of the good shepherds. No one can say why these different prophets had such profound effects within the time at their disposal. Nor can we solve the mystery of how they came into existence across the Euro-Asiatic land mass in diverse cultures at roughly the same time. As Jaspers observes, he who can solve this mystery will know something common to all mankind.

In this difficult era, we are still living in the inspirational light of a tremendous historical event, one that opened up the human soul. But if the neophytes were blinded by the light, so, perhaps, the prophets were in turn confused by the human darkness they encountered. The scientific age replaced them. The common man, after brief days of enlightenment, turned once again to escape, propelled outward first by the world voyagers and then by the atom breakers. We have called up vast powers that loom menacingly over us and we turn to outer space as though the sole answer to the unspoken query must be flight, such flight as ancient man engaged in across ice ages and vanished game trails —the flight from nowhere. The good shepherds, meantime, have all faded into the darkness of history. One of them, Jesus, left a cryptic message: "My doctrine is not mine but His that sent me." Even in a time of unbelieving, this carries a warning. For the sender may still be couched in the body of man, awaiting the end of the story.

When I was a small boy, I once lived near a brackish stream that wandered over the interminable salt flats south of our town. Between occasional floods, the area became a giant sunflower forest taller than the head of a man. Child gangs roved this wilderness, and guerrilla combats with sunflower spears sometimes took place when boys from the other side of the marsh ambushed the hidden trails. Now and then, when a raiding party sought a new path, one could see from high ground the sunflower heads shaking and closing over the passage of the life below. In some such manner, nature's green barriers must have trembled and subsided in silence behind the footsteps of the first man apes who stumbled out of the vine-strewn morass of centuries into the full sunlight of human consciousness.

The sunflower forest of personal and racial childhood is relived in every human generation. One reaches the high ground and all is quiet in the shaken reeds. The nodding golden flowers spring up indifferently behind us and the way backward is lost when finally we turn to look. There is something unutterably secretive involved in man's intrusion into his second world, into the mutable domain of thought. Perhaps he questions still his right to be there. Some act unknown, some propitiation of unseen forces is demanded of him. For this purpose he has raised pyramids and temples, but all in vain. A greater sacrifice is demanded, the act of a truly great magician, the man capable of transforming himself. For what increasingly is required of man is that he pursue the paradox of *return*. So desperate has been the human emergence from fen and thicket, so great has seemed the virtue of a single magical act carried beyond nature that man hesitates, as long ago I shuddered to confront a phantom on a stair.

Written deep in the human subconscious is a simple terror of what has come with us from the forest and that sometimes haunts our dreams. Man does not wish to retrace his steps down to the margin of the reeds and peer within, lest by some magic he be permanently recaptured. Instead, men prefer to hide in cities of their own devising. I know a New Yorker who, when she visits the country, complains that the crickets keep her awake. I knew another who had to be awakened screaming from a nightmare of whose nature he would never speak. As for me, a longtime student of the past, I, too, have my visitants.

The dreams are true. By no slight effort have we made our way through the marshes. Something unseen has come along with each of us. The reeds sway shut, but not as definitively as we would wish. It is the price one pays for bringing almost the same body through two worlds. The animal's needs are very old; it must sometimes be *coaxed* into staying in its new discordant realm. As a consequence, all advanced religions have realized that the soul must not be allowed to linger, yearning, at the edge of the sunflower forest.

The curious sorcery of sound symbols and written hieroglyphs in man's new brain have lured him farther and farther from the swaying reeds. Temples would better contain his thought and fix his dreams upon the stars in the night sky. A creature who has once passed from visible nature into the ghostly insubstantial world evolved and projected from his own mind will never cease to pursue thereafter the worlds beyond this world. Nevertheless, the paradox remains: Man's crossing into the realm of space has forced him to turn and contemplate with renewed intensity the world of the sunflower forest—the ancient world of the body that he is doomed to inhabit, the body that completes his cosmic prison.

Not long ago, I chanced to fly over a forested section of country that, in my youth, was still an unfrequented wilderness. Across it now, suburbia was spreading. Below, like the fungus upon a fruit, I could see the radiating lines of transport gouged through the naked earth. From far up in the wandering air, one could see the lines stretching over the horizon. They led to cities clothed in a blue, unmoving haze of smog. From my remote position in the clouds, I could gaze upon all below and watch the illness as it spread its slimy tendrils through the watershed.

Farther out, I knew, on the astronauts' track, the earth would hang in silver light and the seas hold their ancient blue. Man would be invisible, the creeping white rootlets of his urban growth equally unseen. The cloud-covered planet would appear the same as when the first men stole warily along a trail in the forest. Of one thing, however, the scientists of the space age have informed us: Earth is an inexpressibly unique possession. In the entire solar system, it alone possesses water and oxygen sufficient to nourish higher life. It alone contains the seeds of mind. Mercury bakes in an inferno of heat beside the sun; something strange has twisted the destiny of Venus; Mars is a chill desert; Pluto is a cold wisp of reflected light over three billion miles away on the edge of the black void. Only on earth does life's green engine fuel the oxygen-devouring brain.

For centuries, we have dreamed of intelligent beings throughout this solar system. We have been wrong; the earth we have taken for granted and treated so casually—the sunflower-shaded forest of man's infancy—is an incredibly precious planetary jewel. We are, all of us—man, beast and growing plant—aboard a spaceship of limited dimensions whose journey began so long ago that we have abandoned one set of gods and are in the process of substituting another in the shape of science. The axial religions had sought to persuade man to transcend his own nature; they had pictured to him limitless perspectives of self-mastery. But science in our time has opened to man the prospect of limitless power over exterior nature. Its technicians sometimes seem, in fact, to have proffered us the power of the void as though flight were the most important value on earth.

"We've got to spend everything we have, if necessary, to get off this planet," one representative of the aerospace industry remarked to me recently.

"Why?" I asked, not averse to flight but a little bewildered by his seeming desperation.

"Because," he insisted, his face turning red, as though from some deep inner struggle, "because," then he flung at me what I suspect he thought my kind of science would take seriously, "because of the ice—the ice is coming back, that's why."

Finally, as though to make everything official, one of the space-agency administrators was quoted in *Newsweek* shortly after the astronauts had returned from the moon: "Should man," this official said, "fall back from his destiny . . . the confines of this planet will destroy him."

It was a strange way to consider our planet, I thought, closing the magazine and brooding over this sudden distaste for life at home. Why was there this hidden anger, this longing for flight, these threats for those who remained on earth? Some powerful and not entirely scientific impulse seemed to be tugging at the heart of man. Was it fear of his own mounting numbers, the creeping of the fungus threads? But where, then, did these men intend to flee? The solar system stretched bleak and cold and crater-strewn before my mind. The nearest star was four light-years and many human generations away. I held up the magazine once more. Here and here alone, photographed so beautifully from outer space, was that blue jewel—compounded of water and of living green—that gave us birth. Yet, upon the page, the words repeated themselves: "This planet will destroy him."

No, I thought, this planet *nourished* man. It took 4,000,000 years to find our way through the sunflower forest and, after that, but a few millenniums to reach the moon. It is not fair to say this planet will destroy us. Space flight is a brave venture, but upon the soaring rockets are projected all the fears and evasions of man. He has fled across two worlds, from the windy corridors of wild savannas to the sunlit world of the mind, and still he flees. Earth will not destroy him. It is he who threatens to destroy the earth. In sober terms, we are forced to reflect that by enormous expenditure and effort, we have ventured a small way out into the solar system, but we have scarcely begun to penetrate the distances, no less real, that separate man from man.

Creatures who evolve as man has done bear the scar tissue of their evolutionary travels in their bodies. The human cortex, the center of high thought, has come to dominate, but not completely to suppress, the more ancient portions of the animal brain. Perhaps it was from this last wound that my engineer friend was unconsciously fleeing. We know that within our heads there still exists an irrational, restive ghost that can whisper disastrous messages into the ear of reason.

Today, man's increasing numbers and his technological power to pollute his environment reveal a single demanding necessity: the necessity for him consciously to re-enter and preserve, for his own safety, the old first world from which he originally emerged. His second world, drawn from his own brain, has brought him far, but it cannot take him out of nature, nor can he live by escaping into his second world alone. He must now incorporate from the wisdom of the axial thinkers an ethic directed not alone toward his fellows but extended to the living world around him. By way of his cultural world, he must re-enter the sunflower forest he had thought merely to exploit or abandon. He must do this in order to survive. If he succeeds, he will, perhaps, have created a third world that combines elements of the original two and that should bring closer the responsibilities and nobility of character envisioned by those thinkers who may be acclaimed as the creators, if not of man, then of his soul. They expressed, in a prescientific era, man's hunger to transcend his own image, a hunger not entirely submerged even beneath the formidable weaponry and technology of the present.

The story of the great saviors, whether Chinese, Indian, Greek or Judaic, is the story of man in the process of enlightening himself, not simply by tools but through the slow inward growth of the mind that made them and may yet master them through knowledge of itself. "The poet, like the lightning rod," Emerson once stated, "must reach from a point nearer the sky than all surrounding objects down to the earth, and into the dark wet soil, or neither is of use." Today, that effort is demanded not only of the poet. In the age of space, it is demanded of all of us. Without it, there can be no survival of mankind, for man himself must be his last magician. He must find his own way home.

To Children

(AT THE END OF 1914)

HERMANN HESSE

You know nothing of time,
You know only that, somewhere in the distance,
A war is being fought,
You whittle your wood into sword and shield and spear
And play your game blissfully in the garden,
Set up tents,
Carry white bandages marked with the red cross.
And if my wish for you has any power,
So war will remain
For you, always, only a dim legend,
So you will never stand in the field
And never die
And never rush out of a house crumbling in fire.

Nevertheless, you will be soldiers one day
And one day you will know
That the sweet breath of this life,
The precious possession of the heartbeat,
Is only a loan, and that whatever was lost
In the past, and the heir you long for,
And the farthest future,
Rolls through your blood,
And that for every hair on your head
Somebody endured one struggle, one pain, one death.

And you shall know that whatever is noble
In your soul is always a warrior,
Even though he bears no weapons,
That every day a struggle and a destiny is waiting.
Do not forget this!
Think of the blood, the shambles, the ruin
On which your own future reposes,
And how, even more, upon death and sacrifice is builded
The tiniest happiness.

Then your life will flame out more
And one day gather even death
Into its arms.

PROJECTS

1. The Scranton Report states: "The Constitution protects the freedom of all citizens to dissent and to engage in nonviolent protest. Dissent is a healthy sign of freedom and a protection against stagnation. But the right to dissent is not the right to resort to violence."

(a) How would Truman Nelson ("No Rights, No Duties") respond to this statement?

(b) After reading and evaluating the essays included in this Reader, how would you define or describe the limits of "dissent," of "violence"?

(c) Can you illustrate from your own experience how healthy dissent becomes unhealthy violence?

(d) Is a definition of healthy dissent and unhealthy violence equally applicable to all areas of human violence—biological, psychological, religious, political, and social?

2. Would you agree with the Scranton Report that "no grievance, philosophy, or political idea can justify the destruction and killing we have witnessed"? In what sense would Ardrey, Bettelheim, Niebuhr, Marcuse, Gold qualify this statement?

3. In your opinion could the three issues discussed in the introduction to the Scranton Report—justice and dignity for minorities,

the end to the Indo-China war, and the shortcomings of the American university itself—become "just" motivation for the use of violence? Use an example from one or all of these issues to support your opinion.

4. The Scranton Report mentions the "new" youth-culture as a possible reason for alienation in American society between the generations.

(a) Do you consider yourself a member of this new culture? Why?

(b) Do you agree (whether you are a member or not) with the Report that "among the members of this new student culture, there is a growing lack of tolerance, a growing insistence that their own views must govern, an impatience with the slow procedures of liberal democracy, a growing denial of the humanity and good will of those who urge patience and restraint, and particularly of those whose duty it is to enforce the law. A small number of students have turned to violence; an increasing number, not terrorists themselves, would not turn even arsonists and bombers over to law enforcement officials"?

5. Discuss the Report's exhortation: "Violence must end . . . Understanding must be renewed . . . Reconciliation must begin."

6. Loren Eiseley writes about the necessity for man to be aware of that first world from which he came—the natural world. Robert Ardrey also writes about such a necessity in "The Violent Way." What similarities and differences do you find regarding the insights man gains, according to Eiseley and Ardrey, from such an awareness of his natural origin?

7. "Man's life, in other words, is felt to be unreal and sterile. Perhaps a creature of so much ingenuity and deep memory is almost bound to grow alienated from his world, his fellows and the objects around him. He suffers from a nostalgia for which there is no remedy except as it is to be found in the enlightenment of the spirit —an ability to have a perceptive rather than an exploitive relationship with his fellow creatures." In view of Eiseley's statement, write an essay which develops or denies the premise that all acts of human

violence originated in man's ability to be exploitive rather than perceptive in his relationships with other people.

8. Would you agree with Eiseley that the ultimate violence we commit is that violence we do to the earth itself which promotes, in turn, our violence toward social structures and to other human beings?

9. Discuss Eiseley's statement: "In sober terms, we are forced to reflect that by enormous expenditure and effort, we have ventured a small way out into the solar system, but we have scarcely begun to penetrate the distances, no less real, that separate man from man."

10. Develop an essay indicating how man's realization and reconciliation between his two worlds—the world of nature and the world of his mind—would bring the realization and perhaps the possibility of Hesse's concluding lines in his poem "To Children":

> "Then your life will flame out more
> And one day gather even death
> Into its arms."

FILMS

In addition to the feature-length films suggested in the previous sections, there are many shorter films which have an impact on discussions regarding violence. Divide into groups of five or six, arrange two screenings for each film used, and react to its message not only from your own perspective but also from the perspective of the polemics of violence represented by such writers as Ardrey, Merton, Marcuse, Laing, Bettelheim, Ellul, Niebuhr, Komisar, and others.

From Mass Media Associates, Inc. (2116 North Charles Street, Baltimore, Maryland 21218, or 1714 Stockton Street, San Francisco, California 94133):

1. *Crime in the Streets* (two aspects of the crime problem: police protection and the rehabilitation of juvenile offenders) 60 minutes—rental, $10.00.

2. *Dead Birds* (a study of the nature of man as seen through the ritual activities of West New Guinea tribes) 9 minutes—$45.00.

3. *Follow the Leader* 22 minutes—$15.00.
4. *The Hat* 18 minutes—$15.00.
5. *Living* 8 minutes—$7.50.
6. *The Magician* 13 minutes—$10.00.
7. *Mother May I?* 10 minutes—$15.00 rental.
8. *Neighbors* 9 minutes—$6.00 rental.
9. *Now Is the Time* 34 minutes—$15.00 rental.
10. *Remedy for Riot* 37 minutes—$15.00 rental.
11. *Toys on a Field of Blue* 20 minutes—$7.50 rental.
12. *The Umbrella* 28 minutes—$10.00 rental.

Write to Mass Media Associates, Inc. for a catalogue with its additional description of these films and other possibilities for a media confrontation with violence.

From the American Friends Service Committee (check for local address and rental fees) there are several films worth viewing for discussion purposes:

1. *Time of the Locust* (an anti-war documentary emphasizing the dehumanizing of all involved in violence) 12 minutes.

2. *The Language of Faces* (a sobering view of American life under "a balance of terror," climaxed with a Quaker vigil for the renunciation of violence) 17 minutes.

3. *Who Owns Tony Fargas?* (a black C.O.—confronting a white draft board) 10 minutes.

4. *Walk to Freedom* (the Montgomery nonviolent bus boycott) 17 minutes.

5. *The Holy War* (especially relevant for discussion regarding the religious polemic of violence) 7 minutes.

From Audio-Film Center, two films which will be relevant to the topic of violence as seen in war:

1. *1000 Cranes* (the impact of the A-Bomb on the children of Hiroshima) 24 minutes—$12.50 rental.

2. *War* (visual statement on the violence of war from the beginning of mankind to the hydrogen bomb) 22 minutes—$15.00 rental.

From Contemporary Films, 330 West 42nd Street, New York, New York.

1. *Rondo* (a study of violence between master and servant) 10 minutes—$15.00 rental.

2. *Mammals* (two men tramping in the snow with only one sled for both of them) 10 minutes—$12.50 rental.

3. *Cages* (man's dependence on authority and the consequences when accepted rules are broken) 9 minutes—$11.50.

4. *Labyrinth* (man's loneliness in a desolate urban world) 14 minutes—$20.00 rental.

From Continental 16, Inc., 241 East 34th Street, New York, New York 10016.

Two feature-length films are:

1. *The Balcony* (while a revolution is in progress, the brothel of Madame Irma has its own drama—a group of men act out their wish fulfillments with beautiful women. Their various illusions—to be a judge, a bishop, a general—suddenly thrust the men into the midst of revolution) 84 minutes—$75.00 rental. Compare with the book—Jean Genet's *The Balcony,* Grove Press, New York, 1958.

2. *Dutchman* (a neurotic white girl picks up a young Negro man on the subway in New York and baits him into action which leads to a tragic denouement) 55 minutes—$75.00 rental.

Bibliography

EISELEY, LOREN. *The Firmament of Time.* New York: Atheneum, 1960.

———. *The Immense Journey.* New York: Random House, 1957.

———. *The Invisible Pyramid.* New York: Charles Scribner's Sons, 1970.

———. "The Last Magician," *Playboy,* August, 1970.

———. "The Mind as Nature." New York: Harper and Row, 1962.

———. *The Unexpected Universe.* New York: Harcourt, Brace and World, 1969.

FROMM, ERICH. *Escape from Freedom.* New York: Farrar and Rinehart, Inc., 1941.
———. *Man for Himself, An Inquiry into the Psychology of Ethics.* New York: Fawcett Premier, 1967.
———. *The Nature of Man.* New York: The Macmillan Company, 1968.
———. *The Revolution of Hope, Toward a Humanized Technology.* New York: Harper and Row, 1968.
———. *Sane Society.* New York: Rinehart, 1955.
HESSE, HERMANN. *Poems.* Sel. and trans. by James Wright. New York: Noonday Press, Farrar, Straus and Giroux, 1970.
MUMFORD, LEWIS. *The Myth of the Machine: The Pentagon of Power.* New York: Harcourt, Brace and World, 1970.
ROSZAK, THEODORE. *The Making of a Counter Culture.* New York: Doubleday & Co., Anchor Edition, 1969.
SCRANTON, WILLIAM W., Chairman. *The Scranton Report* (Findings of the President's Commission on Campus Unrest), Washington, D. C.: Editorial Projects for Education, Inc., 1970.
TEILHARD DE CHARDIN, PIERRE. *The Appearance of Man.* New York: Harper and Row, 1965.
———. *The Future of Man.* New York: Harper and Row, 1964.
———. *The Phenomenon of Man.* New York: Harper and Row, 1959.

A B C D E F G H I J 9 8 7 6 5 4 3 2 1